Horace Walpole

Horace Walpole

THE GREAT OUTSIDER

Timothy Mowl

John Murray
Albemarle Street, London

First published in 1996
by John Murray (Publishers) Ltd,
50 Albemarle Street, London W1X 4BD

A catalogue record for this book is available from the British Library

ISBN 0-7195-5619-8

Typeset in 12/14pt Garamond by Wearset, Boldon, Tyne and Wear

Printed and bound in Great Britain by
The University Press, Cambridge

To Sarah, my wife

Contents

Illustrations

The author and publishers would like to thank the following for their kind permission to reproduce illustrations:
Plate 1, The Provost and Scholars of King's College, Cambridge; plates 2, 4, 5, 9, 10, 13, 14, 15, 16, 17, 18, 19, 20, 21, 22, 23, 25, 26, 27, The Lewis Walpole Library, Farmington, Connecticut; 7, 11, 12, Nottingham University; 8, Private Collection; 24, Bristol University, Special Collections. Plates 3 and 6 are from the collection of the author.

Acknowledgements

My first thanks go out to Anna Malicka at the Lewis Walpole Library, Farmington, Connecticut, who answered every obscure enquiry with courteous efficiency. Together with her colleague, Joan Sussler, she made that stay in New England, with the entire Wilmarth Lewis collection at my disposal, the highlight of my research. The study visit was made possible by a generous grant from the Society of Authors (Authors' Foundation), without which I could never have made the trip and completed the book. John Iddon of St Mary's University College was my enthusiastic and informed guide to Strawberry Hill. My interest in the house dates from the 'Gothic Urge' course I taught for his summer school at the college in the 1980s. For my introduction to Rococo–Gothick architecture I must thank Roger White. He first alerted me to the importance of Batty Langley and accompanied me on many excursions to track down little-known Langley-style houses and Gothick garden buildings usually mouldering in romantic decay. My friend and usual co-author Brian Earnshaw was a sounding board for my arguments and particularly helpful over the literary background of the Gothic novel and the editing of the typescript. Joanne Wright shared my enthusiasm for Horace and organized a memorable private viewing of the key Rosalba portrait of Lord Lincoln at Nottingham University.

Dr Simon Corcoran, Assistant Archivist in the Department of Manuscripts and Special Collections at Nottingham University Library, was most helpful over the Walpole letters to Lord Lincoln and quotations from these and other letters in the Newcastle Collection at the Library are made with the permission of the Keeper of Manuscripts. Quotations from the Yale edition of *Horace Walpole's Correspondence* are made with permission from Yale University Press.

Acknowledgements

Many friends and scholars have helped me over the past two years, but I should like to make particular mention of the following: David Alexander, Brian Allen, Bruce Bailey, Hazel Bannister, Reg and Maureen Barton, Andrew Boddington, Geoffrey Beard, the Marquess of Cholmondeley, Susan Cleaver, Catharine Edwards, Annie Grant, Peter Guillery, John Head, Charles Hind, Florence Kaminska, Gordon Kelsey, David Lambert, Michael Liversidge, David McKinney, Steven Parissien, Julian Self, Gillian Sladen, Michael Snodin, Martin Stiles, Baron Walpole of Wolterton.

Sara Menguc, my agent at Murray Pollinger, found me the most appropriate publisher, John Murray, the firm which first took a chance and made a good profit on Horace's *Memoirs* in 1822. Grant McIntyre, Caroline Knox and Gail Pirkis at John Murray have steered the book through to its publication with sensitivity and professionalism. Douglas Matthews has compiled the excellent index.

Lastly I should like to thank my wife, Sarah, to whom this book is dedicated. She has lived with Horace for over two years and has come to accept her husband's dubious fascination with one of this country's most successful sexual outsiders.

Timothy Mowl
Spring 1996

A warning to readers

Anyone who supposes that Horace Walpole was, in any normal sense, a pleasant and acceptable person should consider the following comical anecdote which he included in a letter of 15 May 1752 to his friend, the British minister in Tuscany, Horace Mann:

> A young Mr Winstanley happened to go into a coffee-house in the City, where some grave elders were talking over a terrible affair, that had just happened in the country, where a man broke into a house, ravished the mistress and killed the master. Winstanley said very coolly, 'It was well it was no worse!' The citizens stared, were shocked! An old alderman could not bear it, but cried 'Zounds! Sir, what do you mean? What could be worse?' 'Why,' replied t'other as coolly as before, 'if he had murdered the wife, and buggered the husband' – what would one give to have seen the faces of the company? Adieu.

If the two Horaces – they were distant cousins – found that humorous, then readers should be prepared for a certain moral register and standards.

Walpole wrote the greatest letter sequence of the eighteenth century; wrote more than four thousand letters to chosen friends like Mann, then retrieved as many as possible and edited them to reflect a history of his life and times. This produced an infinitely readable and quotable source for the activities of the English ruling classes over a period of four decades during which the first British

Introduction

Empire was created and lost. No subsequent social or political historian of the period has been able to ignore the treasure trove of anecdote and informed gossip which these letters represent. In addition, with an even more deliberate intention of influencing posterity, Walpole wrote memoirs of the reigns of George II and George III which virtually created that Whig interpretation of English history which later nineteenth-century historians would think they had invented.

No commentator, contemporary or subsequent, has ever quite trusted Horace Walpole as a source. He was a notably effeminate bachelor with a strong vein of malice in his writing; but if he had homosexual tendencies, he appeared to have been too fastidious ever to have given way to them. To compensate, he wrote a celebrated Gothic novella, *The Castle of Otranto*, built an even more famous Gothic castle–villa, Strawberry Hill at Twickenham, gave an impetus to the whole drive of the Gothic Revival and wrote a number of antiquarian tracts, scholarly and contentious, many of them printed on his own private printing-press.

And there, until the 1920s, Horace Walpole's reputation survived: inescapable because he had been so helpfully prolix and so well-connected, the youngest son of Sir Robert Walpole, Britain's longest-serving, though far from triumphalist, Prime Minister. But he remained an indeterminate figure, not quite a literary giant, a ranking historian or an architect; and there remained a tantalizing ambivalence as to his motivation – how precisely had he interacted within his own society?

Then there was a change.

At Farmington, a small town in Connecticut connected with Yale University, in a modest house built by one of Washington's retired generals, an American scholar of great distinction – Wilmarth Sheldon Lewis – a man of eminently conventional sexual identity, made it his life's work, beginning in 1924 and ending only with his death in 1979, to build up a library and a museum devoted to Horace Walpole. The collection Lewis made of manuscripts, letters, books and relics of his subject is awesomely comprehensive. Anyone who wishes to make a serious study of Walpole must go to Farmington.

Introduction

Quite what attracted Wilmarth Lewis to a lifetime of Walpole scholarship is a fascinating question. Lewis was, from all accounts, happily married to a wife who shared his Walpole interests. He was a scholar in the fine gentlemanly sense of that term, born in 1897 and no natural rebel against the assumptions of his age. When he began his collections, he was bidding in a buyer's market. Most collectors of *belles-lettres* were content to have one or two examples of the four thousand-odd surviving Horace letters. Lewis would only have been satisfied with them all. Travelling widely on this side of the Atlantic, he absorbed, like some scholarly chameleon, every sympathetic nuance of the English class system – the arcane assumptions of life in aristocratic country houses, the complexities of rank and the conventions of insular spelling. English lords with packets of Walpole papers lying in rarely opened library cupboards responded favourably to the breadth of his background knowledge and to his cheque-book. The war years and the economic winter of a Labour government, 1945–51, worked to the advantage of an experienced researcher. Today, much of what is significant that Horace Walpole committed to paper or published, together with charming oddments, pictures, prints, scraps of silk, busts, coins and curios from Horace's enormous collection is at Farmington, generously accessible to serious scholars, all catalogued and ordered in a purpose-built, fireproof library behind the original eighteenth-century house.

Lewis's master-work was the Yale Walpole – forty-eight volumes of Horace's correspondence – a publication backed by a large committee of historians and literary men and women. With his eyesight failing, Lewis was still able to scan the typescript of the later volumes. The footnotes are a monument in themselves; virtually every obscure reference was explored to the ultimate, every line was checked against originals, earlier editors like the censorious Berry sisters were corrected, rude words were restored and whole passages printed for the first time. Wilmarth Lewis and Yale University earned the unstinted gratitude of all subsequent Walpole readers for the completeness of the collection and the scholarship which lies behind the text. This book could not have been written without the revealing accessibility of the Yale edition.

Introduction

Whether Wilmarth Lewis was prepared to take in all the implications revealed by that brilliant accessibility, an openness beyond anything Walpole himself intended, is another matter. Walpole censored his own letters rigorously. Lewis in the Yale volumes censored nothing, but may have been less than happy at what he had exposed. No one has ever known nor probably ever will gather so much accurate information about the letter-writer and his circle, yet Lewis never wrote Horace Walpole's biography though uniquely qualified to do so. In a preface to a volume of delightful essays on Walpole, Lewis wrote evasively:

> Over thirty years ago, I started off bravely to write his biography. As I wrote it I asked myself, why should I try to say what he himself has said so much better? I began quoting more and more from him until I had a mere scrapbook of the facts of his life and amusing passages from his letters. Fortunately, I gave it up.

Now that this book is completed I understand his reaction. Walpole is as commanding a figure in English literature as Proust is in French, and even more difficult to absorb. Proust neither intrigued in French politics nor built a house that influenced the development of his country's architecture. Walpole did both but, rather than searching after times past, he caught his present times as they were passing. As Lewis admitted, there was a need for a 'Life': 'in the thirties Mr Ketton-Cremer came twice to Farmington for several months and wrote the biography that makes, I think, another full account of Walpole's life unnecessary.' But in his 1940 preface, Wyndham Ketton-Cremer still wrote, 'It is my hope that Mr Lewis, when he has concluded his edition of Walpole's correspondence, will write his final and definitive biography.' That was not to be and I am sure Lewis never wrote that definitive study because he knew too much about his literary hero and did not like or wish to pass on all that he knew. Wilmarth Lewis 'understood' Horace Walpole. It is inescapable from the forty-eight volumes that Horace was, in so far as openness was acceptable in his time, a homosexual who consorted with other homosexuals and bisexuals of his class. Writing in his introduction to the Yale volumes in 1960, five years perhaps before the sexual revolution, Lewis slides out of the dilemma:

The present age wants to know what evidence there may be of homosexuality in the subjects of biography. The modern reader whose suspicions are easily aroused may misinterpret a few of Walpole's early letters and those of his friends, not realizing that eighteenth-century men expressed themselves and acted with what seems to us today unmanly abandon ... but a handful of letters written in extravagant high spirits in the manner of the time are not proof of it, and none has come to light. The verse written by a friend at Cambridge, who described him as 'untossed by passion', is a description that fits him throughout his life if one means, as the writer did mean, sexual passion.

The 'few' early letters to which Lewis was probably referring were the twenty-five intimate, sometimes passionate and, on one occasion, sexually explicit letters which Walpole wrote to Henry Fiennes-Clinton, 9th Earl of Lincoln and which he was never able to retrieve. Lewis was uneasy about Lincoln. He described him as 'the amorous young man' and admitted that there was 'in Walpole's letters to him an effusiveness, an obsequiousness, that does not appear to anything like the same degree elsewhere'. He also knew of their familiarity at Eton, but drew no further conclusions.

No one expects scholarship to be pure. Lewis was obsessed by Horace Walpole; he came over the years to admire him and, in so far as the dead can be loved, to love him. But being born a Protestant in the nineteenth century and writing in New England, Lewis carried a cluster of moral certainties that made him disapprove of homosexuals. To that extent his scholarship was flawed and he probably made certain that Wyndham Ketton-Cremer's *Horace Walpole* was flawed in exactly the same way. 'Above all,' Ketton-Cremer wrote, 'I have had the benefit of Mr Lewis's criticism and advice, and lately of his revision of the completed manuscript of my book.'

As a result of that 'criticism and advice', Ketton-Cremer produced what has since become the standard biography of Horace Walpole, a bright and crowded canvas. Ketton-Cremer was, like Lewis, a 'Georgian' in the polite twentieth-century sense of that term and his book has those 'Georgian' limitations. He chose to confine Horace and his friends within certain acceptable limits of wit, elegance and sensibility: virtually the world of Jane Austen projected back a few decades and almost as morally circumspect as an Austen parsonage.

The next approach to Horace carried this escapist line even further into the predictable environment of country dances, *bons mots* and tinkling laughter. This was Brian Fothergill's *The Strawberry Hill Set*, a delightful book which nevertheless deflects its reader's attention away from Horace to a selection of his entertaining friends, leaving him to be revealed only in their safe, reflected light.

Whilst valuing these earlier studies, I have altered the focus, unkindly, some might say, to concentrate on the man himself; his friends, eccentric, sophisticated and multiple, have become secondary. This is not another book on Georgian society or an Age of Enlightenment; it aims at what I believe to have been the man and his motivations.

When that has been made clear there remains a further obstacle to a true assessment of Horace Walpole raised by modern political correctness. It is obviously relevant to the style, stance and judgement of a writer, particularly a writer widely used as an historical source for his times, if he was a homosexual. But 'homosexual' in itself is a dangerously imprecise term. Homosexual love and hate take as many different forms and expressions, generosities and perversions, as heterosexual passions. Horace waded deep in contemporary politics and aesthetics. He slept with the enemy, literally, and was not immune to the prejudices that stem from sexual failures and embarrassments. He was a sexual outsider and because of this he was also an aesthetic outsider, and a potent rebel in the heart of a nation's establishment.

So Walpole's sexual nature will be included in this study, not in any sense of moral shock or horror nor with any bias of sexual approval. Some of his adventures were amusing, some were devious and spiteful, some were richly creative in a stylistic sense; but in all his writings and responses to life, his proclivities were relevant, and it will be helpful if both biographer and reader remain open-minded and alert.

Everyone has prejudices, biases and viewpoints, biographers as much as their subjects, so let me state mine now. I am an architectural historian but, with interests in fine arts and literature, no more disposed to relate to Horace's building activities than to his gloriously overwhelming literary leavings. If readers suspect that a writer like myself, happily married to a second wife and the experienced father of a school-age son, has no business analysing the subtleties of homosexual attitudes in the eighteenth century, then they are probably unaware how much homosexual activity and internecine conflict is commonplace in the world of architectural historians. My profession has been a perfect preparation, and this I report in no spirit of complaint, for the Strawberry Hill set. If Horace behaved often in ways that would be described today as 'camp' and some of his friends acted like 'screaming queens', this needs to be said; the 'gay' world is anything but politically correct in private. The enchanted castle of Strawberry Hill should be conceived of not only as an exercise in public relations, but as a large Gothick 'closet' to which Horace Walpole could sometimes retire when he wished to express his true persona with intimate friends. 'The weather grows fine,' he wrote to Richard Bentley, 'and I have resumed little flights to Strawberry. I carried G. Montagu thither, who was in raptures, and screamed, and whooped, and hollaed, and danced, and crossed himself a thousand times over.' George Hardinge, writing as a disapproving outsider, came near to the truth when he remarked, 'There was a degree of quaintness in Mr Walpole's wit, but it was not unbecoming in *him* for it seemed a part of his *nature*. Some of his friends were as effeminate in appearance and in manner as himself and were as witty. Of these I remember two, Mr Chute and Mr George Montagu. But others had effeminacy alone to recommend them.'

Horace's life was a case of privacy turned inside out. His taste as expressed in Strawberry Hill was one of a deliberate rebel counter-culture. He was proud of it and turned his retreat into a public showplace. He was delighted by his own identity and concerned, like a public relations expert, to communicate it to us down the years, but in a form carefully censored to conceal any overtly homosexual implications. It will appear from the following chapters that Horace Walpole was one of the most successful deviant infiltrators that the English establishment has ever produced.

CHAPTER ONE

The first clear object of his wishes

Horace Walpole's childhood, those years before he went, aged nine-and-a-half, to Eton, are unrecorded. No contemporaries noted the youngest child of the most influential politician in the country because he was out of the public eye. In eighteenth-century terms, his parents were divorced: separated by mutual consent but making no emotional or legal fuss over their disengagement. The effect on their last son was to leave him architecturally underprivileged. Sir Robert was pouring his money into a Palladian palace, Houghton, the family seat of the Walpoles on the barren heaths of the Norfolk coast, and into Richmond Lodge in Richmond Park just up the Thames from London. He did not own the Lodge but still spent £14,000 on it as deputy to his eldest son who was officially the Ranger of the park. Houghton could have given Horace a familiarity with classical grandeur, orderly proportions and conventional taste, but when his father entertained his Norfolk friends in lavish house parties at Houghton or hunted with the king at Richmond, the hostess was his mistress, Maria Skerrett, not his wife Catherine, so both houses were morally and socially out-of-bounds to Horace.

Instead he was brought up in plain London town houses – 10 Downing Street, Arlington Street and a slightly more rural house in the stable-yard of the Royal Hospital at Chelsea. The Hospital is, admittedly, an impressive brick palace by Christopher Wren, but in function it is only a dormitory for old soldiers and its stable-yard was not the most distinguished of addresses. Sir Robert was an indulgent father, but he had two other sons, sixteen and eleven years older than Horace, and on them his hopes for the family succession rested. Horace's mother had lost two daughters by the common illnesses of childhood. Horace himself was a frail, undersized child who, as he later wrote, 'so engrossed the attention of my mother that compassion and tenderness soon became extreme fondness'. So he was reared almost as the only child of a single parent family, but always with the comfortable awareness of the Walpole wealth and the awesome prestige of his father's position.

One of the rare personal anecdotes from these years that he recalled in later life is malicious, humorous and snobbish. In extreme old age and half-blind, the Duchess of Tyrconnel, a one-time supporter of King James II, called on his mother to ask for financial help. Looking out of the window onto the blank wall of a yard, the poor old soul congratulated her hostess on the beauty of her garden. Would such pathos and irony have been appreciated by the average small boy? Or was it rather the first instance of a quite unusual relish for the frailties of the human condition, especially when the human involved had a title and a past?

It is always assumed that Horace doted on his mother and that she doted on him. Nevertheless, she was ready to put him out a little into the world even before he went to Eton, sending him to live with his Townshend cousins and their tutor at Bexley in Kent when he was eight. William Cole, older than Horace and already three years at Eton, was brought in during school holidays to share drawing lessons from Bernard Lens, so he was not a particularly sheltered child. Indeed he never gives the impression of having the need of a careful upbringing, for all his poor health and feeble physique. An inner toughness and a social consequence as a son of Sir Robert seem to have carried him happily through years that could have been fraught with bullying.

He had been at Eton less than a month, at the end of May 1727, when he brought off a social *coup* that is likely to have shaken and subdued any older boys at the school who might have been inclined to take out on him the sins of his father. Horace expressed a wish to have a private audience with King George I. Writing years later, he pretended that 'female attendants in the family' put the idea into his head, but it was an obvious master-stroke of defensive tactics in his new environment. One evening, soon after he had made his request, he was brought to St James's Palace and introduced to the amusing cartoon cast of German women who kept the old king reasonably happy in a strange land. Melusina von der Schulenburg ushered him into a royal ante-room, the nine-year-old kissed hands and exchanged, or so he later claimed, a few words with a king who spoke little or no English. And that was that. Etonians could take note. A fortnight later, King George died of a stroke on his way back home to Hanover, but Horace had a social scalp safely tucked away.

To appreciate the visual impact of Eton on a small, self-satisfied little boy from Chelsea, it is rewarding to walk the Thames tow-path, across the river from the College, in early spring before the tourists are afoot. The river of water and the river of history flow together there inescapably. Across the Thames, beyond the flow-ering may and the fresh willow leaves, the white stone pinnacles of the College chapel rise above a pleasant huddle of cloister yards and ranges, human in scale, of mellow brick. On the near side of the river Windsor Castle rears up on a steep hill with a long confusion of towers and state apartments above hanging woods. Two cathedral-sized royal chapels stand almost within catapult-shot of each other. The whole setting is Gothic, Picturesque and Romantic, not ordered or classical; the past is made visible in an emotionally appealing nursery for youth of the élite.

To the young Walpole, it was paradise achieved and the College buildings were the ideal form of Eden – asymmetrical, jumbled, a place of dark corners and sudden courts, a male world and his 'mimic republic'. Mooning nostalgically about the place only a year after he had lost it, he claimed hyperbolically to George Montagu: 'Alexander at the head of the world never tasted the true pleasure that boys of his own age have enjoyed at the head of a school'. And what were those 'true pleasures'? Montagu, though four years his senior, had been a friend at Eton and was to remain for many years the recipient of some of his most intimate letters. Possibly Horace had been his fag, so the two would be frank with each other. Ketton-Cremer, guided as he wrote his biography by Wilmarth Lewis, was not. Quoting from this important letter, he actually cut out the key passage from Horace's appreciation of his school, leaving only a row of dots. What, according to Horace, made Eton a time of true pleasures for boys, was that it provided 'the season when they first felt the titillation of love, the budding passions and the first clear object of their wishes'.

That clear recollection of schoolboy crushes may have offended puritanical scholarship, hence the row of dots. But the letter continued in an allusive pastoral vein, one natural enough to someone who had recently been a sixth-former translating, in a standard Eton exercise of familiarity with the classics, the doubtful loves of Virgil's shepherd boys and Quintus Horatius Flaccus's bisexual passions for young athletes. 'Dear George,' it continued, 'were not the playing-fields at Eton food for all manner of flights? At first I was contented with tending a visionary flock and sighing some pastoral name to the echo of the cascade under the bridge.' These were not the usual associations of the playing-fields of Eton, but Horace made no apology for having been 'never quite a schoolboy,' nor is there any mystery about those pastoral names over which he sighed. Horace was 'Celadon', Thomas Gray was 'Orazmades', Richard West was 'Favonius' or sometimes 'Zephiron', and Thomas Ashton was 'Almanzor'. Years after they had left Eton behind them, these precious four of the 'Quadruple Alliance' as they called themselves were still using these pastoral names when they wrote to each other. Scorning 'a match at cricket' or 'an expedition against bargemen' – punch-ups with the locals – the effete foursome discussed classical poetry with each other 'in Egeria's hallowed grove', some private corner of the school grounds, Eton's equivalent of 'behind the bicycle sheds'. Though Horace does admit obscurely, 'I was sometimes troubled with a rough creature or two from the plow.' Agars Plough was a farm across the road from the school and its young labourers would not have known when they threw clods at him that the small schoolboy with a mincing bird-like walk was the great Sir Robert's son.

Horace's friends at Eton are usually described as formalized into two groups: the 'Quadruple Alliance' named above and the 'Triumvirate' of Horace, Montagu and Charles Lyttelton, but these groupings exclude both his first cousin and closest friend, Henry Conway, and his 'intimate', Lord Lincoln. Of the rest, only Gray of the 'Alliance' and Montagu of the 'Triumvirate' went on to play significant roles in Horace's maturity. Lyttelton became an antiquary and eventually Bishop of Carlisle, but he remained always on the periphery of Horace's acquaintance. There were two other Etonians, Richard Edgcumbe and George Selwyn, in another group, the 'Out of Town Party', but this was formed later as a dining club. Both Edgcumbe and Selwyn were professional libertines, Edgcumbe an amateur artist and a depressive, infatuated with prostitutes, and Selwyn a waster who gambled with his friends' money, profaned the sacrament in Oxford and made a hobby of attending executions. Selwyn had been Lord Lincoln's closest friend at Eton and was, curiously, Wilmarth Lewis's favourite among the more raffish members of Horace's circle. 'Frivolous, undependable, cynical, the wit of wits, he remained a good friend,' Lewis wrote, and then quoted Horace's 'few knew him so well, and consequently few knew so well the goodness of his heart and nature'. Contemporaries accused Selwyn of 'sentimental sodomy' on account of his close, platonic friendship with Lord March.

It was with the members of the 'Quadruple Alliance' that Horace was most closely engaged in the years immediately after leaving Eton, and what emerges from their correspondence is that the College had been a very happy and successful educational environment. Its ex-pupils loved what they had learnt, they liked or loved each other and they continued to express that affection through the same passages of wit and classical reference that had been standard class-room practice. Before they graduated to those morning exercises when sixth-formers had to turn Homer's Greek into correct Latin in front of a critical audience of fifth-formers, they had regularly imitated Martial's terse epigrammatic put-downs of Roman society with their own neat Latin jokes about their contemporary world. An anonymous example, aimed at Horace's father, has survived:

Sapere est fari
si sapiant taceant alii, Walpole diserte
nunquam si sapias tu tacuisse velis

To know is to speak.
Others, when they know, are silent; you, oh learned Walpole,
When you know, always wish to speak

and the pattern was hard to throw off. Echoes of modern satire: a Roman *Private Eye*, a stab of wit revolving around dry antithesis, recur often in Horace's and George Montagu's letters. The classics taught well can shape the linguistic patterns of native English and at Eton at that time the classics were taught very well indeed.

Throughout Horace's stay, the under-master was Francis Goode, 'a most easy and good-tempered man ... much beloved by his scholars' who had anticipated the modern belief that education can be fun. Because of his 'easy and pleasant way of instilling his instructions', his boys 'seemed rather to be entertaining themselves with their familiars than at school while he was explaining Ovid or Terence to them'. This clearly brilliant teaching must explain why all four members of the 'Quadruple Alliance' went up to university with vague notions of becoming poets on their own account, regardless of the fact that they were now studying law, theology, mathematics, natural sciences or astronomy. Their letters overflow with Latin and English verse and with serious analysis of the nature of the poetic impulse. One of the four did eventually become the first English poet of his century to make a major lyrical escape from the deadening habit of the heroic couplet, so not all their earnest self-importance was in vain.

Curiously, since Horace Walpole was later to develop into an unusually sharp critic of contemporary follies, there is no mention in his letters of the chaos, bad discipline and sharply declining numbers that Eton actually experienced while he was there. Horace had arrived in Henry Bland's last year as headmaster, a man 'of a becoming gravity, allayed with a sweetness and amiableness of temper peculiar to himself, having a continual smile upon his countenance'. This benign Buddha was succeeded in 1728 by William George, soon nicknamed 'Dionysius the Tyrant', who was 'not only foolish, but proud, ill-mannerly and brutal'. In George's second year there was a rebellion, 'the whole government of the school in a state of anarchy', with the Head's reactions to the riot 'so weak as to invite another'. He was a pedantic misogynist whose response when a young lady quoted Latin verse in front of him was:

> Madam, if you were in the lowest form of the Upper school I should lay you upon our block for that recitation, which contains in three lines two false quantities and the same number of concords equally false.

His pompous buffoonery in a class-room was so entertaining that Frederick, Prince of Wales, is supposed to have been smuggled in to witness it. Once a year it was an Eton custom to release a ram in the grounds for the boys to chase and bludgeon to death with clubs, an amusement the young Duke of Cumberland, a future hero of Culloden, enjoyed. But one year, during William George's headship, the ram escaped across the river and was battered down bloodily in the streets of Windsor. To avoid any repetition of this scandal, George ordered that all future rams should be hamstrung so that they would not run too fast or too far. Not surprisingly, in the first three years of his bizarre rule Eton's numbers shrank from 370 boys to 212, so the school was not only Gothic for the young Walpole in its architectural setting, but Gothic in its wild mood and behaviour. Possibly, since he never commented critically upon the disorder, he enjoyed it. Horace speaks appreciatively of 'little intrigues, little schemes, and policies'. His only reaction to the appalling ram-bashing was a typical antiquary's footnote that the custom had come to the College from a Norfolk parish which had been a fifteenth-century endowment confiscated from the alien priory of Bec in Normandy.

Horace developed his strong and enduring homosexual attachment to the Earl of Lincoln, subsequently 2nd Duke of Newcastle, while still at Eton. Many years later, Horace admitted to Horace Mann that 'The Duke [as Lincoln had then become] and I have been intimate from our school-hood'. In the light of Horace's subsequent devious contriving, the relationship probably began when

Horace, three years older than the Earl, had the glamour of a sixth-former about him and Lincoln was still in the fourth form. The link would have been temptingly symmetrical to a boy of Horace's political awareness and sexual disposition. His father, Sir Robert Walpole, had for years depended upon the wealth and rotten boroughs of the Duke of Newcastle for his control of the House of Commons. Newcastle was the uncle and guardian of the orphan Earl of Lincoln, who was eventually to succeed to some of his rotten boroughs and to his dukedom. His uncle had changed the title, with royal consent, from that of Newcastle-upon-Tyne to Newcastle-under-Lyme, expressly in order for his nephew to inherit a new title. What more satisfying prospect could there be for Horace than to establish on his own account a sexual relationship parallel to his father's strictly political alliance? There would have been the additional bonus of the Earl's striking good looks. A manipulative charmer, dark-haired, well-built and always ready to strip down to his breeches for a sporting contest, he would be described in a few short years by George II as 'the handsomest man in England'. To Horace, always inclined to confuse affection, physicality and politics, he could have seemed very attractive on those playing-fields.

Lincoln had a private tutor at Eton, the Revd John Hume, later Bishop of Bristol, then of Oxford and finally Salisbury, who wrote regular reports on his charge to the Duke. Hume was to follow the Earl in the same capacity to Newcastle's old Cambridge college, Clare, where he continued his reports. When the Earl went on to complete his education on the Continent, at Dijon and Turin, another tutor, Joseph Spence, the Oxford Professor of Poetry, took over, still reporting regularly to a concerned, interfering but genuinely affectionate guardian.

There is an intriguing consistency in these reports, though they were written by two different tutors and over a period of eight years. It is apparent that the tutors were putty in the hands of the wilful, charming young man they were supposed to be controlling. From Eton to Turin, they made excuses for him and the equally malleable Duke absorbed those excuses. In July 1733, when the Earl was thirteen, Hume's report began:

I am to make my Lord Lincoln's excuses for not writing, which considering all things a'n't bad ones. He has twice as much book and desire to play as ever he had in his life, and cant find a moments leisure. From construing and pearcing Greek he is gone to make verses, and from verses to prose, and from prose to Greek again; what time for letters? And what a change from Claremont? [The Duke's enormous house in Surrey] Nevertheless the number of boys in the same case with himself makes the pill go down, tho 'tis a bitter one.

The Revd Hume assured the Duke that his charge was well placed in the fourth form of the Upper school and should not be hurried into the more intense academic testing ground of the fifth and sixths, where Horace was presiding over the last year of a united 'Quadruple Alliance'. If Hume had also in mind the wisdom of keeping his student distant from Horace Walpole, three years his senior, then he had not reckoned with the enduring constancy of an attachment which would in most young men have been no more than a schoolboy crush.

CHAPTER TWO

Brideshead half-visited

In the autumn of 1734 the 'pastoral' friends were scattered, Gray and Ashton to Cambridge, West to Oxford. Horace, for reasons never made clear, gave himself a sabbatical, neither Eton nor University, but socializing in London. He would only go up to Cambridge in March 1735, just over a year before the Earl of Lincoln arrived there from school. It may have been pure coincidence that Horace's college, King's, was then still on its old site immediately across the narrow Trinity Hall Lane from the Earl of Lincoln's college, Clare, but as the coincidences of proximity and meetings build up they need to be noticed. Walpole was nothing if not subtle and ingenious in adjusting events to his advantage. He was always to take a delight in plotting.

As Horace's school contemporaries moved on and their letters, with firsthand evidence of states of mind, began to accumulate, it is interesting to note how Wilmarth Lewis reacted to that evidence. Lewis must have had his suspicions about Horace's sexual identity and relationships. He accepted that 'the feminine element in his personality was a strong one, as it has been in all great letter-writers'. The information was there, from which he could have drawn conclusions. The footnotes of the Yale Walpole volumes alone are a rich source for anyone with a mind to follow leads. In his denial of any real homosexual tendencies in his hero, Lewis admitted that 'some of Walpole's youthful letters, especially those to Lord Lincoln and Conway' were high-spirited. But Lewis believed what he wanted to believe.

Warren Hunting Smith, the editor, after Lewis's death, of the last Yale volumes, describes this personal involvement and critical blindness almost as a virtue:

> Towards Walpole himself, Wilmarth Lewis had an almost mystical feeling of identification; in fact he wrote that at one period he had to be rescued from a real obsession with this idea. He felt a very special guidance whenever he entered a room and turned towards the very cabinet where 'a bit of the True Cross' was concealed.

Lewis suffered from a 'mother complex' which he had openly admitted in one of his books. Therefore Horace Walpole must also have suffered from a 'mother complex'. But Lewis was not, perish the thought, a homosexual; therefore Horace could not have been a homosexual either. 'This feeling of identification with his subject,' Smith continued, 'sometimes made him impervious to certain suggestions.' Smith cautiously does not reveal the nature of those suggestions; Lewis 'simply *knew* how Horace Walpole would have talked and acted, even if the evidence for it was not entirely convincing.' Everyone edits within the temper and constraints of their times. One lesson to be drawn from Lewis's partiality is that it is as unhelpful to press one view of Horace's sex life as another; 1996 is as open to bias of one kind as 1936 was to its opposite.

If he ever had suspicions over the relationship between Horace and his favourite cousin, Henry Seymour Conway, Lewis was almost certainly mistaken. It was fond but it is unlikely that it ever edged over into the sexual, although it was a very intense mixture of the affectionate and the political. Horace's politics were deeply emotional. Years later, in 1776, when Henry Conway, by that time an ex-Secretary of State and a respected general of the British army, had suffered a mild stroke with facial paralysis, Horace visited him on his sick bed and was shocked into an extraordinary confession in a letter which he wrote to another old Etonian, William Cole. All the scheming and political plotting of the last forty years, Horace now realized, had been motivated only by his love for Conway. The realization had come 'like a mortal distemper in myself, for can amusements amuse, if there is but a glimpse, a vision of outliving one's friends?' Horace often claimed that he had no political ambitions for himself, but seeing the twisted, distorted face of a once handsome friend had brought out the truth. 'I have had dreams in which I thought I wished for fame – it was not certainly posthumous fame at any distance; I feel, I feel it was confined to the memory of those I love. It seems impossible for a man who has no friends to do anything for fame.' How this denial of 'posthumous fame' squares up with the *Memoirs* and letters which he left to be read long after his death is not easy to explain. But what this emotional outburst reveals is that Horace had all the time seen himself, for all his effete ways and faintly ridiculous image, as following in his father's footsteps, hoping to become a power-broker, leading, with the beloved Conway, a coalition to rule the country. Perhaps, in an ideal scenario, Lincoln's influence and the Newcastle pocket-boroughs would have been a third element in a consummated political passion.

In the university interlude between leaving school in 1734 and his Grand Tour which began in April 1739, Horace's relationship with four friends developed interestingly and can be followed, one-sidedly at least, in the letters which they wrote to him. Most of his letters to them are lost. The friends were Conway, George Montagu, Richard West and Thomas Gray, four aspects to the multi-sided Horace. No letters to or from Lord Lincoln were suffered to survive, so there is no proof that any were written. Conway stands naturally as the first of the four, as Horace would have been close to him in those London-based eight months between Eton and Cambridge. His cousin was heading not for the university but for the army and while he hesitated over which regiment to join, which commission Sir Robert Walpole's influence could best secure for him, he was free to enjoy the social round of London. He did not join a regiment, Lord Molesworth's Dragoons, until 1737 and even then regarded the next few years as more a part of his education than a time to be dedicated to serious soldiering.

Conway's unguarded letters to Horace explain why Wilmarth Lewis was uneasy about their relationship. Henry Conway was in a not uncommon adolescent condition, poised between two identities: in his case, that of a high-camp socialite, and that of a career officer with parliamentary ambitions on the side. Like Horace, Conway loved dressing up for a masquerade, and dressing up as a young girl was a great thrill. Horace demanded a full account and got one. Conway wrote back:

> We love to flatter our vanity, you know, not a little so that I can't help troubling you with a few of my adventures. I picked all my peacock's plumes out of my sister Jenny's wardrobe which I ransacked without reserve; when I was sufficiently decorated, it was necessary, they said, for the sake of my reputation, to put myself under the protection of a moral lady; this I willingly submitted to, and was no sooner got there than I was surprised with a thousand extravagant encomiums on my shape and beauty, for which I was entirely obliged to a loose sack and a black silk mask.

One masquerader dressed as a Dominican friar chatted him up 'after much lewd conversation', while a military masquerader 'immediately invested me, and after several vigorous attacks, finding he could not carry me by storm, made a blockade of it'. What Conway meant by writing 'at last I withdrew the garrison and left him to take possession, if he pleased, of the empty citadel' is not explained.

From Conway's faintly embarrassed responses, it is obvious that some of Horace's letters to him had been effusive; he mentions 'the many kind professions of friendship and engaging frankness with which your last was penned'. But Horace could not have failed to notice where his friend drew the moral line. Conway would quote admiringly some lines of homosexual love from the Latin:

> *Te per gramina Martii*
> *Campi, te per aquas, dure volubiles*
> [You, hard-hearted one, exercise on the playing-fields and swim the strong currents].

But he would then hastily express his moral distaste for such attitudes: 'the avowing a passion for a youth (though not an uncommon thing with the Greek and Roman poets), is so notoriously impious and contrary to nature, as well as morality and religion, that it is impossible not to be offended at it.' At times it is difficult not to label Henry Conway as a prig. In one letter he announced: 'I have met with the most terrible accident that could possibly befall me.' A lady whom he had long yearned after in secret 'inconsiderately let drop an expression too gross for me to name, and almost for you to imagine'. This had left him with 'a strong garrison of anti-venereal thoughts which I much question if I shall ever be able to dislodge'. Tantalizingly, and surely deliberately, he signed himself off with the flirtatious: 'Yours, my dear Horry, much more than hers, Strephon II.' He also frequently promised to dedicate any laurels he might gain on a field of battle to Horace, a Grecian gesture that could easily be misinterpreted. Conway's signing himself off as 'Strephon', the lovelorn shepherd, indicates that he was at least an honorary member of the 'Quadruple Alliance'. It would be interesting to know who had played Strephon I in their pastoral games.

Lacking a psychiatrist's couch on which to disentangle his ambivalences, Conway confided his revealing dreams to Horace 'more to give myself ease, than, I doubt, it can possibly afford you pleasure'. He had dreamt that, after attending a performance of a particularly chaste, moral play, *The Orphan*, he had gone off to a bawdy tavern. This had turned into a brothel where all his 'jolly dog' companions 'each retired with his respective lady' and where one young lord boasted of having ten mistresses a month. What disturbed Conway about the dream was the contrast between the romantic pieties of the play and the carnality of 'the other people bringing themselves upon a level with the brute creation', to 'act purely to satisfy their bestial lust, entirely excluding the more refined sensations of the mind'.

It is possible that Horace may have been a little disappointed, certainly wryly amused, by his friend's prim conclusion: 'Whichever gate my vision flew out at, you may be sure my principles are not shaken, but that I still remain the same H.C.' There is, however, a sense of emotional vulnerability and sexual uncertainty about the letter that his reader could well have found hopeful. When Horace wrote a poem prematurely praising Conway's martial ardour, Conway promptly replied that he had no such combative spirit but begged him 'not to divulge a secret which I have imparted to you in confidence, and which if known must entirely spoil my fortune in the army'. Like Horace's other friends, Conway, who would later fight bravely at Fontenoy but miss Dettingen, was far more interested in discussing poetry than military matters.

In 1737 Horace was asked to accompany two other friends, George Montagu and Lord Francis Conway, Henry's brother, on a trip to Italy. Horace politely declined. When he eventually set off in 1739 on his Grand Tour he took as his companions Thomas Gray, of whose abject love he was confidently assured, and joined in Paris Henry Conway, whom he found physically attractive and, after those dreams and confessions, emotionally promising. It was typical of Horace that he contrived then to divert his travels with these two ill-assorted friends into a predatory quest on the trail of a third love-object, the Earl of Lincoln.

George Montagu cannot, however, be dismissed casually as a rejected travelling companion. He was the most mysterious and unpredictable of Horace's friends, a fat, lazy Northamptonshire squire who would suddenly quit his bucolic idleness to take public office in Ireland or to act as private secretary to Lord North. High camp in his affectations, he was another lifelong bachelor. He had been four years Horace's senior at Eton, which is a long gap in schoolboy terms; Horace never shook off that air of being the doting junior fag in their relationship.

The first letter which Horace wrote to Montagu and then demanded to have returned is dated 2 May 1736. This is, in a scholarly sense, the most important of all Horace's many thousands that have survived. It proves that, while he was still only eighteen, he had fixed his eye upon futurity and decided, first, that he wanted to be remembered for ever, and second, that he wanted to be remembered for a light, easy style and for accounts of the commonplace incidents of daily life. It was this deliberately modest ambition which gave him his immortality. Born into a century of formal writing he had noticed a literary gap and moved in to fill it.

Montagu had provoked his resolve by sending him a lively account of the recent wedding of the Prince of Wales, but then ordering Horace to burn it. 'You desire I would burn your letters,'

Horace wrote back angrily, 'I desire you would keep mine.' He then tried to shame Montagu into writing longer letters by offering to send him sheets of blank paper. Over the next thirty-four years there would always be this tension between the two friends. It was Horace who made the running, forever cajoling or abusing the older man for rapid replies of a satisfying length and in an affectionate register. 'I hope,' he wrote, 'for the future our correspondence will run a little more glibly, with dear George and dear Horry, not as formally as if we were playing a game at chess in Spain and Portugal; and Don Horatio was to have the honour of specifying to Don Georgio by an epistle whither he would move.'

Confidence was Horace's strength. He had confidence to be himself, to be relaxed and easy. Given his frail physique and a sexual apartness of which he must already have been aware, that confidence could only have come from his birth into a family of power and the affection and respect that had surrounded him during his childhood. He may have been an outsider because of his sexual inclination, but he was only ever an embittered and belligerent outsider when that sexuality was threatened by a marriage which excluded him or by a public 'outing'. Normally he was happy with society and with his place in it.

This determination to treat letter-writing almost as a career indicates something more than mere confidence. At eighteen, and with a Prime Minister as father, politics would have been the more obvious course for which a younger son should have been preparing. Instead, Horace was already aiming in 1736 at a literary immortality which would demand a gallery of obedient friends, all ready to play the Horace game with little hope of any reward. He would have to become a 'professional friend', a remarkably detached and calculated concept for a young man.

It would present problems. His liveliest and wickedest friends, men like Selwyn and Edgcumbe, were the ones least likely to play the literary game by his rules, reply regularly and return his own letters. Then again, how scandalous could he afford to be? There is proof that Lord Lincoln wrote regularly to him while their affair was most active, but not a single Lincoln letter of 1739–44 has been allowed to survive, nor would even one of Horace's to Lincoln have been preserved if Horace had been able to get his hands on them. His half-sister Mary and his heiress, Mrs Damer, destroyed all his letters to them. Horace Mann, writing faithfully from Florence for forty years and returning Horace's letters at intervals, was apparently ideal. Yet with no physical meeting between the two friends over all those years, even Horace's literary invention sank low in human interest. A major holocaust of Scottish peers or a coronation at Westminster was needed to revive it.

Horace was never perfectly in control. He might select his correspondents but that would not necessarily produce good letters either from him or from them. When Horace Mann died, Horace went on writing, as if nothing had happened, to his nephew (confusingly, another Horace Mann) but the resulting letters were mechanical and unimportant. The great letter sequences and the occasional soaring rockets of fire arose from an emotional warmth and a vulnerability between Horace and his correspondent. In the following chapters it will become apparent just who struck off sparks and who did not, and there will always be the limitation of censorship (as in so many early letters to Gray) and the sheer luck of survival. Many of the wonderfully pompous and wary letters that passed between Horace and the Marquis of Hertford were discovered by Wilmarth Lewis in Ceylon, of all unlikely places. That piece of literary detective work restored a stimulating emotional counterpoint built up during 1764–5, with Horace presenting one face to Hertford – politic, manipulative, exhilaratingly false – and another, all despair, frustration and danger, to Montagu. Can the literature which was created be described as deliberate or serendipitous?

Only when there was this tension, which could grow out of delight as well as anger, could Horace's letters approach great literature and become not only a record of his times, but the rough and vital outline of a novel based on the life of an artist–politician who half failed in both art and politics.

*

Nothing illustrates the importance of Horace's recipient more clearly than the contrast between what he wrote at this time to lazy, indifferent, but visually sophisticated George Montagu and what he wrote and endured from Richard West. West was the reader and correspondent Horace would have been better without at that vulnerable stage in his adolescence. A confident, high-spirited young man like Horace could carry one melancholic, would-be-poet friend with ease and even impel him into real creativity, but two depressed versifiers were excessive. Thomas Gray, resident at Peterhouse throughout Horace's time at King's, Cambridge, had at least come to terms with the black dog of melancholy, possibly even valued its moods; but Richard West, separated from the other three at Christ Church, Oxford, was a gloomy pedant and a bore. He is significant only because Horace was obviously impressed by him, put up with his tedious correspondence and valued his flattery. The exchanges of letters during the university years have all been ruthlessly edited at one time or another as Horace prepared his reputation for future consumption.

Whatever he wrote to Conway and Gray, and there is internal evidence that he wrote often, must have come to seem emotionally inappropriate when he was middle-aged. Those 'many kind professions of friendship' that Conway mentions would have caused embarrassment once Conway had become a moderately successful Secretary of State and a fairly gallant general. As for the Horace–Gray exchanges, so many of Gray's letters can be read as desperate pleas for notice, love letters from a hyperliterate, that Horace's lost replies must either have been the verbal equivalent to buckets of cold water or equally and responsively passionate. His exchange of letters with West was quite different: eminently proper in emotional tone, tiresomely academic and literary in content. Hence very few of Horace's letters to either Henry Conway or Thomas Gray between 1734 and 1739 have been suffered to survive, but his replies to West are generously represented, no doubt also because Horace still felt proud, many years later, of their precocious pedantry.

Richard West was the orphan son of a successful lawyer who had been briefly Lord Chancellor of Ireland and then supposedly been poisoned by his wife when his son was only ten years old. But that melodramatic circumstance is the kind of event Richard West would have relished and might easily have invented. In 1734, when he left Eton, West seems already to have been dying of tuberculosis: a Hamlet in terminal self-pitying decline. Encouraged by his tutors at Eton, and probably by his 'Quadruple Alliance' friends, he believed he was a poet and his letters are a mix of prose-wit and derivative verse deliberately modelled on Petronius's writings. Scholarship trickles out with the ink from his pen. Worse still, in his replies Horace imitated this pedantry, concealing his natural gift for clear expression and sharp communication in mere artifice.

West would begin a letter in a pedantic jumble of English and Latin that should be savoured:

> My dearest Celadon
> > *Crimine quo merui juvenum placidissime -*
> After a long and tedious melancholy silence comes a letter, or rather the shadow of a letter, so short – I thought it a dream indeed.
> > *Tu querar, ah Celadon, (nisi differat aura querelas)*
> > *vel scripsisse parum, vel siluisse nimis.*
> Suffer then my poor little desponding letter to make its appearance before all like a ghost wrapped up in a white sheet, and to make its apology thus –

Then follows an interminable quibble about the merits of Statius. Horace, infected by this verbiage, would reply in the same vein. Here he is railing priggishly about his studies in Cambridge:

> I have been so used to the delicate food of Parnassus, that I can never condescend to apply to the grosser studies of Alma Mater. Sober cloth of syllogism colour suits me ill; or, what's worse, I hate clothes that one must prove to be of no colour at all. If the Muses *coelique vias et sidera monstrent*, and *quia vi maria alta tumescent* why *accipiant*: but 'tis thrashing, to study philosophy in the obstruse authors.

Bombarded with bad verse, English and Latin, from West, Horace would open with a straight lie, 'I don't think I am at all a poet, but from loving verses, try to make some now and then.' Such Rococo efforts as:

First when pastorals I read;
  Purling streams and cooling breezes
I only wrote of; and my head
  Rhymed on, reclined beneath the treezes:
In pretty dialogue I told
  Of Phoebus' heat, and Daphne's cold.

But the warm bath of West's flattery induced such offerings: 'I own I ought to be deterred from tacking verses to the end of my letters,' West wrote, 'since I have read yours, where the prose and the poetry are both so exquisite that for the future I shall never venture to send you either except when I am in a dream as at present', after which came a version of *'O fons Bandusiae'*, followed by a little critical theory.

To the end of his life Horace Walpole believed that he was not only a letter-writer but also a poet. If in critical retrospect he is to be allowed a talent for light verse and brisk, rhyming pornography, then it was West who in these years convinced him of his ability. 'I can never forget,' Horace wrote affectionately, 'the many agreeable hours we have passed in reading Horace and Virgil'. This was more true than he realized; the blight upon eighteenth-century poetasters was their classical education. Saturated at school with Roman poetry, they naturally transposed its style, its images, inversions, figures of speech, vocabulary, even at times its metres, from one language to another, with deadly results. Yet West had not only read Shaftesbury's contemptuous analysis of his contemporaries in his *Characteristicks*, but had actually quoted some of it to Horace: 'there is hardly anywhere to be found a more insipid race of mortals than those whom we moderns are contented to call poets, for having attained the chiming faculty of language, with an injudicious random use of wit and fancy.' Which was an exact description of the verbal junk the two young men were exchanging. West claimed that poets must respond to Nature 'in a superior light to other mortals', but when Horace politely suggested a few lines on his father's Thatched House in Richmond Park, West poured out 127 lines resembling Milton's *Il Penseroso* crossed with Thomson's *Seasons*, in just that 'chiming faculty of language' that Shaftesbury had scorned.

In another poem, called *'Ad Amicos'*, to the severed friends of the 'Quadruple Alliance', West began,

> Yes, happy youth, on Camus sedgy side,
> You feel each joy that friendship can divide;

and concluded, 'and this I send you and my friends at Cambridge, not to divert you, for it cannot, but merely to show them how sincere I was when sick'. Gray replied wickedly: 'If what you sent me last be the product of your melancholy, what may I not expect from your more cheerful hours?' Gray was treacherously ambivalent about the Walpole–West friendship. While his letters to West are full of 'esteem and admiration', he would write to Horace, 'I have had a letter from West with an elegy of Tibullus translated in it t h u s l o n g.' On another occasion Gray wrote maliciously to his 'dearest Horace': 'I received a long letter, mighty pretty, in Latin from West yesterday, partly about buttered turnips, partly about an eclipse, that I understood no more than the man in the moon; he desired his love to you in English.' So West's Petronian effusions were becoming something of a joke in Cambridge, or, if they were not, Gray was trying to project them as such.

But Gray and West were in reality two of a kind. In those days of 'Tar Water' and 'Joshua Ward's "Drop and Pill"' cure, neuroticism was allowed to run its natural, sometimes useful, sometimes fatal, course. Today they would both have been dosed with anti-depressants. Neither had ever quite recovered from the safe enclosing environment of Eton and the life of scholarly fantasy that Horace had spun around them there. When they left they clung instinctively to Horace as if to a pledge that the days of poetry, Petronius, wine and roses might return again. The remarkable achievement of Horace was that in Gray's case those days did, in some measure, come back.

To turn from West's letters to Gray's is to move from the moribund to the living. West needed Horace; Gray also needed Horace, but in addition he loved him. In those first two Cambridge terms, when Gray and Ashton had gone up but Horace was diverting himself in London, Gray's letters burn with impatience, his rapturous affection and longing only half-hidden by humour, as in his pastiche Levantine love letter to Horace in the style of *The Turkish Spy* which he had just read:

> I have beheld thee in my slumbers, I have attempted to seize on thee ... We were as two Palm-trees in the Vale of Medina, I floursh'd in thy friendship & bore my head aloft, but now I wander in Solitariness, as a traveller in the sandy desarts of Barca, & pine in vain to taste of the living fountain of thy conversation ... When the Dew of the morning is upon me, thy Image is before mine eyes; nor, when the night overshadoweth me, dost thou depart from me. Shall I e'er behold thine eyes, until our eternal meeting in ye immortal Chioscs of Paradise?

And when, after a whole winter term Horace was still only expected, Gray wrote:

> I, Orazmades, Master of the noble Science of Defence, hearing of the great reputation of thee, Timothy Celadon, do challenge and invite thee to attend with me at long-love, great affection, or whatever other weapon you shall make choice of, in Kings-College Quadrangle, a Week hence precisely. *Vivat Rex.*

But the week passed, as did another term, and still there was no Horace. Hiding his despair in mock heroicism, Gray ranted: 'Don't believe that I would refuse to do anything for your sake, since at this present I am starving for you, & losing my dinner, that I may have the better opportunity of writing.' At times, as March 1735 approached and Walpole would actually pay his college a call, Gray's impatience began to sound a little like Juliet's 'Gallop apace, you fiery footed steeds':

> Well! be it as it will, you have got my soul with you already; I should think 'twould be better for you to bring it hither to the rest of me, than make my body take a journey to it ... I hate living by halves, for now I lead such a kind of I don't know how – as it were – in short, what the devil d'ye mean by keeping me from myself for so long? I expect to be paid with interest, and in a short time to be a whole thing.

Where West was all dry Latinisms, Gray's language is brilliantly

Saxon, contemporary and alive: 'I can no more think of Logick &
Stuff, than you could of Divinity at a Ball, or a Caudle and
Carraway Confits after having been stuffed at a Christening.' One
of his fellow students from London he described as looking 'like
toasted Cheshire Cheese, strewed with brown sugar'.

Even the poems he wrote – for, to compete with West, there had
to be poems – used living language that almost escapes the gin-trap
of Dryden–Pope diction. One description of a park in Heaven
oddly foreshadows Rupert Brooke's *Grantchester*:

> Here spirit-beaux flutter along the Mall,
> And shadows in disguise skate o'er the iced canal:
> Here groves embowered, and more sequestered shades,
> Frequented by the ghosts of ancient maids
> Are seen to rise: the melancholy scene
> With gloomy haunts, and twilight walks between
> Conceals the wayward band: here spend their time
> Greensickness girls, that died in youthful prime.

Its last lines conceal truth under flippancy:

> Believe that, never was so faithful found
> Queen Proserpine to Pluto underground,
> Or Cleopatra to her Mark Antony
> As Orazmades to his Celadony.

West turned to Virgil and Petronius for models, Gray to
Shakespeare and to playwrights like Congreve and Wycherley.
Gray was alive and in love; he thought that Eton was going to be
renewed in Cambridge and he expressed his feelings by writing to
Horace Walpole with the breathless enthusiasm of John Keats's let-
ters to Fanny Brawne.

Being English and upper-class, Horace inevitably snubbed Gray
when the much anticipated reunion finally took place. After March
1735 Gray's letters are never quite so eager. He was reminded of
his place as Horace flitted fashionably back and forth from
London. Horace, conscious of his power, played cruel games with
him. He pretended that there was a possibility he might get married. This left Gray almost incoherent with dismay:

You are a very different person behind the scenes, and whatever face you set upon the matter, I guess – but perhaps I guess wrong: I wish I may for your sake; perhaps you are as cool as you would seem: either way I may wish you joy: of your dissimulation, or philosophy.

He ended the letter humbly, falling back into the safe animal imagery of childhood:

Bear I was born, and bear, I believe, I'm likely to remain; consequently a little ungainly in my fondness, but I'll be bold to say, you shan't in a hurry meet with a more loving poor animal, than
Your faithful creature, Bruin

Though conscious of the class gap between himself and Gray, Horace never became indifferent to Gray's command of language or the promise of his style. There would be treachery, disappointment and jealousy ahead but, for all the bitterness of their later quarrel in Italy, Horace would come back for a reconciliation and urge Gray to publish and achieve his potential. Poetically, Horace was never unfaithful to the one-time lover, even when that hopeful young man had turned into an eccentric and retiring don, old before his time.

Apart from these friendships, Walpole's Cambridge years appear to have been a time of wasted opportunity. He never concealed the fact that he found the place wanting and also architecturally inferior to Oxford. In his day, the Backs were still largely commercial, with none of their present coherence and flowery charm. Cambridge's colleges were of brick and uncleaned. The amazing Gothic certainties of King's Chapel had been counterpointed in 1723 by the blank classical statement of the Gibbs Building. Walpole later made a point of his preference for Oxford because it retained 'the true Gothic *un-Gibbs'd*'. Cambridge also represented academic failure for Horace. He claimed in his *Short Notes on the Life of Horace Walpole* to have streamed tears of humiliation when his half-blind professor of mathematics dismissed him as unteachable. Then he studied music for a while, only to be bored by it; he listened to lectures on anatomy that seem only to have given him a lifelong mistrust of doctors, and his conventional Christian faith was turned into the standard, blasé eighteenth-century deism by the theologian Conyers Middleton.

Horace's religiosity is best described as a 'purple area', one wholly illogical and inconsequential. Middleton taught him that prayer was a delusion and that large sections of the Old Testament were nonsense. There was a favourite Middleton lecture on the links between ancient pagan practices and the modern rites of the Roman Catholic church in Italy. All this Horace absorbed readily enough, as it allowed him to feel superior. But aesthetically he found Catholic church services with their music, vestments, incense and ceremonial irresistible. While he was in Italy he behaved as an honorary Catholic, still claiming to despise priestly authority and corruption. Back in England he felt unthreatened by Catholicism and even starved of its pomp. An occasional Church of England service, like the funeral of George II, pleased him well enough, but he still needed to play-act Catholicism with incense and candles in a private chapel at The Vyne, Hampshire where he enthusiastically assisted the improvements of his friend John Chute and was a frequent visitor. Eventually he added a pseudo-chapel, the Tribune, a cross between a church and an art gallery, to Strawberry Hill.

A man with Horace's love of the past and his delight in ruins and old churches could never be a complete deist. By making him an infidel, Dr Middleton set up a basic contradiction in Horace's mind between what he believed and what his natural instincts directed. The intensity of this internal spiritual conflict should not be underestimated. The success of evangelical sects in his contemporary society did not merely disturb him, it enraged him, particularly when, as in the Countess of Huntingdon's Connection, the proselytizing was successful among the aristocracy. If Horace had any real belief, it was the belief that 'Enthusiasm' was an evil.

His more positive influences during this period were the letters he received from Lord Hervey and a new Cambridge friend and mentor, usually referred to in the whimsical Etonian style as 'Plato'. From these letters it is clear that as early as 1735 and 1736 when he was just out of school and only eighteen or nineteen years old, Horace was already a stylistic rebel and a natural eclectic, but attracted at that time not to Gothic, or to the mainstream classicism of the day, but to the exotic potential of chinoiserie.

Lord Hervey, *cicisbeo* to Queen Caroline and the courtier who contrived to pass Sir Robert Walpole's political needs on, via the queen, to King George II, had recognized in Horace a fellow spirit. In 1735 Jean-Baptiste Du Halde's four-volume *Description géographique, historique, chronologique, politique et physique de l' empire de la Chine* had been published in Paris and Lord Hervey gave the volumes to Horace as a present. Horace was instantly taken by them and wrote back a lost but apparently enthusiastic letter of thanks. Hervey's reply to this was remarkably wise and prescient. 'You describe,' he wrote, 'in a very entertaining manner the change it has made in you,' but, he continued, 'nothwithstanding my partiality to China, I advise you if you can to continue an Englishman.' And that, of course, was exactly what Horace was to do. After a few years of dabbling in the Chinese fringes of Rococo design in the 1740s, he realized that he was in a stylistic dead-end and moved out into the much wider and satisfyingly nationalistic fields of Rococo–Gothick. He continued an Englishman, in Lord Hervey's words, while remaining an eclectic rebel.

Du Halde's book was an expensive and thoughtful present. This suggests that Horace and Lord Hervey were already well acquainted. Hervey was exactly the older, worldly-wise and sophisticated man whom Horace would have been likely to choose as a role-model. He was physically small and delicately pretty, given to malicious wit and epigrams. Though married, Hervey had conducted sexual affairs with Stephen Fox, later Lord Ilchester, and with Count Algarotti: a combination of sexual deviancy with rank which Horace would have found sympathetic. From his central position in court and politics, Hervey had written detailed and amusing memoirs of the reign of George II, but ended them abruptly with the death of Queen Caroline in 1737. It is likely that when Horace began his *Memoirs of the Reign of George II* he was consciously taking up the task which Hervey had laid aside.

That was all a decade away. Hervey's letter was dated 21 October 1735; a few days earlier Horace had received a cheerful, joshing letter from 'Plato' offering in a more practical form the same advice as Lord Hervey had given: put England first and China second.

Some mystery has been made over the identity of 'Plato'. He is mentioned in letters from Horace, West and Gray; he was clearly another Etonian but, as his nickname indicates, a superior figure, a guide and a philosopher though given to hard drinking and hearty eating. He was John Whaley, a fellow of King's College since 1731 and Horace's private tutor; he had been a sixth-former at Eton for two years when Horace had been in the lower school. William Cole, who had been his contemporary at both Eton and Cambridge, described him as a very suspect character with a 'turn for a dissolute and debauched kind of life ... yet as he was reckoned a man of genius and a poet, a good jolly companion, a singer of a good song, and rather a genteel person, his company was sought after, and he spent his time in a continual scene of jovial amusements and mirthful society.'

There is more than an element of sour grapes in Cole's attack. Whaley was obviously in the grand tradition of Cambridge – and more particularly of King's College – tutors: sophisticated and charming bachelors who delight in the company of young men and gather them up into a circle of self-indulgence and influence. John Whaley's particular line was to take one or two favoured students off on antiquarian and topographical jaunts exploring the English countryside and visiting the houses of the aristocracy to discuss their architecture and art collections. It was while he was leading one such tour in the Long Vacation of 1735 that he had written the anti-Chinese letter to Horace.

This was addressed 'From the Devil's Arse', a cave outside Buxton which Whaley's party had explored by candlelight. After a brisk account of the Derbyshire scenery and the glories of Chatsworth, a house which he compared to Milton's Pandemonium, Whaley ended with the hope that this might take Horace's mind off the Chinese and 'break off your devotion while you are sticking a pig with a mandarin on the top of a mountain in the province of Quenton'. The bait proved successful and next Easter Whaley took Horace and his friend John Dodd on a

Midlands tour of Wrest, Althorp, Easton Neston, Oxford and Blenheim. What is remarkable, however, in the written responses to these two tours – Whaley's to the earlier and Horace's to the later – is the superiority of Horace's writing. Whaley is superficial, topographical in the Defoe manner; Horace is richly descriptive, sensitive to textures, to the details of portraiture and the charm of decay. Whaley had fired his interest in the decorative arts, architecture, ancestry and the atmosphere of old houses, but already Walpole was his tutor's superior in his eye for detail and in his style.

Horace's very first topographical letter was written to George Montagu on 20 May 1736 in the gossipy vein of so many revealing accounts to come. First came a spiteful comment from the 'Mrs Housekeeper' at Wrest, the Duke of Kent's house: the portrait of the Duchess was 'too handsome; her Grace's chin is much longer than that'. Then came the feminine detail: 'old Dame de Greys, in a gown of her own work, embroidered all over with little flowers of all colours, like the border of an under-petticoat, round her head is a kind of hoop-petticoat of gauze.' At Cornbury he noted 'a prodigious quantity of Vandykes' and was irritated at being hurried past them, his cataloguing instinct already alert. At Easton Neston, in a perceptive visual flash, he noted that 'in an old greenhouse is a wonderful fine statue of Tully, haranguing a numerous assembly of decayed emperors, vestal virgins with new noses, Colossuses, Venuses, headless carcasses and carcassless heads, pieces of tombs and hieroglyphics'. With a precocious eye for quality, he had spotted nothing less than the Arundel Marbles, neglected and undervalued.

It was this appreciation of textured decay, this delight in the inappropriate accidents of time that would make him such a perceptive antiquary and adventurous aesthete. At twenty years of age, his style was already the perfect servant to his taste. All he needed, and at that time found in an idle George Montagu, was a sympathetic reader and partner in feeling. Somewhere along the line he would find John Whaley inadequate and too obviously set on using him to gain preferment from Sir Robert Walpole, but in these early Cambridge years, in spite of his 'dissolute and debauched kind of life', Whaley was a valuable and positive influence.

*

It was during Horace's university years that he began to appreciate his father and move tentatively into a new role as a dutiful son. In 1737 his mother had died. According to his friends, Horace was ravaged by grief, but he would never be a person to underplay an emotion or miss a chance to dramatize sorrow. The only letter that survives to indicate any reactions to his mother's death, one to Charles Lyttelton, is remarkably stoic, praising 'the surprising calmness and courage which my dear mother showed before her death'. He noted that 'few women would behave so well, and I am certain no man could behave better. For three or four days before she died, she spoke of it with less indifference than one speaks of a cold; and while she was sensible, which she was within her last two hours, she discovered no manner of apprehension. This, my dear Charles, was some alleviation to my grief.' Written on 18 September, when his mother had died on 20 August, this letter does not suggest a mind almost unhinged by grief as some of his friends claimed to fear. As Henry Conway sensibly told him: 'Don't think what a mother you have lost but how good a father you still have, than whom as nobody is more able, so I am sure nobody is more willing to make you happy.'

Horace needed no prompting. He had begun to visit Houghton as early as 1735 and his response to what must have been among the most vulgarly glittering and sumptuous Palladian palaces in Europe was remarkable. He ignored entirely the great building, then nearing completion. Instead he struck up a pose: 'I spent my time at Houghton for the first week almost alone; we have a charming garden all wilderness; much adapted to my romantic inclinations.' At such moments Horace in his wilful perversity sounds like Evelyn Waugh's Sebastian Flyte, but if he had not developed this early habit of contrary responses there would never have been a Strawberry Hill or the whole episode of Gothic exhibitionism.

Towards his father, the apparently permanent Prime Minister of Great Britain, Horace's letters at this stage were carefully worded and strictly conventional. Thanking him after a brief visit in 1736, Horace implied that the real attraction of Houghton was that it was his father's creation, a tactful evasion of his indifference to the architecture of the house. He ended quickly, 'I will not detain you by endeavouring to express in a long letter, what the longest could never do, my duty and admiration. I beg these short lines and all my actions may convince you how much, I am, Sir, Your most dutiful son, Hor. Walpole.' This solemn mask of filial devotion was only one of several – passionless aesthete, earnest poet, man-about-town – that Horace, a natural masquerader, chose to put on. Soon, on the other side of the Alps, these masks would begin to fall.

CHAPTER THREE

Waiting for Lincoln

Emotionally, Horace's Grand Tour was the most important episode in his long life. It was not, if honestly appraised, a Grand Tour at all in any normal sense. It was a pursuit of love. Neither architecture, facility in foreign languages nor political experience was Horace's prime motivation as he ranged about Europe; it was the love, in very varying degrees, of three men – Thomas Gray, Henry Conway and Lord Lincoln. Whether they intended to or even knew they were doing so, they directed his itinerary, inspired his contriving and caused his quarrels.

These years and these travels occasioned one of the first great expressions of Romantic feeling for landscape; they emotionally crippled Thomas Gray for life and at the same time set him on a certain course as a poet. They left Horace himself with a sense of guilt at his treatment of Gray so striking that he felt obliged later to compensate by projecting this lost friend into successful publication. More obscurely, the experience of these years left Horace, after initial success in love and ultimate rejection, bitterly biased in the influential commentaries which he was to write about the intrigues and manoeuvring of England's ruling élite over the next twenty years. As an historical source for the period he is, as a result, deeply suspect. That being noted, it is reasonable to enjoy the unfolding of the loves of Horace as a wildly romantic episode that could vulgarly but quite fairly be described as one of the great love stories of the eighteenth century; one that all previous commentators on Horace Walpole have either failed to register or found it expedient to ignore.

As Horace and Gray were preparing, in the Spring of 1739, for a curiously limited tour only of France, Lord Lincoln was coming to the end of his term at Clare College, Cambridge. His private tutor, the Revd John Hume, had been with him at Cambridge to preside over his moral welfare, and more particularly over his health. This concern was understandable. Lincoln's father, the 7th Earl, had died in 1728, and his wife had taken her four children, two boys and two girls, to live with her at Vigan in a supposedly healthy, Protestant area of southern France. Unfortunately her children were frail. Her elder son, the 8th Earl, died in 1730 and Lady Ann, the elder daughter, in 1734. Lord Lincoln, the 9th Earl, was assumed also to be delicate. His uncle, Thomas Pelham Holles, Duke of Newcastle, had no children to succeed to his huge estates in Sussex and Nottinghamshire, and Newcastle's brother, Henry, an equally potent political figure, had only two very young sons and a number of daughters. So, apart from his naturally affectionate, not to say fussy, concern for his nephew–ward, the Duke of Newcastle was anxious to keep Lord Lincoln alive for dynastic reasons.

He was certainly concerned. Something of a family wrangle developed over the young Earl's taking, or not taking, Dr Hubst's powders, a medical regime that was supposed to be strengthening. The Revd Hume in his regular reports to the Duke noted detail as trivial in his charge as 'a little redness in the eyes', and the Duke was a figure of such consequence in the state that even the Master of Clare, Dr Wilcox, was recruited in a process that seems designed to turn a sociable, lively young man into an abject valetudinarian. 'He has no ill, or disorderly Inclinations,' the Duke reported in a letter of early 1739 to Dr Wilcox, 'but, I am afraid, is sometimes led away by Company, which he has not always Resolution to resist. I have laid before him all the Consequences.' There followed a string of trite moral adages, a regular feature of the ducal letters, with a final warning that 'an irregular way of living would not only bring him into the greatest inconveniences; but, as his constitution is very tender and weak, would soon put an end to his days'.

A letter from Lord Lincoln to his concerned uncle ended 'I am your Grace's most affectionate and dutiful nephew,' but insisted, 'I can not take Dr Hubst's prescription,' though he promised to 'take it without interruption' at a future date. Lord Lincoln was already the master of a technique of mingled conciliation and defiance which was to surface again in his Italian letters. He had inherited very little money with his title and was living, out of term-time, at Claremont, that interminable Great Wall of China of a house that John Vanbrugh had designed as an appropriate seat for the dignity of the Pelham Holles dynasty. So his relationship with his guardian was necessarily delicate.

On 17 May 1739, while Horace was suffering Paris society for the first time, the Revd Hume and the Duke were considering a third stage in Lord Lincoln's education that might correct his Cambridge experience which had included friendship with a socially suspect Horace. 'He continues taking his powders which seem to agree with him, and is in general very well,' Hume reassured the Duke. 'He is a little unfortunate in ye choice of his companions, but is drawn into less mischief by them than might be apprehended, his vivacity and parts incline him naturally to gay companions, like himself in one particular, but not in his other good qualities.' Unfortunately Hume does not particularize this 'one particular', but the young lord's 'good qualities' clearly included charm. Between them, Hume and the Duke decided to send Lord Lincoln off to the Continent, not on a conventional Grand Tour, but for a course of gentlemanly instruction abroad. This had been in the air for some time but the details and precise destination had not been finalized.

Meanwhile, Horace was now in France, behaving with characteristic perversity. At Dover he had been seen off by the mayor and on his second night in Paris dined with Lord Waldegrave, the English ambassador; after that, nothing. The French ignored him. Back in England, when dining with his father at Richmond, he had been able casually to introduce Cardinal Fleury, virtual ruler of France for ten years, to his friend West, but in the French capital he complained, 'We have seen very little of the people themselves, who are not inclined to be propitious to strangers, especially if they do not play, and speak the language readily.'

Piqued at this social cold-shouldering of a Walpole, he determined to find all things French inferior. Paris opera was then, as now, a 'penance': 'their music resembles a gooseberry tart as much as it does harmony.' He sat through Moliere's *L'Avare* but could not 'at all commend their performance of it'. The Place Louis le Grand (Vendôme) was 'not so large as Golden Square'. The abbey of St Denis got good marks for its stained glass but the ceremonious funeral of a Marshal of France only pleased a malicious Horace because the friars who were supposed to be praying over the hearse fell asleep, candles set fire to the drapes, the lead coffin melted and the corpse had its feet burnt off. Horace's account to West of this débâcle is a foretaste of his talent for exposing the realities behind the pretensions of an age of façades. To write amusingly and impartially about society, it helps to be an outsider at heart.

For all his expressed disdain for the clothes the French wore, the rouge with which their womenfolk were plastered and their obsession with card games, Horace stayed on in Paris at the Hôtel de Luxembourg in the Quartier Saint-Germain for two months, almost twice as long as he had intended. What is most interesting in all his frigid reactions to the place is his rapturous account of what was one of Paris's least imposing Gothic complexes (it was demolished in 1776), the Chartreux, home to the capital's Carthusians. Horace turned to it after dismissing Versailles, in yet another long letter to West, as 'a lumber of littleness, composed of black brick, stuck full of bad old busts, and fringed with gold rails'. The Chartreux, in contrast, was 'a place of another kind, and which has more the air of what should be, than anything I have yet met with'.

This phrase 'the air of what should be' reveals Horace reaching out towards his aesthetic and spiritual ideal. The Chartreux of Paris stands midway between Eton College and Strawberry Hill in Horace's creative pilgrimage: a place Gothic and faintly melancholy, but human in scale and the confused accretion of several centuries. From an early age Horace Walpole had been a natural rebel against order and regularity of form. He was eventually to subvert Thomas Gray, who had been delighted by the garden front of Versailles, into a similar, though more nervously tentative, appreciation of romantic chaos.

At the Chartreux, sited in the back garden of the Hôtel de Luxembourg where he was staying, Horace found 'all the conveniences, or rather (if there was such a word) all the *adaptments* are assembled that melancholy, meditation, selfish devotion, and despair would require. But yet 'tis pleasing. Soften the terms, and mellow the uncouth horror that reigns here, but a little, and 'tis a charming solitude.' And that is exactly what he would do a decade later at Strawberry – soften the terms, mellow the uncouth horror and produce a charming suburban solitude, Twickenham instead of Saint-Germain. For a natural bachelor like Horace, a man devoted to the ancestry of his family yet perversely determined never to produce a son to continue a faltering family line, the domesticity of the Carthusians' life was very appealing. Once they had penetrated a gloomy chapel, 'some dark passages', 'a large obscure hall, which looks like a combination-chamber for some hellish council' and then the cells, they met a middle-aged monk, Dom Victor, who was permitted to talk to visitors though not to fellow monks – a realization of the Horatian ideal. He had 'four little rooms, furnished in the prettiest manner and hung with good prints. One of them is a library, and another a gallery.' This amiable recluse bred canaries and cultivated 'good tulips in bloom, flowers and fruit trees'. 'We have promised to visit him often,' Horace wrote.

If Henry VIII had not severed the ties with Rome, Horace would perhaps have ended up as Abbot of Glastonbury or, for the sake of the scenery, Fountains. As soon as he and Gray landed at Calais they were attending high mass in the 'Great Church' there and buying knitted knick-knacks from Mrs Davis, an English Dominican nun. Immunized against faith by Dr Middleton at Cambridge, Horace could afford to luxuriate in all the outward pomps and mysteries of Catholicism, and did. Strawberry Hill was to be his Chartreux realized. For him an ideal residence had to grow piecemeal.

As their stay in Paris lengthened, Horace grew ever more short-tempered and Gray more perplexed. The whole expedition had from the start been left deliberately unplanned. There had never been any intention of making a conventional Grand Tour down

through France with a year in Italy and a return through
Germany. That would have required the usual 'bear-leader', a
learned clergymen to 'govern' Horace's whims and direct their
itinerary: the last thing he wanted. He had sold the project to his
father as a stay in France to perfect himself in the language, with a
month in Paris and then several months in an appropriate French
city. Rheims had been recommended by Conway's brother, Lord
Hertford, who had stayed there himself. No 'bear-leader' would
be needed and Gray would be a safe companion of proven pliabil-
ity. From the start Gray was only a cover and a cruelly misused
dupe.

Horace had learnt in Cambridge from Lord Lincoln that he was
going to the Continent to complete his education. If Lincoln's own
wishes had been decisive he would have returned to Vigan in the
far south of France, a town where he had friends and to which he
was sentimentally attached after passing a happy childhood there.
Lincoln did, in fact, eventually reach Vigan with Horace in tow,
but that was to be two years ahead. Meanwhile the Revd Hume
was ripe for episcopal promotion after a long and not wholly successful stint with a self-willed charge. His place was to be taken by
the Revd Joseph Spence. When Spence had last acted as a 'bear-
leader' to Lord Middlesex in 1731, he had gone down from Paris
to Dijon where Lord Middlesex had spent the winter at an academy, followed by a stay in Lyons. That was all Horace had known
when he set out in April. His plan was to make for Paris and then
wait. Unfortunately for him, the Duke of Newcastle was wary and
while Horace hung irritably around a city that failed to appreciate
his social importance, Newcastle and Spence had planned a different itinerary. This was based upon education at a strict academy in
Turin where the young aristocrats were locked in at night. Spence
had approved Turin on a previous visit – 'I never saw anything in
my life so regular' – and regularity was what the wilful Lord
Lincoln was believed to need.

Gray, who had initially been intoxicated by the foreignness of it
all, began to grow querulous. Henry Conway and Gray were not
natural associates. Eton linked them, class and profession divided
them. Gray regarded Conway as a military blockhead who had

seen nothing of Paris until the other two began their church crawling. Horace had been afraid to tell Conway, when he had been arranging their rendezvous in the city, who his companion was going to be. Later, when he was in Geneva, Conway would end his letters to Horace with a rude 'ta to Gray' or an abrupt 'service to Grey', spelling his name incorrectly. For Horace, with his addiction to 'selfish devotion', the charm of both young men was their readiness to follow his lead and their proven record of love for him. Their mutual dislike was probably a social asset, as Horace would always be the beloved arbiter of any complaint. Already the tensions were building up. Gray grumbled in a letter to Thomas Ashton that they were to spend a month or two improving their French in Rheims 'and then return hither again', which in the end they did not do. 'This is our present design,' he continued, 'and very often little hankerings break out, so I am not sure, we shall not come back tomorrow.' Even more disturbing had been a hint from Horace that they might be going down 'to seek out cool retreats among the scorch'd rocks of Provence'. When winter came, Gray added scornfully, 'we shall take a trip to Muscovy'.

Waiting for an arrival that could not decently be revealed to either Gray or Conway produced an unhappy atmosphere. 'We are exceedingly unsettled and irresolute,' Gray wrote, 'don't know our own Minds for two Moments together, profess an utter aversion for all Manner of fatigue, grumble, are ill natured and try to bring ourselves to a State of perfect Apathy in which [we] are so far advanced, as to declare we have no Notion of caring for any mortal breathing but ourselves.' When Gray wrote 'we', he obviously meant Horace. Whether he appreciated the reason for all the procrastination is questionable, but Gray was an intelligent young man and he had been at Cambridge for three years with Horace and Lord Lincoln.

Eventually, as the heats of summer were settling in on the tedious flat plains of Champagne, the ill-assorted trio set off for Rheims, a notably dull French town with a sublime cathedral, inexhaustible stores of sparkling wine and very little else. Their stay in the city lasted more than three months, from 3 June to 7 September, and from their letters it is plain they were dreadfully bored there. When Horace returned to France in the 1760s his

French was still inadequate to the requirements of polite society, so Rheims had not even served its purpose as a language school. Three bored Englishmen staying in a French city will spend far too much of their time talking to each other in English to be able to pick up good colloquial French; though Gray claimed in one letter that they had become so irritable with each other that they had resorted to sign language. Many years later, after Gray's death, Horace was shown one of the letters he had written to West from Rheims. 'I had disgusted him,' Horace observed, 'but my faults were very trifling and I can bear their being known, and forgive his displeasure.' The letter was, however, destroyed: a measure of that forgiveness.

So little of any interest occurred in the long Rheims summer of card parties and evening collations that Horace spent a whole letter to West describing a morning when a wild young Irish mercenary surprised him in 'his trim white night gown and slippers' and insisted on discussing military tactics. 'I hope our memoirs will brighten,' Horace ended, 'at present they are but dull, dull as Your humble servant ever, HW.'

Against expectation, it was Gray, not Horace, who wrote the description of an impromptu episode, evocative of *A Midsummer Night's Dream* or some Fragonard painting, in a garden in Rheims. Supper was served on the grass 'by the side of a fountain under the trees'. A woman of the party began to sing, 'From singing we insensibly fell to dancing, and singing in a round; when somebody mentioned the violins, and immediately a company of them was ordered: Minuets were begun in the open air, and then came country-dances.' Finally, as dawn approached, they all went home still singing and dancing in the streets.

A week later Horace tried to repeat the alfresco elegance, but the moment had passed. This was the Rococo sophistication, pastoral, casual yet refined, that Horace was to enjoy again and memorably describe one May day of 1763 at Esher Place, William Kent's Gothick conversion of a Tudor gatehouse in Surrey. At its best, the Gothick had always an informal Rococo spirit clinging about its shoulders; its essential form, as Horace would first practise it, was amateur and romantic.

An unexpected visit to Rheims by the two world-weary Georges, Selwyn and Montagu, Etonian friends inevitably, prolonged the stay there for four wearisome weeks. Horace had intended, and this was an essential part of his plot, to leave on 20 July. Burgundy was to have been their destination, 'in our way only,' wrote a suspicious Gray, 'as it is said to Provence, but People better informed [by which he presumably meant Henry Conway] conceive that Dijon will be the end of our expedition, for me, I make everything that does not depend on me, so indifferent to me, that if it be to go to the Cape of Good Hope I care not.' From his resigned tone, it is plain that Gray was becoming the victim of the enterprise. Lured by the promise of travel in luxury with the son of a Prime Minister, he was finding himself in a false position. His own deep affections for Horace were no longer meeting with any response, only sign language and evasions. Henry Conway was good-looking, uncongenial and aristocratic, also there was some unseen and mysterious unknown whose movements were dictating the ill-matched trio's travels about France.

That enchanting account of a night of music and dancing at Rheims is a reminder to a side of Thomas Gray that can easily be forgotten behind the repressed and depressive poet–don of his sad maturity. Until Horace betrayed his affections and left him the mortified spectator to an upper-class love duo, Gray had, despite his gloomy turns, an infectious, near manic zest for life. Horace may only have taken him abroad to satisfy his father that he had a respectable companion and to give cover to his real intentions, but he would still have been aware of Gray as the dancer in the streets of Rheims, the man who had arrived at Calais seasick but still found it 'a very pretty town'. The opera in Paris which Horace had dismissed sourly as 'a greater penance than eating maigre', had been for Gray a delightful hoot, a 'grand Orchestra of Humstrums, Bagpipes, Salt-boxes, Tabours and Pipes'. His, and at the time almost certainly Horace's, reaction to the 'absurdity' had been 'to express it by screaming an hour louder than the whole dramatis personae'. After love, shared laughter is a very binding response.

At last, released from the chore of entertaining the two Georges and with the news that Lord Lincoln would soon be crossing the

Channel, Horace's party hurried south from Rheims to the supposed 'end of our expedition', Dijon, arriving there on 9 September. Horace wrote no letters between July and late September; Gray had reacted positively to the pastoral charm of the Marne valley. Dijon with its skyline spiked by towers and its fine town houses he found 'one of the gayest and most agreeable little cities of France', a place 'to make us regret the time we spent at Rheims'. Horace did not find it agreeable. Lord Lincoln was not expected at Dijon after all.

What was to have been their destination now only kept the trio four days. There was time for a visit to the local Carthusian abbey, something of a theme now in Horace's wanderings, and then they were off to Lyons. Gray found this 'the dismallest place in the world, but the number of people, and the face of commerce diffused about us, are, at least, as sufficient to make it the liveliest'. It had also been the next port of call after Dijon when Joseph Spence had been bear-leading Lord Middlesex seven years earlier. There, as Gray reported, the only company was from English travellers passing through on the standard route over the Mont Cenis to Italy. But at last in Lyons, after an otherwise inexplicable nine days in an ugly industrial city, the paths of Lincoln and Spence crossed with those of Horace. Lincoln had arrived in Calais on 14 September and dined ritually in Paris with Lord Waldegrave, the ambassador, on 17 September. He and Spence reached Lyons on 24 September but naturally spent only one night there before hurrying on over the still clear and open Alpine passes to reach Turin on 2 October.

For Horace, it was a disaster. At least he now knew Lincoln's destination but he had only asked his father, Sir Robert, for permission to travel in France. A European war was brewing and the son of a Prime Minister had to move with politic caution. So, instead of chasing over the Alps before the winter snows fell, Horace was obliged to hang about around Lyons, explaining the complete change of plan to a half-delighted, half-puzzled Gray and waiting until Sir Robert gave the word for an Italian extension to his journey. Henry Conway could be escorted to Geneva, where he had commitments, but Horace decided to make a dog-legged detour on that trip to take in the father-house of all Europe's Carthusian monasteries, St Bruno's greatest foundation, the Grande Chartreuse high up in the mountains of Savoy. Perhaps he was hoping to find a complex as Gothic, picturesque and congenial as the Chartreux in his Parisian back garden. What actually resulted was the most aesthetically significant event of the whole Continental tour and one refreshingly apart from its otherwise insistent emotional preoccupations.

At Les Echelles on the Guiers Vif the young men abandoned the *chaise* that had carried them that far and took to horses, or perhaps mules, to follow the ominously named Guiers Mort into the real Massif de la Chartreuse. For all three, being southern English, it was the first baptism in wild Nature and perfectly scaled to impress without horrifying. A month later Horace and Gray would cross the Alps with none of the stunned exhilaration they had experienced in this six-mile ride up from St Laurent du Pont to the Grande Chartreuse. That route up the gorge, not greatly changed today, offers the sublime in digestible portions. It shook Horace from his self-absorption and gave him a new visual dimension which he never lost. 'But the road, West, the road!' he exclaimed in a first letter after a long literary silence. 'If I could send you my letter post between two lovely tempests that echoed each other's wrath, you might have some idea of this noble roaring scene, as you were reading it.'

They climbed, he wrote, 'winding round a prodigious mountain, and surrounded with others, all shagged with hanging woods, obscured with pines or lost in clouds! Below a torrent breaking through cliffs, and tumbling through fragments of rocks! Sheets of cascades forcing their silver speed down channelled precipices, and hasting into the roughed river at the bottom.' Unlike the true Alps, this Massif is acceptable, just, to an eye trained by the paintings of Claude or Poussin. Its limestone rocks are delicately sculpted, not broken, thousand-foot cliffs are softened by trees, the water of the river runs clear and green, not grey and ugly with snow-melt. And here and there the gorge gives a hint of a landscaped park feature, as Horace eagerly noticed: 'Now and then an old foot-bridge, with a broken rail, a leaning cross, a cottage or the ruin of a hermitage.'

As the gorge turned left, opening into a valley, the monastery itself came into view. It was an anticlimax. The buildings were not Gothic but seventeenth-century and notably well ordered. A courteous guest-master set an austere meal before them and offered lodging for the night, but Horace had been caught up in a more natural rapture of rocks and rushing waters. The Grande Chartreuse was far too grand for his ideal retreat. After two hours they were on their way back down the gorge, under the overhanging cliffs, past the soaring Pic d'Oeillette to recollect in tranquility. 'Did you ever see anything like the prospect we saw yesterday?' Horace demanded. 'I never did.'

It is fascinating to speculate whether Horace fired Gray to enthusiasm over this episode or whether Gray fired Horace. Gray described the gorge in a letter and a journal at the time, then a month later penned the celebrated reflection: 'Not a precipice, not a cliff, but is pregnant with religion and poetry. There are certain scenes that would awe an atheist into belief, without the help of other argument. One need not have a very fantastic imagination to see spirits there at noon day.' Later, on his forlorn return journey to England, he went out of his way to visit the place again. But it was the monastery itself, not the gorge, that was the primary attraction for him, exactly the reverse of Horace's reaction. Gray wrote a Latin poem in the guest-book on this second visit, yearning for a secluded life and 'the enjoyment of these enviable halls and the sacred law of silence'; but by that time, after the meeting in Reggio, he had given up on human love. If he wrote anything else besides the Latin verse, it has been lost. In response to enquiries the present Père Archivist gives a sweet smile and says that the monks destroyed the visitors' book in the nineteenth century because Voltaire had written such a rude entry. So should faith always triumph over scholarship!

As for the question of who enthused whom, the letter-writer or the poet, Walpole wins on points. His response has an intoxicated commitment lacking in Gray's nervous reaction. Horace will take risks with precipices; Gray measured the width of the road exactly and was uneasy to find it 'commonly not six feet broad'. To Horace it was sheer visual excitement, for Gray a theological argument. Henry Conway's feelings were not recorded but a gallant young officer would no doubt have laughed nonchalantly at danger. Horace at least seems always to have envisaged Conway as a soldier hero of romance.

Horace and Gray left him at Geneva, a Protestant welfare state, 'small, neat, prettily built', which delighted Gray's orderly, essentially unromantic mind, and returned to Lyons. Sir Robert's permission for an extension of their tour to Italy had come through, so the scheme of wintering in the south of France was laid aside. They had left it late for crossing the Alps but Horace assured Gray that when they reached Turin they would rest after the fatigues of the journey. Gray's comment on that assurance is lost, edited out of the letter by one of Horace's later friends, the Revd William Mason.

Even allowing for their dramatic exaggerations, Horace and Gray had a hard crossing. The valley of the Arc which they followed up towards the Mont Cenis pass is particularly ugly. Clumsy giants appear to have quarried the slopes and left their ruins lying around the stream-bed at the bottom. Gray wrote of 'the savageness and horror of the place'; there was no repetition of their exhilarating experiences at the Grande Chartreuse. Instead there was a grotesque incident. Horace, always emotionally self-indulgent, had taken with him to the Continent a pet, a black-and-white King Charles spaniel called Tory, 'the prettiest, fattest, dearest creature'. On this occasion, Tory had been let out of the *chaise* for an airing:

> And it was waddling along close to the head of the horses, on the top of one of the highest Alps, by the side of a wood of firs. There darted out a young wolf, seized poor dear Tory by the throat, and, before we could possibly prevent it, sprang up the side of the rock and carried him off. The postillion jumped off and struck at him with a whip, but in vain. I saw it and screamed, but in vain ... It was shocking to see anything one loved run away with to so horrid a death.

Gray's reaction was characteristic. He described the assailant as 'a great wolf' and was frightened because it might have attacked the horses and resulted in the *chaise* pitching over a precipice. Informed of the incident in a letter, Henry Conway was facetious: 'that little bark pierced my heart with grief! and was more moving

than if he had made a dying speech of an hundred pages.' Tory, he
urged, might now be acting in Olympus as Diana's cupbearer.
Conway ended his letter of cold comfort with an obscure PS indicating that Horace might have taken him into his confidence about
Lord Lincoln and the purpose of the journey: 'tell me dear,
whether you're in earnest about Tosh. You fright I.' If 'Tosh' was
Eton slang for Lord Lincoln, then Conway was wise to be apprehensive.

With their *chaise* dismantled, their feet bound up in bearskins,
furs on their heads and seated in rough carrying chairs, the two
effete young men were carried up over the snows of the Mont
Cenis by drunken quarrelsome porters, two to a chair since they
were only lightweights. Four miles up and six miles down brought
them into Italy and the Kingdom of Sardinia, in whose capital,
Turin, the object of Horace's journey was studying, not too assiduously, the pursuits proper to a gentleman.

CHAPTER FOUR

Meeting at Reggio

If the impression has been given that Horace Walpole was a thoughtless, arrogant homosexual in pursuit of a typical 'queer's victim' – a much younger, frail, handsome youth, unaware of the perils of seduction and helpless in the coils of a predatory schemer – then that impression needs to be corrected. Horace was a small man, delicately built with a face that could, as Rosalba Carriera's pastel drawing convincingly illustrates, be made to look pertly handsome. He walked in a peculiar mincing fashion, in Laetitia Hawkins's description, 'like a peewit', his legs splayed out from his knees and stepping 'on tip-toe as if afraid of a wet floor'. If he had a good feature then it was his eyes which were large and lustrous in a narrow face. As several quotations have already suggested, he was given, in moments of animation, to screaming.

Lord Lincoln, on the other hand, was a charming tearaway, a widow's son with a real gift for manipulation. In 1733, before he went to Eton and when he was only thirteen, he was living away from his mother at Montpellier, bilingual and self-confident, better employed, or so his mother earnestly assured him, writing letters to her 'than roving any streets either in France or England'. The boy playmates he had left behind him in Vigan 'have never been merry since you went'. One of them, little Villars in particular, 'can't forbear crying when I joke with him about it' and had to be eased by the gift of a ring with Lord Lincoln's hair entwined in the metal. Eton seems to have been as turbulent for Lincoln as it was idyllic for Horace. 'I suffer much more whenever you commit a fault than is possible for you to do in the punishment of it,' his mother wrote. And punished he certainly was, flogged in fact. 'I hear you have been engaged in some battles lately and come off victorious, tho' not without danger of civil discipline,' his mother thrilled in another letter; 'I was not displeased to hear of your exploits, tho' I'm afraid your poor B— suffered for it.' 'Pray tell me sincerely,' she quizzed, 'wch of the boys you love best and are most inclined to side with in case of disputes.' With a mother like that, the young lord could hardly fail to grow up manipulative. He did not mention Horace's name as one he loved, though he did name Horace's friend George Selwyn who was three years his senior.

At the age of fourteen Lord Lincoln was being rationed by a nervous mother to two plays and one opera on his visits to London. She was also trying to arrange for a Mr Laroquette to watch over him on his excursions to bull-baiting. In 1735, the year before she died, leaving him entirely to the care of his guardian uncle, Newcastle, Lord Lincoln's physical charms had been modified by an illness, possibly ringworm, and he was having his head shaved regularly. His mother desired 'you will not neglect it being done constantly once or twice a week'. She was impatient 'to see how you do, and whether the medicines agree'. Her death brought no relief from this fretful cosseting, nor did removal to Italy. 'I must beg you not to run the risk to your health, in order to remove a pimple out of your face,' Newcastle fumed, and urged, 'it might not be amiss if you would take Sir Edward Hulse's medicine now. Alternative physick being particularly good at this Season of the Year.'

But if he was spoilt, Lord Lincoln still had the wit to remain loveable. Letters of calm defiance would end 'I will certainly be guided entirely by my dearest uncle's advice' and his 'dearest uncle' would open a letter: 'My dearest boy, never was so much goodness and affection as in your dear letter which I received this day.' After the first week of his new charge, the Revd Joseph Spence reported 'Ld Lincoln I find so sensible, so agreeable and so obliging', like Lord Middlesex but not 'of so strong a make'. Carriera's pastel, drawn in Venice, explains this chorus of rapture: there are captured the long aristocratic nose, the blue eyes, wavy black hair falling to a black ribboned queue down his back, a faultless complexion, that pimple long banished, and full sensual lips; it is a face almost epicene but rescued by humour, self-confidence and a slight malocclusion.

This was the man whose friendship Horace was proposing to renew at that dangerous point when education years are almost over and a man's role is beckoning. Whether the two had ever made physical love at school or university has to be mere speculation. Outstandingly beautiful men are always more likely to have a bisexual past or a bisexual potency simply because they attract the attentions of both sexes. Love to them tends to be the natural and half-acceptable tribute paid to their looks. The plain are usually reassuringly normal in their sexual proclivities. Whatever the obscurity of the Lincoln past, the next five years were to be well documented in letters; but here a fascinating paradox arises: the bisexual earl was proud of the long attachment and seems to have treasured every revealing and often brilliantly written letter that Horace sent him. Horace, the guilty homosexual intent about his posthumous image, destroyed all the earl's letters to him, though judging by references in those that Horace wrote, many of the earl's letters were both affectionate and reassuring. Only two brief notes survive written by Lord Lincoln in the 1760s, long after the affair had been ended by his marriage to Catherine Pelham, a first cousin. In Horace's faintly contemptible later years when he was scurrying about snipping and scissoring incriminating passages from some fine letters and completely destroying others, like Horace Mann's early Roman letters to him, Horace could hardly have imagined that the beloved earl of long silences, a stranger now for thirty or forty years, was still hoarding a time bomb for future detonation and a grave embarrassment for Wilmarth Lewis. For the Pelham Clinton family of Clumber, Nottinghamshire, Lord Lincoln's descendants, kept those Walpole letters, either by natural integrity or mere indifference, and handed them over to Nottingham University which, in its turn, supplied Lewis with clear photocopies for volume thirty of the Yale edition. This he declared regretfully in the introduction was 'not the pleasantest volume of the *Correspondence*'.

And so down that straight avenue of trees, nine miles in length, to Turin, laid out to the delight of the Alp-weary Gray on a classical grid after the destruction of a recent siege. There, in the mixed but superior company of a Sardinian marquis, a Polish earl, a Swiss nobleman and an Irish gentleman, Lord Lincoln was attending an academy abutting onto the grounds of the royal palace 'where my Lord learns to Ride, Fence and Dance'. As if the threesome of Horace, Gray and Lincoln were not emotional confusion enough, at Turin a fourth element became involved: the Revd Joseph Spence, tutor–governor to the earl. Spence's role in the forthcoming events is best explained by looking ahead to a letter which Spence wrote his one-time charge in 1751. It begins 'I love you better than any-body else in the world'. Lord Lincoln seems to have had that impact on other men. The point of Spence's letter was that Lord Lincoln should be grateful to him as he had done his utmost in the past to persuade Lincoln not to marry Lady Sophia Fermor. Spence had been paid by the Duke of Newcastle to guide Lord Lincoln's moral conduct, watch over his health and return him to London free from entanglements. So here was someone with whom Horace had to reach an understanding, such a *modus operandi* as he appears to have achieved with the earl's previous tutor, the Revd Hume.

Horace and Gray rested at Turin for twelve days from 7 to 18 November 1739. Lord Lincoln and Spence had been there since 2 October and they would remain in residence at their academy until 15 September 1740, delayed by a bad sprain to Lincoln's leg. Horace wasted no time in being introduced to the Sardinian court where Lincoln was already a great favourite, admired for his skill, or so he claimed, at handling hounds on the hunting field. For all his delicate beauty, the earl was an out-of-doors aristocrat and sports-man, always ready to strip down and join in competitive athletics. The leg-sprain that incapacitated him was sustained in a jumping contest. Horace was attracted by opposites though ever ready to gig-gle and scream in the company of fan-waving 'decadents'. Lord Lincoln's eager lusts for women made him more, not less, attractive in the eyes of Horace, who already had some experience, with Eton friends like Richard Edgcumbe, in playing the game of sympathetic confidant to other men's heterosexual love affairs.

Twelve days in Turin were long enough for Horace to appraise the impossibility of the situation from his selfish point of view. Lord Lincoln's strict academy kept its students hard at work studying languages in the morning and practising the gentlemanly skills of fencing and riding in the afternoon. As in an Oxford or Cambridge college, they had to be in early at night behind locked doors. In addition, the Revd Spence was on the alert for any attempt to subvert his lordling. He would have been warned by the Duke of Newcastle that bad companions had been the problem in Cambridge and as yet Horace had not had time to flatter his vanity and win him round to more compliant attitudes. Eventually there would have to be a price for Spence's tolerance of the affair between his charge and Horace. Meanwhile Turin had no night-life, even Gray was bored by the place, so a frustrated Horace decided to enjoy the Grand Tour which had been sprung upon him unexpectedly.

From Genoa, Horace's next stopping-place, he wrote, on 21 November 1739, his first letter to Lincoln, trying to persuade him out to that dazzling half-amphitheatre of marble palaces pitched steeply up to face a western sea: 'Here are a thousand inducements; a glorious town, delightful situation, a dear Doge, a French play, and an English Lord Granby; millions of pretty women beside.' Their relations were at that phoney stage, 'we-men-on-the-town-together'. A careful compliment was passed on to the intrusive Joseph Spence, 'he is so much in the way of Mr Hume, I am quite fond of him'; it was essential that he keep on the right side of a possible fellow homosexual, a man of inferior rank but troublesome potential. Then, as was to become a habit with Horace, came a little fling of naughtiness in the PS: an epitaph supposedly noted in leaving Turin:

> Here lies L— L—; Death had wondrous luck
> To overtake him, – *for he was a buck.*

Followed by the arch 'I forebear writing the name at length, because the person is living on whom the epitaph was made. Goodnight, my dear Lord.'
    It seems fair to describe the tone of the letter as intimate, if a lit-

tle clumsy. Lord Lincoln did not follow Horace to Genoa and Spence makes no mention of Horace's stay in Turin in his weekly, gossipy letters to his old mother back in Winchester, though both Walpole and Gray are listed in his notebook of people encountered at their various stopping points. Gray loved Genoa – 'gardens and marble terraces full of orange and cypress trees, fountains, and trellis-works covered with vines' – but Horace gave him only a few days there; Lord Lincoln was not following. They moved on, church visiting through Reggio, Modena and Bologna, marvelling at the purity of castrati voices in the choirs, still grumbling about the awfulness of the Paris opera, and came down over the rainy Apennines to Florence, with Gray observing in his usual appreciative form how tremendous the prospect of the city would have been, if only they could have seen it through the clouds.

Horace was in no such positive mood. He had enjoyed only a few days with Lincoln at Turin under the Revd Spence's chaperonage and with no time to come to an accommodation with Spence, even if that had been possible. The course at the Turin academy, which Spence likened in its strictness to New College, Oxford, would last until the summer. Horace had only left England with one purpose: to end up in the south of France at Vigan. Italy was an accidental afterthought and where classical architecture was concerned, Horace was no tourist.

'I have left off screaming Lord! this! And Lord! that!', he confided in a letter to West. 'To speak sincerely, Calais surprised me more than anything I have seen since. The farther I travel the less I wonder at anything: a few days reconcile one to a new sport, or an unseen custom: and men are so much the same everywhere. The same weaknesses,' he droned on, 'the same passions that in England plunge men into elections, drinking, whoring, exist here.' With the eye of frustration, he saw happy homosexual couples, or *'Corydon ardebat Alexis'* as he described them in his mannered Etonian style, at every street corner. He was stuck with Gray, fond but unattractive and almost certainly sexually virginal, possibly also more than a little resentful by that time about the purposes of the quest. Horace was coming to see himself as a romantic hero: 'I know the causes that drove me out of England,' he declared in another letter to a probably mystified West, 'and I don't know that they are remedied. But adieu! When I leave Italy, I shall launch out into a life, whose colour I fear, will have more of black than of white'.

It must have taken a considerable effort of will to feel gloomy in Florence at carnival time. The Grand Duchy of Tuscany was in a power vacuum; it was a pro-British Ruritania, committed principally to pleasure. The last Medici Grand Duke had died in 1737. Maria Theresa's husband, Francis of Lorraine, was now the absentee ruler, distant in Vienna and absorbed in Austria's problems. In his place a Marshal of France, the Prince de Craon, was viceroy, though a corrupt Comte de Richecourt, the Finance Minister, really governed. A dreadful old bat from the Walpole attics, Horace's sister-in-law Lady Walpole, long estranged from her husband, Horace's eldest brother, was a Florentine resident pursuing an on-and-off affair with Richecourt while still living with the lover, Thomas Sturgis, with whom she had eloped. But for Horace, the key figure was the acting British Minister, his remote cousin, Horace Mann.

Mann reads like a comic invention. He was a plump, good-natured thirty-eight-year-old bachelor, clinging gamely to the underpaid bottom rung of the diplomatic ladder and making ends meet by running a lodging-house, the Casa Ambrogi, and dealing in antiques. Spying was an integral part of his duties but he had no reliable agents and there was a rival British spy, far more efficient, in the same city. This was a formidable, one-eyed homosexual, the Prussian Baron Stosch. He also was an antique-dealer. Mann, for that matter, was also a homosexual but an inactive one; he suffered terribly from headaches and piles, so no one would have described him as formidable, though Mrs Thrale, Dr Johnson's patron, spotted him as a ' "Finger-twirler" meaning a decent word for Sodomites'. Mann's most surprising role at this stage of Britain's war with Spain was as acting, temporary, unattributable and unpaid Admiral of the Fleet with the power, under certain ill-defined circumstances, to direct Admiral Haddock's squadron, which was coasting off Leghorn to deter a Spanish landing.

Both Horace and Gray took instantly to this eighteenth-century prototype for Our Man in Havana. Mann, for his part, courted Horace assiduously. As the years went by he was to owe his permanent posting, a baronetcy and the Order of the Bath to Horace's influence. The price for these favours was having to respond over a forty-six year period to just under 1800 often rather dull letters. Wilmarth Lewis devoted six volumes to them. At intervals, Mann had to return Horace's letters to be stored away in a trunk as an historical commentary. The two Horaces liked each other but love was not involved. Walpole had simply decided, in his calculating way, that Mann was ideal for a role in the grand design of 'Horace for Posterity'.

Florence became Horace's base for idling around Italy waiting for Lord Lincoln. He was sincerely and obsessively in love with Lincoln and never took advantage of his Italian stay to enjoy the homosexual pleasures that were, as he noticed, so readily available in Florence. He appears never in his life to have been promiscuous. Sexually as well as architecturally, he was a romantic. Now he and Gray lodged first at the Casa Ambrogi, from 16 December 1739 to 21 March 1740. Then, after a ten-week trip to Rome and Naples, they returned to an apartment overlooking the Arno in Mann's grand new ministry, the Palazzo Manetti (from 5 July 1740 to 25 April 1741). After that date Horace was caught up in his own contriving and zigzagged wildly from Florence to Reggio and Venice, then back across the peninsula to Genoa, leaving Italy finally by sea on 28 July 1741, at seven in the morning.

Had it not been for his failure at Turin, there was much about Florence that should have charmed him. The viceroy and his wife were impressed by him and gave an open invitation to sup with them. Their son, the Prince de Beauvau, urged that *'quand même toutes les flottes d'Angleterre auraient coulées à fond toutes celles de France, vous pouvez toujours me regarder comme votre très humble et très obeissant serviteur'*; [even if the English fleet had sunk the entire French fleet, you would always be able to think of me as your most humble and obedient servant]; while his mother praised Horace's friendship above *'tous se qui se trouve precieus en engleterre den la chine et aus indes'* [all that is most precious in England, in China and the Indies].

*

For the reputation of a closet homosexual, the Italian institute of a *cicisbeo* was perfect cover, as a lady's *cicisbeo* could be either sexual or platonic in his affections. Horace swiftly picked up a pretty young married woman, Elisabetta, Marchesa Grifoni, who was very pleased with his undemanding attentions. Horace, for his part, could always imply by a nod or a wink that he was having a great time in bed with her. Until his dying day, he kept her portrait by his bedside at Strawberry Hill as a certificate of sexual propriety. The tone of his letters in this first Florentine period evokes a world of romantic musical comedy: 'I have done nothing' he wrote, 'but slip out of my domino into bed and out of bed into my domino'. Florentines, he claimed, did not use the concealment of a mask to 'catch at those little dirty opportunities of saying any ill-natured thing they know of you ... or talk gross bawdy to a woman of quality'. Gray, the inveterate sightseer, was less pleased by aristocratic high life and wrote after Horace's ceremonious reception by the aged Electress Palatine Dowager, standing under a black canopy, 'so she passes her life, poor woman'. Because it was all new to him and he was untroubled by distractions, Gray wrote home infinitely more descriptive letters than did Horace. Gray was a natural bourgeois outsider who could note at a grand Roman reception the Old Pretender's 'rueful length of person, with his two young ones, and all his ministry about him', while 'I sat in a corner regaling myself with iced fruits and other pleasant rinfrescatives'.

To Horace, it was all high politics and desperately serious. He knew that his father was no natural war minister and that if hostilities with Spain spread to an all-out European war this would give the Old Pretender his first real chance since 1715 to invade Britain and recover the throne for the Stuarts. That would mean, at the best, exile and poverty for all Walpoles, Horace included. It was vital for London to be kept informed of the movements, not only of the Old Pretender, but of his far more dangerous son Prince Charles, the Young Pretender. Charles would eventually surprise not only the British, but his own allies the French by his daring landing in Scotland and the initial successes of the 'Forty-five'.

The trip to Rome to witness a papal coronation was thus a genuine cover to the more serious business of spying on the Stuart court. It was not, however, a success. Any spy mission organized by Mann with Horace Walpole as special agent was likely to be a fiasco. Rome was Jacobite in sympathies and Horace twice sent couriers flying off across Europe by letters to Mann in which he claimed that Prince Charles was on his way to invade Britain, when in reality he was only out in the Campagna shooting quail. On another three occasions Horace tipped Mann off as to the identity of the next Pope and got it wrong every time. Predictably Horace was not impressed by Rome: 'The Cassian and Flaminian ways were terrible disappointments; not one Rome tomb left; their very ruins ruined . . . everything is neglected and falling to decay; the villas are entirely out of repair and the palaces so ill kept, that half the pictures are spoiled by damp.'

Only three things, very oddly assorted, caught his interest on this excursion to Rome and Naples: the excavations at Herculaneum, which he recognized as being of great scholarly importance; a little ruined garden in Rome around the temple of Minerva Medica; and, symbolic of his prevailing mood, a depressing halt on the post road from Florence to Rome:

> Lord! Such a place, such an extent of ugliness! A lone inn upon a black mountain, by the side of an old fortress! No curtains or windows, only shutters! No testers to the beds! No earthly thing to eat but some eggs and a few little fishes! This lovely spot is now known by the name of Radicofani.

As if it responded to a streak of desolate nihilism in his life, he sent another description of the place to Henry Conway. 'I must write to you. 'Tis the top of a black mountain; a vile little town at the foot of an old citadel: yet this, know you, was the residence of one of the three kings that went to Christ's birthday; his name was Alabaster, Abarasser, or some such thing; the other two were kings, one of the East, the other of Cologn'. He meant Balthazar of course. Something in the superstitious piety of the place enraged him, that attraction and repulsion which Catholicism can hold for a confirmed but romantic deist. The rest of the letter is a rant against the local Carthusian convent's hoard of relics: 'a bit of the worm that never dies, preserved in spirits; a crow of St Peter's cock, very useful against Easter; the crisping and curling, frizzling and frowncing of Mary Magdalen, which she cut off on growing devout.'

Yet he rarely missed an opportunity to witness any of the great festivals of the Catholic church. Earlier in their tour at Genoa, Gray had reported smugly but with more than an element of truth, 'I believe I forgot to tell you, that we have been sometime converts to the holy Catholic church.' While during the impressive Easter celebrations at St Peter's where both Horace and Gray pressed to the front of the church to inspect 'a great piece of the true cross, St Longinus's spear, and St Veronica's handkerchief', Gray records that Horace 'saw a poor creature naked to the waist discipline himself with a scourge filled with iron prickles, until he had made himself a raw doublet that he took for red satin torn, and showing the skin through. I should tell you,' Gray added in their usual camp self-mockery, 'that he fainted away three times at the sight, and I twice and a half at the repetition of it.'

Horace was quite unashamed of this mixed attraction and repulsion. In Bologna, where they had no introductions to houses of quality, he wrote, 'Now and then we drop in at a procession, or a High Mass, hear the music, enjoy a strange attire, and hate the foul monkhood!' Prolonged foreign travel often has this power to isolate a traveller from reality, undermining any normal analysis. E.M. Forster made it a theme of *A Passage to India*: a dreadful introspection and a desolating lack of purpose. 'Everybody out of town,' Horace wrote when, tired of waiting for the cardinals to choose a new Pope, they had returned to Florence. 'I have seen nothing but cards and dull pairs of *cicisbeos*. I have literally seen so much love and pharaoh [faro was a popular card game] since being here, that I believe I shall never love either again as long as I live. Then I am got into a horrid lazy way of a morning. I don't believe I should know seven o' clock in the morning again, if I was to see it. But I am returning to England and shall grow very solemn and wise! Are you wise? Dear West, have pity on me, who has done nothing of gravity for these two years, and do laugh sometimes.'

Emotionally deserted by Horace, Gray was building up towards the pressures and state of mind that were to surface in Reggio: 'I have struck a medal to myself,' he confided in a letter to West, 'the device is thus O, and the motto Nihilissimo, which I take in the most concise manner to contain a full account of my person, sentiments, occupations, and late glorious successes. If you choose to be annihilated too, you cannot do better than undertake this journey. Here you shall get up at twelve o'clock, breakfast till three, dine till five, sleep till six, drink cooling liquors till eight, go to the bridge till ten, sup till two, and so sleep till twelve again. We shall never come home again,' he concluded in lotus-eating mood, 'a universal war is just upon the point of breaking out; all outlets will be shut up. I shall be secure in my nothingness.'

It was always poor West, not cheerful, soldierly Conway, who got the full blast of both Horace's and Gray's self-revelations. But West himself was collapsing into a sympathetic neuroticism, confiding his distaste for the law and his despair at finding any purpose in life. Even a military career was beginning to attract him. 'Have you learned to say Ha! Ha!' Gray mocked, 'and is your neck clothed with thunder? Are your whiskers of a tolerable length? And have you got drunk yet with brandy and gunpowder? Adieu, noble captain!' With friends like that it is easy to understand why Richard West would shortly choose to die alone and without their consolation.

Horace killed time with 'small collections – some bronzes and medals, a few busts, and two or three pictures: One of my busts is to be mentioned; 'tis the famous Vespasian in touchstone, reckoned the best in Rome except the Caracalla of the Farnese: I gave but twenty-two pounds for it at Cardinal Ottoboni's sale. One of my medals is as great a curiosity: 'tis of Alexander Severus, with the amphitheatre in brass.' While in Rome he had ordered a statue which would not be finished until September 1741. In these dead days of out-of-season Florence one breeze of artificial animation had blown into Mann's new home, the Palazzo Manetti. This was the arrival of that ultimate in eighteenth century high camp, John Chute, and his party.

*

At this point, with Horace on tenterhooks as Lord Lincoln and Spence's arrival was inexplicably delayed, Chute was only a distraction, possibly an unwelcome one as a whole group of overt, finger-twirling deviants might be expected to have an alarming impact upon newcomers. John Chute was, however, to become one of the most significant and influential of Horace's many friends, so his presence must be registered in an already complex social scene.

Chute was one of those feminine homosexuals who delight in flaunting the most outrageous behaviour, challenging the world to accept them or throw them into a pond. Tall, with a long prominent nose and a recessed chin, he was not easily ignored in company as he waved his fan against the heat and gushed with aggressive *joie de vivre*. Strictly speaking, he was travelling as a paid companion to a washed-out young man with hearing problems called Francis Thistlethwaite, but the impression given to the world was that Thistlethwaite travelled in Chute's train. Against all probability Thistlethwaite, who had changed his name to Whithed in order to inherit a fortune, was a heterosexual who later sired a child in a Florentine love affair. Again and again the events around His Britannic Majesty's Ministry in Florence, or the King's Arms, as Horace called the Palazzo Manetti, read more like an invention by Ronald Firbank than real life.

Chute's influence in the sequence of Italian events should not be underestimated. In the twentieth century he would have fought in the Stonewall riot by homosexuals against the police in New York and marched in Gay Pride weeks. He was as old as Horace Mann and may well have given Walpole the confidence to act as boldly as he did, before and after Reggio. His letters certainly hint, in their arch innuendoes, that he knew more about the Lord Lincoln attachment than Horace Mann ever did. Someone at this time, in late 1740 and early 1741, pushed Walpole, a man usually delighted by women's company provided no sexuality was involved, towards an extreme and even scabrous misogyny. But that could have been influenced by more than one event and by more than one person in Florence that autumn and winter: by Lady Mary Wortley Montagu, the Countess of Pomfret or Pomfret's elder daughter, Lady Sophia Fermor. All three women came to be seen by Horace as obstacles, real or potential, to his love affair with Lord Lincoln.

The Pomfrets were a formidable family group. They had arrived in Florence on 20 December 1739, only a few days after Gray and Horace, and rented the very grand Palazzo Ridolfi with eight acres of garden, a popular trysting place. Lord Pomfret was a nonentity; it was his wife who made the decisions and held weekly 'Conversations' to discuss literary and political topics. She had two daughters, the beauty, Lady Sophia Fermor and the scholar, Lady Charlotte. Horace always claimed to prefer Charlotte, describing Sophia as 'very beautiful and graceful, much prejudiced in favour of her own person, but not to the prejudice of anyone that liked it'. Lady Pomfret had decided that it was time for Sophia to cash in on her good looks and make a favourable marriage, so their Italian tour was not only an education for her daughters but a fishing-trip for husbands.

Lady Mary Wortley Montagu was a very different case. Later on in his life Horace could, and indeed did, take the romantic fifty-one year old adventuress and feminist in his stride, enjoyed her eccentricities and even cultivated her friendship. At this stage, however, she brought out a particularly vindictive and unattractive side to his nature. He already hated his sister-in-law, Margaret Walpole and, by association, her friend, the calculating bluestocking Lady Pomfret. Lady Mary joined the group on 22 August 1740. 'On Wednesday,' Horace wrote, 'we expect a third she-meteor. Those learned luminaries the Ladies P and W are to be joined by the Lady M.W.M. You have not been witness to the rhapsody of mystic nonsense which these two fair ones debate incessantly, and consequently cannot figure what must be the issue of this triple alliance: we have some idea of it. Only figure the coalition of prudery, debauchery, sentiment, history, Greek, Latin, French, Italian and metaphysics; all, except the second, understood by halves, by quarters or not at all. You shall have the journals of this notable academy. Adieu, my dear West.'

By September Lady Mary was in fine form, bringing out the best, that is to say the most spiteful, in Horace's writing:

Her dress, her avarice, and her impudence must amaze anyone that never heard her name. She wears a foul mob, that does not cover her greasy black locks, that hang loose, never combed nor curled, an old magazine blue wrapper, that gapes open and discovers a canvas petticoat. Her face swelled violently on one side with the remains of a pox, partly covered with a plaister, and partly with white paint, which for cheapness she has bought so coarse, that you would not use it to wash a chimney.

Henry Conway relished this description which does indeed flaunt Horace's genius for the concrete and the actual. By October Lady Mary, or 'Moll Worthless' as Horace called her, was cutting out Margaret Walpole on the dance-floor in rivalry, or so Horace claimed, for the affections of an unnamed young Englishman. 'Lady Mary is so far gone,' he told West, 'that to get him from the mouth of her antagonist, she literally took him out to dance country dances last night at a formal ball, where there was no measure kept in laughing at her old, foul, tawdry, painted, plastered personage. She played at pharaoh two or three times at Princess Craon's, where she cheats horse and foot. She is really entertaining.'

If Horace could have seen ahead and known that Lord Lincoln would be equally taken by Lady Mary's personality and sex drive, he might have bitten back that last sentence. What he may well have anticipated was a more serious threat to the Earl's affections from the lovely Lady Sophia Fermor. It was in these last months of 1740 that a complexity of passions and pressures began to build up in Florence, Rome and England. Horace, Gray, Lincoln, Spence, the Pomfrets and even the Duke of Newcastle were all involved, as was Lady Mary, though only peripherally. The crisis would come in May 1741 in Reggio, the second city of the independent Duchy of Modena. But precisely what happened in the first twenty days of that month at Reggio's fair and opera festival will never be worked out because Horace saw to it that all the relevant letters between him and Mann were destroyed.

So many parties were involved in the affair and so much was concealed that all Horace's biographers have been satisfied to accept Lord Lincoln's arrival at Reggio as a happy coincidence that saved Horace from a serious bout of tonsillitis. They have ignored the clear evidence that the two men had been affectionately involved with each other in the seven months previously, that Lincoln's arrival had been planned by Horace weeks before and that for the next three years the two men conducted a clandestine off-and-on love affair after what was, to all intents and purposes, a honeymoon on the French Riviera.

After that warning of events to come, it is necessary to go back a little to follow the frustrations of the Revd Joseph Spence in Turin. Lord Lincoln had become a very much more significant figure in the political and dynastic calculations of the Pelham brothers, Henry Pelham and Newcastle, when Henry's two little sons had died, within a day of each other, in November 1739. Lord Lincoln was now the sole male heir to their titles and fortunes. Lincoln's health thus became of obsessive importance to his two uncles, and not only his health but his marital prospects. The Revd Spence's prime responsibilities were therefore to ensure Lincoln's health and his freedom from unsuitable attachments to women of no fortune. In both he proved a complete failure.

For a start, Spence became quite excited by reports of Lady Sophia Fermor's presence in Italy and of her beauty. This excitement naturally communicated itself to an amorous and competitive young male like Lord Lincoln. Then Spence allowed his charge to injure his leg seriously in a bout of competitive athletics. Lord Lincoln was a very reluctant letter-writer, but on this occasion Spence persuaded him to write a long letter to his uncle Newcastle, explaining the incident. The letter merits quotation because it reveals much of Lord Lincoln's simple but engaging personality. He had been invited to a July house party at the Marquis de Riversols' villa, got drenched to the skin riding out there, stripped and borrowed clothes far too big for him. The accidents continued:

> Walking in the garden after dinner whilst they were preparing every thing for ye Ball, ye Prince proposed jumping with me, for ye diversion of ye Company. Upon that you may be sure I was not a man to refuse a challenge so accordingly we immediately stript and went to it. Among the Piedmontese I made a very considerable figure, happy shd I have been if I had contented myself with ye applause I had just acquired, but greedy of Glory I needs must take up another Champion ... my honour fell in ye dust and I was carried off the field of battle

only to remain in bed for the next month, just when a much agitated Spence had been hoping to be in Rome enjoying the ruins.

More than a week had to be spent at the baths of Aqui near Alessandria, treating a seriously sprained leg. Like most athletes Lincoln spent a good deal of time being hospitalized. But by 27 September Spence was looking forward to meeting Lady Walpole, who was an old friend of his, in Florence and meeting on his way down to Rome the celebrated Lady Sophia. 'Heaven defend the heart of J. Spence' he signed himself off in his weekly letter to his mother.

It was not J. Spence's heart that needed defence. They reached Florence on 21 October and in his next letter Spence reported, 'I was this morning with Lady Walpole (with whom I am a sort of favourite) and this afternoon with Lady Pomfret and her two fair daughters; with whom I should be very glad to be a favourite. My Ld is gone with them to an Assembly.' So, under Spence's complacent gaze, the very relationship which he had been employed to prevent – a love match with a girl of no fortune – was set in train. Horace's feelings are not recorded but he fought back: 'We have got Mr Walpole here again,' Spence wrote in his next letter 'and dine with him almost every day.' So at long last Horace was making the social contact with Lord Lincoln which had been his basic motive for venturing abroad in the first place.

After a month of this three-sided courtship, Lord Lincoln and Spence set off on 28 November for Rome, struggling through the worst floods for many years to settle in lodgings on the Spanish Steps. It was then that a seemingly slight but highly significant incident took place. Lord Lincoln wrote to Horace before Horace wrote to Lincoln. The lord, not Horace, was making the running. It was not an obvious case of an older man pursuing a reluctant youth; the affair was mutual and only Horace's pusillanimous destruction of the earl's letters has half concealed the truth, that and evasive American scholarship.

Lord Lincoln's letter reached Horace in time for him to transform the tone of his own letter with an exuberant postscript. 'You make me extremely happy,' he wrote, as if hardly able to believe his luck, 'with letting me think my endeavours to please you were not lost, and that you saw I had the inclination if I had not the power. 'Twould have been a great satisfaction to me to have kept you longer here; my dear Lord, wherever I am you will always command my affections; I did not love you without thinking; and not believing you will alter, I never shall.' Love eternal, in fact.

The letter now took a spiteful turn, with an account of how Lady Sophia 'the Adorable has been ill of a fever and swelled face' and 'had a whole dish of chocolate flung over her last night' which Mr Dashwood had made a great business of wiping down. 'I wish you were here,' Horace ended, 'do, wish a little so too.' But then the Earl's next letter revealed, like a red rag to the proverbial bull, that the bisexual and by commonplace standards, over-sexed young man had met Lady Mary in Rome and been very excited by the experience. We know this from a surviving letter which he wrote at the time to his uncle the Duke. He had found Lady Mary 'as extraordinary as my imagination had fancyed her (which by ye by is not saying a little) I am so happy as to be mightily in my kinswoman's good graces. Lord knows what would happen if it were not for ye closeness of blood.'

Horace aimed an instinctive but contemptible blow back at Lady Mary: 'I hear the master of the house where Lady Mary lodged at Rome complains he did not imagine so old a woman could have spoiled his bed with her flowers.' In his next letter after a few professions – 'Believe that I love you sincerely, and that I think you deserve it' – he returned snarling to battle in jealous and (the word has to be used) bitchy, fury:

I did not doubt but Lady Mary would be glad of having you flesh of her flesh, but did not imagine she would try to bring it about by making you of her blood; of her poxed, foul, malicious, black blood! I have gone in a coach alone with her too, and felt as little inclination to her as if I had been *her son*. She is a better specific against lust than all the bawdy prohibitions of the Fathers.

In a last, perverse stroke of malice, Horace set out to make Lincoln jealous of Lady Sophia by ending the letter with a poem in French which the Prince de Craon had written to her. He will have heard that the Pomfrets were soon to follow Lord Lincoln to Rome to see the sights and give Lady Sophia another chance at an advantageous marriage, so he intended the Prince's poem to act as an apple of discord. It began:

Nous vous voyons, belle Sophie,
Dans l'âge heureux où les plaisirs
S'offrant en foule à vos désirs
Doivent bannir de votre vie
Et la tristesse et les soupirs

[Lovely Sophie, we see you in that happy, youthful prime when there is a whole host of pleasures around which you should be taking advantage of to banish the sighs and sadness from your life.]

which was neither tactful nor, psychologically, very clever.

Meanwhile Horace had also written a letter of arch duplicity to Spence to assure him, 'in my own proper person, that I shall have great pleasure on our meeting in England to renew an acquaintance which I began with so much pleasure in Italy.' Worse still, he went on: 'I shall always be proud to own you as my master of the antique, and will never let anything break in upon my reverence for you, but a warmth and freedom that will flow from my friendship.' His true assessment of Spence, confided later to the antiquary William Cole, rated him 'a good natured harmless little soul, but more like a silver penny than a genius ... that had read good books and kept good company, but was too trifling for use, and only fit to please a child'.

Every letter which Horace wrote to Lincoln at this stage included some fawning compliment to Spence or an epigram to flatter his scholarship. A protestation to Lincoln, 'Believe I love you sincerely and that I think you deserve it. I will never change,' would be followed closely by an even more ingratiating message for his 'governor':

Is Mr Spence enough at liberty among his antiquities to think of me? I deserve a little for I have a vast esteem for him ... I naturally love anyone that has so real an esteem for Lord Lincoln, yet I hope you won't put all my friendship to his account. When we meet in England, I hope we shall be vastly well together.

Such language was quite out of Horace's usual character and pure hypocrisy, but it explains what he was hoping to achieve. In ideal circumstances, he would never have chosen to make his once-in-a-lifetime Grand Tour of Italy with Thomas Gray, but neither would a conventional Grand Tour under the control of a middle-aged clergyman have appealed to him. Now, almost within his reach, was an ideal Italian sojourn with the handsome aristocrat he had fancied since his schooldays. Lincoln was more than half willing, only the Revd Joseph Spence stood in the way. With his permission, Horace could join them and then all the delightful intimacies of travel would be his to take advantage of: picnics by the wayside, evenings of carnival, foreign inns and late suppers with Lincoln flushed by wine.

It was worth playing for, but Spence was wary as well as vain. He was directly responsible to his employer, the Duke of Newcastle, and Newcastle could dispense bishoprics, had indeed done so to Lincoln's last tutor. If Horace was to have his way, Spence would need a good excuse, a crisis of some kind, a sudden illness perhaps, leaving Horace helpless, frail and in need of company. Even then Spence would be reluctant and his silence would have to be bought.

Time was running out. One purpose of the letter which Horace had written to Spence was to find out if Lord Lincoln had, like him, been ordered back to England as there was a very real danger that the Spanish, who had easily evaded Admiral Haddock's squadron and Horace Mann's spy network, might invade Tuscany. Sir Robert Walpole had told Horace that on his way home he 'might pass some time in France'. If Lord Lincoln was also returning to England, then why should Horace not keep him company? The Duke of Newcastle did, in fact, write to his nephew Lincoln on 16 March, not only telling him to come home quickly, but recalling a family project to get him married off to a rich heiress in England. Horace is unlikely to have heard of this but he had shrewdly perceived that Spence the enemy could be turned into Spence the ally. If Lord Lincoln married Sophia, then Spence was in trouble with his employer, the Duke of Newcastle, but if Lincoln rejected Sophia and the Pomfrets, and returned to England with Horace, the son of Newcastle's political master, Sir Robert, then what could be more respectable? If Spence kept his mouth shut about the liaison then there remained only one problem: Thomas Gray. Horace might conduct a romantic affair with another man while a complaisant clergyman looked the other way, but not with another jealous young man as the fourth party.

At this point the action becomes complex, even at times impenetrable, because of Horace's later mendacity and censorship. On 8 April Lord Lincoln wrote a long letter, desperately confused and confusing, to his uncle admitting 'I love Lady Sophia more yn words can say', but then asking for advice. After hoping that his uncle would not 'be angry at my not leaving Rome quite as soon as we intended', he promised 'once more to endeavour as much as possible to conquer my passion, but at least if I can't do it I will certainly be guided entirely by my dearest uncle's advice'. Lincoln was capable, when circumstances demanded, of describing himself as 'your humble Servant Linki, who loves nothing in this world or aims at nothing so much as pleasing his dear uncle'. Newcastle, however, still urged a speedy return to England. Lord Lincoln had thoughtfully covered up for Spence by telling his uncle that Spence had heaped him with sound anti-Sophia counsel.

That was probably no more than the truth as the Revd Spence had begun to appreciate the perils of the situation. Then, on 18 April, Horace played his last card. He wrote to Lincoln, a known lover of opera, telling him that he had 'made a most agreeable party to go to the fair at Reggio' where some of the best singers in Italy would be performing at a festival. He begged the Earl to reply fast, 'write me a line, it will find me here and give me vast satisfaction.' He signed off touchingly: 'My Dear Lord may you always be happy, and may I sometimes contribute a little, however little, to your being so.' In the event the Earl's reply missed Horace by hours when Horace, Gray and two others left Florence for Bologna and Reggio on 25 April. Mann readdressed it and Horace received it in Bologna. From that city he wrote again to Lincoln on 29 April, another firm letter to say that he could not meet Lincoln in Venice on Ascension Day (11 May) because he would still be in Reggio. He sympathized with 'a separation' that the Earl had mentioned, obviously from Lady Sophia.

'I trust,' he continued, 'we shall meet soon in England, and that you will then give me leave to be sometimes of your company: you

will never meet any man more sincerely desirous of your friendship; you have promised it me and I do not doubt of it.' He then
asked for another letter in reply and promised, 'I will endeavour to
make my motions square with yours.' And that is exactly what he
did. Lincoln received this, dashed off a reply, lost like all his
replies, which persuaded Horace to stay on at Reggio alone. He
delayed at least twelve days after the quarrel with Gray, which took
place between 5 May, when they arrived, and 8 May when Gray
left. Lord Lincoln would not arrive with Spence until 20 May.

Meanwhile, in Rome, Lincoln continued to wine and dine the
Pomfrets generously. Lady Pomfret must have thought that he was
as good as caught for her daughter. The Pomfrets were due to leave
Rome for Loreto and Venice on 18 May. Nothing would have
been easier than for a doting Lord Lincoln to accompany them to
Venice and so on to England and wedding bells, via Germany.
Instead he bolted. On 13 May he dined with the whole family; on
the 14th he took his formal leave and on the 15th he and Spence
left Rome for Reggio 'where', a perplexed Lady Pomfret noted, 'I
am told there is a very fine opera', and where there was also a very
devious and ruthless Horace Walpole waiting impatiently.

Reggio was then, as now, 'a dirty little place' of drab brick houses,
their walls flaking with buff plaster, dusty streets, two baroque
church facades, an octagonal stone tower doubtfully attributed to
Giulio Romano and two surprisingly grand theatres to maintain its
tradition as a cultural centre. The precise sequence of the events
which took place there from 29 April to 27 May will never be
known because Horace later destroyed all the relevant letters. John
Chute was intimately involved, as he had joined Horace and Gray
at Reggio on 5 May and it was he who was to shepherd a traumatized Gray off to Venice before 8 May, to leave the field clear for
Horace and Lincoln. All the evidence as to Horace's health in
Reggio and his meeting with Lord Lincoln depends upon the witness of the Revd Joseph Spence and this is a tissue of lies because
Spence was one of the plotters. When he eventually reached
England, he would be given on 28 April 1742 a pension for life of
£100 a year by a legal document which Horace signed as a witness.

That effectively guaranteed his silence. Only one of the letters which Spence would write during the slow return from Genoa, through Antibes, to Paris, would mention Horace's presence in the party, and that very briefly.

What happened was that, before 8 May, Horace staged a quarrel with Gray in Reggio. This would be easy to arrange. Gray had been in a distressed state of mind for months, idling about in Florence. Now, to find that they were waiting again for Lord Lincoln to join them would have brought his jealousy to the boil. Gray had been writing throughout the tour with unwise candour to Thomas Ashton, describing Horace's whims and tantrums in unflattering terms. Ashton, always a natural toady, had passed these criticisms on in his own letters to Horace who brought them up now to accuse Gray of ingratitude. When he was reporting it all to Mann, Horace appears to have made one particular letter a prime cause of the whole dispute. The wrangle was bitter but Gray was not totally dependent on Horace for funds and an understanding John Chute was there to ease him away to Venice. A letter which Horace wrote to West on 10 May makes no mention of Gray, only details carefully the social round of 'such a dirty little place as Reggio'. The letter is a cool, composed, and even self-satisfied document, but equalled in these frigid qualities by the only other letter from Reggio that Horace allowed to survive, one of 18 May to Mann. There is not the slightest sign of a nervous breakdown or of ill health in either, though posterity has been led by Spence to believe that by 22 May Horace was at death's door. 'I pass most part of the opera in the Duchess's box,' Horace told West, meaning the reigning Duchess of Modena, 'who is extremely civil to me and extremely agreeable'. He spoke of returning to England 'myself', not 'ourselves', via Germany. So Horace was apparently still not sure of his hold on Lincoln.

The first letter which Horace wrote reporting the quarrel and its causes to Mann was censored out of existence, probably because it was unconvincing. Certainly it puzzled Mann. In his next letter of 18 May to Mann, Horace began firmly 'I will not mention any more the affair, that has happened . . . I will write you now a thousand trifles', which he did. The ducal family had showered him with champagne and compliments 'and Madame Benedette [a daughter of the Duchess] sent me such a glass of Barbadoes that I was choked'. Curiously placed among these civilities was the news which 'Lord! I forgot to tell you,' his dog, 'poor Bettina tumbled out of the balcony into the street this morning and died in three minutes – was it not shocking – and is it not cruel to have all one's creatures come to such untimely ends?' Was Horace unlucky with pets or were his pets unlucky with Horace? Whatever the cause, it was a disturbing incident and possibly betrayed some inner tension.

Poor Mann was distracted throughout these crises days by a series of very dangerous and painful operations on his anal fistulas. He was 'cut' three times and was living on a diet of boiled chicken and gooseberry tarts. Therefore he was never able to intervene effectively in the quarrel. Horace told Mann that he had made a token gesture to effect a reconciliation with Gray.

Gray, alarmed by the false report of Horace's desperate illness, came all the way back from Venice, a four- or five-day journey, for an interview at Reggio on about 30 May. Horace's letter describing the meeting has, predictably, disappeared. Gray never mentioned it. But Mann professed to be 'astonished to see the terms and the reproaches, and much more that he could withstand your entreaties to return with you to England'. This attempted reconciliation is probably pure invention by Horace, anxious to seem to have been the healer in an unfortunate rift. It came to nothing and Horace salved his conscience by passing funds to Gray via Mann. Years later, when Gray was dead and his biographer, the Revd William Mason, quizzed Horace about the events at Reggio, Horace was brilliantly persuasive in his cover-up, with never a mention of Lord Lincoln, only an admission that Gray 'freely told me of my faults. I declared I did not desire to hear them, nor would correct them': all true enough. 'The fault was mine,' Horace admitted, but never named forbidden love as that fault; 'I was too young, too fond of my own diversions', not too fond of another man. Then a little sincere repentance was allowed an airing: 'I treated him insolently; he loved me, and I did not think he did. I reproached him with the difference between us, when he acted from conviction of knowing he was my superior'.

It was all magnanimous, generous and very slightly condescending – nothing to harm the reputation of Horace Walpole. A much earlier cover-up had been written in two letters from Reggio by Joseph Spence to his mother. These have since become famous and accepted at face value. They are probably inventions from beginning to end. In the first, dated 22 May, Spence and Lincoln have been in Reggio since 20 May, completely unaware of Horace's presence in the town, even though Lincoln had come there expressly to meet him. That, for a start, is completely implausible in such a small place. Spence reported that the opera was splendid, 'we last night heard four of the best voices in Italy . . . we shall pass four or five days here very agreeably and then we return to Bolognia. Lord Lincoln is extreamly well.' But then in a letter of 29 May sent from Bologna, having left Reggio on 27th, Spence breaks the exciting news of how he had saved the life of 'one of the best natured and most sensible young gentlemen that England affords'. Unfortunately we have only Spence's word for it. Neither the local doctor nor Dr Cocchi, brought in post-haste from Florence by a message from Spence, seem to have been much concerned by Horace's attack of tonsillitis or a quinsy.

Cocchi had been Horace's doctor in Florence, described as 'a plain honest creature with quiet knowledge'. He set out from Florence on 25 May, arriving in Reggio on the 27th. Mann, who had to pay for this supposed emergency call, questioned Cocchi closely as to Walpole's real condition and dismissed it when writing back to Horace not as a quinsy or tonsillitis but a simple 'cold'. Dr Cocchi was clearly annoyed at having been dragged all that way for nothing when Mann was genuinely suffering. 'If Cocchi had not the greatest regard for you,' Mann rebuked Horace, 'he would think me extreme troublesome in my demands about you.' There had been no fever.

According to Spence, he and Lord Lincoln, learning of Horace's presence in the town, 'after we had been there a day or two', visited him on his sick bed and then, still unconcerned, attended the opera. But in the middle of the night Horace's coach was sent round to their lodgings with a message for Spence, not Lincoln, to come immediately because 'Mr Walpole was extreamly worse'.

Spence found him 'scarce able to speak', raised the alarm and had
doctors brought in. Up to that point Horace had not been sick
enough to require any medical attention and by 27 May he was
sufficiently recovered for Lincoln and Spence to leave him in
Reggio.

What really took place in this obscure incident is that Horace,
Lincoln and Spence had been together at Reggio from 20 May. In
order to give the impression that Horace was a semi-invalid who
would need to be accompanied back to England, and therefore join
Lincoln on the remainder of his Grand Tour, they grossly exagger-
ated his sore throat. This would have had the advantage of putting
Gray in the wrong as a man who deserted a dangerously sick friend
and benefactor. Gray, as Mann related, borrowed ten zecchini to
return to Reggio, not as a result of Horace's proposal for a reconciliation, but because Gray had been worried by reports of
Horace's health. To understand Gray's state of mind, it is necessary
to recall a letter which he wrote to Horace from Cambridge before
Horace began to use him so shamelessly:

> You can never weary me with repetition of anything that makes me
> sensible of your kindness: since that has been the only idea of any
> social happiness that I have ever received.

Nothing can excuse Horace's behaviour at Reggio and significantly
none of his friends ever attempted to excuse it. What can be said is
that in later years he helped to make Gray a celebrated poet as
some measure of compensation.

Horace may have had a Florentine friend, Francesco Suares,
with him throughout this pseudo crisis and this has confused later
editors. As Mann tried to ferret out what really happened, he suggested in a letter to Horace that Gray had been sincere and had
previously confessed to him with tears that Horace was losing confidence in him, whatever that might mean. 'As to the oddness of
his behaviour with C— and the particulars you mention and
Bologna,' Mann concluded, 'they surprise me very much, and
would almost induce me to give another turn to the whole.' So
Gray had behaved oddly with 'C—'. Wilmarth Lewis suggested
that 'C' could stand for 'Cecchino', a friendly nickname for the

cavaliere Francesco Suares de la Concha. But on the same page of the letter Mann refers to him as Cecchino, not as 'C', which could as easily stand for Clinton, Lord Lincoln's surname: Lewis ignored that possibility.

On 4 June Spence and Lincoln arrived in Venice; on the 6th the Pomfrets arrived, still in pursuit. On 10 June Horace arrived and stayed in the same lodgings as Lord Lincoln. A letter to Mann ends with a relaxed note of almost domestic possessiveness: 'Lord Lincoln is this instant come in, and desires his compliments to you: so good night my dearest child.' Horace was in an exceptionally mellow mood, even religious; he had concluded, 'God gives us everything to use.' Chute and Whithed were still with them and the whole party enjoyed the carnival, though Horace did not mask. It was open again to Lord Lincoln to follow the Pomfrets up through Germany. Instead he took an affecting farewell. On 17 June Lady Pomfret recorded, 'Mr Walpole, Mr Whithed and Mr Chute came to take leave of us for they remain at Venice. Lord Lincoln took leave, as setting out tonight for Padua. We intend to do the same tomorrow for Padua.' On 18 June she writes from Padua, 'Here we found Lord Lincoln and Mr Naylor, who supped with us. Farewell to Padua.'

Farewell indeed. The Pomfrets made their way towards Milan and the Alps. Lady Pomfret may well have hoped that at the last minute Lord Lincoln would follow them. Lincoln himself may have been hesitant rather than preparing an emotional parting. Instead he returned to Venice, joined Horace and remained in the city until 10 July. Against all the odds, Horace had won. He now had almost a month with Lincoln in Venice where they both sat to Rosalba Carriera for those two remarkable pastel portraits: Lincoln's on the edge of the epicene, Horace looking self-satisfied. They are conceived as twin portraits, one looking at the other, both lovers wearing the same splendidly embroidered coat as a token of their togetherness.

John Chute's presence tended to bring out the high camp element in Horace. At this time the Empress Maria Theresa's youngest sister was being hawked around Europe as a prospective bride. Horace proposed that his white Roman spaniel, Patapan, might take her on as a husband. In default, Horace wrote, 'He shall go to England where I shall get him naturalised and created a peer by the title Viscount Callington.' Horace's parliamentary constituency was to be Callington in Cornwall. Mann joined more macabrely in these flights of fancy, suggesting that Patapan, being widowed by Bettina's death, might be depressed and commit suicide in the Po. A case perhaps of the wish being father to the thought.

Understandably a censorship fell upon Horace's letters for the next few months. From his letter of 19 July from Genoa to that of 11 September, written from Calais, all the letters to Horace Mann recording his voyage and journey home have disappeared, apart from three scissored fragments of a letter written from Paris. They would all have concerned Lord Lincoln and betrayed the relationship. In default we must depend upon a few reflective scraps in Mann's own letters and upon the serviceable Joseph Spence's regular, if unrevealing, letters home to Winchester. If Horace and Lord Lincoln's slow return to Paris could be accurately retold, it would read like the happy ending of a romantic novel for older homosexuals. This was Horace's idyll. He had fought for it ruthlessly and now he intended to enjoy it.

The journey from Venice over the hills to Genoa was appropriately gloomy with Lord Lincoln 'quite melancholy' at what he had given up: a lovely young woman and a mother-in-law, Lady Pomfret, who was a granddaughter of Judge Jeffreys of the Bloody Assize. In that last letter from Genoa, Horace told Mann that Lord Lincoln rode a horse while he and Spence 'went together in the *chaise*' playing a game, 'spot the loaded mule', straight out of an *I-Spy* book. Their count in one day was 857, so Horace was in high spirits. Lord Lincoln was still working out ways to marry Lady Sophia; ' 'til now,' he declared, 'I never wished for riches.' Horace pitied 'his determination of marrying much more than his present pain'. In Genoa, the city poor Gray had admired so much, they met Lady Mary Wortley Montagu again; by this time, however, Horace was confident enough to find her rants and plottings amusing. Lord Lincoln wanted three pairs of golden scissors as presents for the bereft Pomfrets. Horace wrote to Mann to order them from a silversmith in the Palazzo Vecchio, 'and put it to my account'. It was a small price to pay.

There followed an episode that reads like the purest fiction. Hiring two feluccas, they set out from Genoa in perfect July weather and sailed for two days with favourable winds down that enchanted coast, untainted by tourism but enlivened by the presence of Catalan privateers who would have been only too pleased to capture the son, albeit the youngest son, of Britain's First Lord of the Treasury. For Horace the arrangement was perfect. He and Lincoln sailed in one felucca and the Revd Spence in another. Lord Lincoln said he saw Spanish boats anchored in Arassi harbour and later claimed to have traversed seas 'full of Spanish Vessels'. Spence in his felucca was untroubled. 'We had so fair a wind,' he told his mother 'that we came near a hundred mile the last day; and the whole voyage was to me as agreeable as ayring in a pleasure boat on the Thames.' He had, in addition, that £100 pension to look forward to. After they had doubled the Cape of Monaco, they dined 'in an arched cave just by Nice and drank of the Spring that runs out of into the sea'. Lord Lincoln could hardly have resisted stripping off in his usual style at that point to enjoy the cool blue waters of the Mediterranean.

CHAPTER FIVE

Horace in love – 'Not the pleasantest volume of the *Correspondence*'

For Wilmarth Lewis, his ultimate editor, the 1740s were Horace Walpole's 'low dishonest decade'. It was a period best packed away into one distasteful volume thirty, where letters from catamites, whores, rakes and loose-living women of fashion could be crammed in together with an account of John Chute as a hysterical, bullying woman-hater, a pornographic poem in which the Speaker of the House of Commons is sodomized by a black-amoor and, as a sobering makeweight, Horace's last will and testament.

This is a pity, for scattered away among all these seedy but intriguing pages is a record of Horace in love, not happily but sincerely; and if he had really been, as Lewis desperately tried to persuade himself, innocent throughout a long life of any sexual relations with either man or woman, he would have been rather less of a letter-writer. A love affair can have surprising backdraughts of emotional awareness and charity towards the human condition, while a Walpole unloved and unloving could so easily have become the most frightful reactionary prig. Instead, his deep and thoughtful affection for Lincoln, a love that in strict law still merited the death penalty, made him just enough of an outsider to question on occasions the society and the politics with which he would otherwise have conformed. By instinct a jingoistic patriot with an appetite for victories, he would nevertheless oppose a declaration of war against France in 1744, and in Britain's central crisis of imperial identity in the mid-century he would sympathize with the

American rebels. Intelligence services are wise to mistrust homosexuals. Being rejected by society at one level, they tend to stand apart at others. And Horace's homosexual love was no trivial dalliance with a cunning street arab; promiscuity never tempted his fastidious nature, but snobbery raised his sights. He aimed not just at an earl, but a 9th Earl, and not merely a 9th Earl, but one who was the nephew of the two most powerful politicians of the era following Sir Robert Walpole's premiership. Give Horace his due: even in secret, he did things in style.

That letter, already briefly quoted in an earlier chapter, written to Mann from Venice as the disconsolate Pomfrets retreated, leaving Horace victorious and Lord Lincoln returning to the lodging-house and bed, contains an astonishing paragraph of enlightenment on the penal codes together with thoughts on the deity that come remarkably close to a generous orthodoxy. Such a mood of grateful content might not last but once experienced it could never be quite forgotten.

The state of Venice had beheaded that morning a poor man 'for stealing a cup out of a church' and Horace was still outraged. He had been unable to sleep for thinking of the unhappy creature. 'Had he murdered, or broke open a house he might have escaped; but to have taken from the church was death *without the benefit of clergy.*' It was a perfect case for righteous radical rage and Horace rose to it. 'Only think,' he wrote, 'some dying usurer or superannuated old whore gives God a pair of silver candlesticks, and if a famished poor creature takes away one, he is to die for it.'

His adjustment of the facts is instinctive: whores and bankers must have given the silver and the thief had to be starving. He had already a Radical's fixation with the defence of the underdog. But then, unpredictably, he mellowed into nostalgia:

> I remember an old superstitious parson by Cambridge who met his daughter one night going up to bed with a farthing candle in her hand; he asked her where she was going? She replied, to bed. Well, says he, and you design to say your prayers first, I'll warrant you! Yes, Sir. Yes, Sir, and are you going to talk to God with only a farthing candle? If any foolish visitor or gossiping madam was to come

to you, you would light up two tallow candles – pray go light up two to say your prayers by.

Lord Lincoln is this instant come in . . .

It is vintage Horace Walpole: direct, unexpected, ambivalent, with a faultless ear for dialogue. He wrote few of his great letters in the 1740s. In that respect Wilmarth Lewis's instinct was correct; but this is one of them: a wretch beheaded, the Christian Church as oppressor, and then the domestic chiaroscuro of a Cambridge vicarage, love of God linked to light and to respect; and lastly, in comes Lord Lincoln. The economy and the compression are effortless.

Lincoln is the key to these shiftless years of Horace's life between 1741 and the purchase of 'Chopp'd Straw Hall' in 1747. When his father was thrown from power in February 1742, the question which disturbed Horace the most was: how would Lord Lincoln react now that his uncles held the reins? Richard West, emotional confidant of the Italian years, died of consumption that spring, but Horace never once visited him or showed great concern. Lincoln was the star around which his social life revolved. The circle of friends into which Lincoln drew him are best described in Bertie Wooster terms as 'rotters'; but because they were Lincoln's cronies Horace was uncritical and even admiring. There was Richard Edgcumbe, long entangled with a prostitute he both loved and despised; Lord Strafford, the Roman Catholic expert in pornography; Thomas Winnington, whose morals 'seemed imbibed from the most profligate courts that ever existed', Sir Charles Hanbury Williams who 'poxed' his wife and wrote lewd verses; and the shameless Lady Townshend, who lay with 'an hundred other men' but still took comfort in the Blessed Sacrament. Finally there was Lord Lincoln himself, who filled the gap between despairing love for Lady Sophia Fermor and a rich marriage to his first cousin, Catherine Pelham, by an affair with a London courtesan called Peggy Lee, and, as a little bit on the side, by his affair with Horace.

Exactly what that last affair amounted to in physical terms can only be deduced from Horace's letters and perhaps from that copy of Horace's portrait by Jonathan Richardson which Lincoln owned and kept at Clumber. This may represent Horace as Lincoln wanted to see him. Horace described the portrait as 'round and fair and blooming and about eighteen', when he thought of himself as merely 'long and yellow and towards eight and twenty'.

Horace was so infatuated after the sail along the Riviera and the slow journey up through France that he wrote Lincoln a letter while they were still both staying in Paris at the Hôtel de Luxembourg, on different floors. 'My Dear Lord,' he began, 'It is an age since I saw you, and above three months since I had a letter from you. I should have wrote to you above a quarter of an hour ago, but I did not know in what room you was; and was unwilling to have my letter fall into other hands, especially in the present situation of affairs, when it is scarce safe to write from one storey to another'.

In modern terms Lincoln was, apparently, a bedspring bouncer, very vigorous in the sexual act. 'I heard some time since you were at Paris, by the noise you made under me,' Horace continued, to show that he knew precisely what Lincoln had been doing in the night with some French courtesan. For him, though, it was all part of the sexual machismo a bisexual holds for an inexperienced homosexual. 'I wont keep you any longer from your breakfast,' Horace ended cosily, 'or myself from my own, having before me some charming bread and butter, of which you know nobody is so fond of as, my Lord, your Lordship's Very humble servant and sincere friend Captain Rolls.'

It was Horace's habit to sign himself off with one of the pair's in-jokes. Captain Rolls was the Revd Spence's detested half-brother, mention of whose name made Spence foam with jealous rage. At other times Horace was 'Percy Plunkett', in memory of a criminal who had caused legal problems for Lincoln's father, the 7th Earl. Trivial, light-hearted and confidently intimate, this Paris letter captures the relationship between the two men at that point, remote from England and realities. But nothing is quite as telling as the fact that Lord Lincoln kept what its author had so clearly intended should be ephemeral. The attraction was not one-sided, but mutual.

Anxious to avoid an embarrassing reunion with the Pomfrets at King George's birthday reception in October, Lord Lincoln stayed on in Paris. To demonstrate the social clout of even a junior Walpole, Horace was arranging for him to be introduced to the Marquise de Matignon, one of those middle-aged ladies of rank whose acquaintance Horace unaccountably always seemed to value. There were also those other ladies whom the Earl had been noisily pleasuring in the room below. Horace's predictably faint and refined sexual profile was beginning to emerge. He saw 'my Earl's' heterosexual lustiness not as a threat but as an attractive and manageable proof of virility. A handsome face, a distinguished pedigree and the thrill of concealment were his prime requirements in an affair. Sex came last and in a particular form.

Then he was off to Calais and England; but before he had gone many miles beyond Canterbury he was writing again to his 'Dearest Lord' from Sittingbourne. This time it was to give Lincoln, who was always short of money, a blank cheque to draw what he pleased from Horace's banker, Charles Selwyn, in Paris. He asked forgiveness for 'not writing more, or my writing at all, when I had nothing to say, but that I am ever by inclination and by gratitude for all your goodness to me, my dearest Lord Yours sincerely Hor. Walpole'.

It was a masterly token of submission: recklessly generous and abject, with a joke, a smutty little *double entendre* in the PS, where Horace was often at his most relaxed. A clergyman had prayed in church for a prospective bride 'as going to take a great affair in hand'. Horace liked the joke so much that he repeated it to both Mann and Henry Conway in other letters. For the next few years in the company of Lincoln and his circle he would become perceptibly coarser in his wit. As one of Nichols's *Literary Anecdotes* was to observe, 'Though he was elegant and polished, he was not, I think, well-bred, in the best view of that phrase.'

Back in London, refreshed by the 'small beer and newspapers' which he had missed so much on the Continent, Horace settled down to wait for the first sitting of an ominous new Parliament in December. His father's power-base of placemen, committed to support the 'Old Corps' of the Whig party, would only command a wafer-thin majority. If the Tories could link up with the 'Patriot Whigs' and the other group of ambitious dissidents who gathered around Pulteney and Carteret on some convincing issue of confidence, then twenty-one years of the Walpole balancing-act would be at an end. Meanwhile, society was returning from the country to the capital and those emotional manoeuvres that Horace loved to record could be played out now on home ground. He tried hard to cultivate the Pelhams and the Clintons but neither the Duke of Newcastle nor Lincoln's much-loved sister, Lady Lucy Clinton, was 'at home'. Lincoln's other uncle, Henry Pelham, the man who was to dominate English politics for the next twelve years, was cornered and, so Horace reported, 'was excessively pleased with all the *white truths*, which I could not help telling him of you – Dodd [an old college friend] says I talk of nothing but Lord Lincoln'.

On reading that catalogue of indiscretions Lincoln would surely have taken some alarm. Whilst Horace was coyly advising him that, according to London gossip, he and Lady Sophia were already married, Lincoln had, in fact, just written to his uncle Newcastle from Paris to say that 'it would be unhappy both for myself and her to carry that affair so far as I might otherwise have wished'. Lady Sophia, still hopeful, was back in London on 8 October and Horace, confident now that he could handle the participants, gave her advice on what clothes she should wear to look 'well dressed and nobly genteel'. He reported to Lincoln that she had 'asked extremely after a Lord at Paris'.

All this time, Horace's old friend Henry Conway had been virtually forgotten in the sequence of letter-writing, but he was aware of the snub and making a determined effort to reassert himself. He too was in love, with Lady Caroline Fitzroy, a daughter of the Duke of Grafton, but, like Lord Lincoln, had no money to support the match, and Lady Caroline, while beautiful, was a calculating flirt. It was a situation made for Horace to take advantage of but, for the time being, he kept it in reserve.

In mid-November Lincoln was back to make his official appearance at Court. When Lincoln and Sophia eventually met, Horace observed that 'he turned pale, spoke to her several times in the evening, but not long; and sighed to me at going away'. In an excited, gossip-crammed letter to Mann, Horace gushed away like a lovesick girl. 'He came over all alive; and not only his uncle–duke, but even Majesty has fallen in love with him. He talked to the King at his levée, without being spoken to – that was always thought high treason – but I don't know how, the gruff gentleman liked it.' Accused of many faults in his time, George II was never known to fancy anyone of his own sex, but it was on this occasion that the King declared, according to a doting Horace, 'Lord Lincoln is the handsomest man in England.'

At Sir Thomas Robinson's ball on 2 December there occurred a perfect social contretemps for Horace to savour. Lord Lincoln, Henry Conway and the Ladies Sophia and Caroline were all present in a glittering company of some two hundred guests. 'Out of prudence', Lincoln partnered Lady Caroline in country dances, leaving Conway to partner Lady Sophia. 'It was an admirable scene,' Horace recalled, 'the two couples were just mismatched, as everyone soon perceived, by the attentions of each man to the woman he did *not* dance with.' Afterwards a small group of young bloods, including Lincoln and Horace, but not the reserved Henry Conway, got drunk, roistering on until seven in the morning on thirty-two bottles of wine. It was not Horace's usual scene and he ended up, deservedly, with a violent headache.

That ball just before the new Parliament met was probably the last point for a number of years at which Horace could have considered himself to be in control of events. Parliament, where Horace represented his pocket borough of Callington, moved chaotically from one artificial crisis to another. The opposition scented blood, Sir Robert was a sick man and well aware that he was not a natural wartime First Minister. Shrewdly perceiving that, if he were to sacrifice himself, then the 'Old Corps' of Whigs, led by the two Pelhams, would still be able to soldier on, Sir Robert slid gracefully into retirement in the second week of February 1742. For him it was a concealed triumph. The King wept at losing him; he took the title of Earl of Orford to spite Lord Sandys, a political enemy, who thought the title belonged in his family; Sir Robert's bastard daughter Maria was given the rank of an earl's daughter while he remained the respected adviser behind the scenes. All this while he was still able to enjoy the bucolic pomps of his Palladian palace at Houghton in his native Norfolk. Only for Horace was it a disaster.

The pleasures of influence and the possibilities of office had been snatched away from him after a few turbulent weeks. Worst of all, his and Lincoln's roles had been reversed. The new First Lord of the Treasury, Winnington, was a cipher. Lincoln's two Pelham uncles were the new power-brokers and Lincoln was their heir presumptive. Power is an aphrodisiac and Horace had lost it. To cap his misery, Lincoln took a mistress, Peggy Lee, who, in 1743, would bear him a daughter. It was not at all what Horace had been planning. He had been growing to admire and even like Lady Sophia, to assess her as a prospective Lady Lincoln alongside whom he could live amicably, but now he knew from Lincoln that the match was definitely off. Horace had arranged a little triumph for himself on 17 February at the Duchess of Norfolk's masquerade, with all the royal family present and the streets illuminated and bonfired. He attended dressed as Aurengzebe, the Mogul emperor, but no one noticed him and even the piquant accident by which Lord Lincoln and Lady Sophia both appeared in Spanish costume failed to cheer him.

On 22 March he wrote a letter to Mann which, when it was returned to him, he censored almost to nothing. Whatever its contents had originally been, they disturbed Mann dreadfully. He had written back:

> But my dear child you have made me quite miserable by hinting to me only that you are not happy; you have just given me a glimpse of a scene of which I could have no idea and which torments me extremely, as I am too well convinced by the strength of your expressions that you must have met with usage you did not expect – and yet your not having at all explained yourself leaves me too much in the dark to say aught about it.

From Mann's reportage of Horace's dark hints, it sounds as if someone in his new group of friends had acquainted him with the rumour that he was not his father's legitimate child, but the result of an infidelity between his mother and a brother of Lord Hervey.

Sir Robert never showed any sign of suspicion and the marked physical likeness between Horace and his father's illegitimate daughter Mary makes the story even more improbable. The imputation had, however, wounded his relations with another person whom he greatly loved and respected: Lord Lincoln, in all probability. That was the price to be paid for going about town with a group of scurrilous and disreputable young men. Such a life-style had, however, a lighter side. One night at the opera in the Haymarket Lord Lincoln 'was abused in the most shocking manner by a drunken officer, upon which he kicked him, and was drawing his sword, but was prevented'. Horace, sitting on the other side of the theatre, rushed to the rescue, 'climbed into the front boxes, and stepping over the shoulders of three ladies, before I knew where I was, found I had lighted into Lord Rockingham's lap'.

Slapstick incidents could not compensate for the hard social reality of being presented to Frederick, Prince of Wales and his wife, a couple whom Horace had always despised, but receiving not a single polite word from either of them. Then, to emphasize the fall, in July Horace's father was ordered to quit 10 Downing Street and allow the hated Samuel Sandys to take up residence. A long exile in the country loomed ahead. The Walpoles retained a town house, but the years from 1742 to 1745 were Horace's Houghton time.

Throughout his life Horace was to carry the burden of a strong feeling of family loyalty to a large group of relations with whom he had little in common and whose company bored him to tears. The only respectable male member was his father's brother Horatio, after whom he had been named and whom the Pelhams later made Lord Walpole of Wolterton. A serviceable politician, he was, in social terms, a Norfolk bumpkin who 'now and then drops a sharp sentence against the King of Prussia even in the middle of a field of turnips'. Horace's eldest brother, Robert, 2nd Earl of Orford, would die in 1751, leaving a son, George, the 3rd Earl, who had probably been sired by another man in one of the dreadful Lady Margaret Walpole's affairs and who was, in addition, periodically mad and incapable. His other brother, Edward, never married but raised a family by his mistress, Dorothy Clements, a dressmaker. Three girls from this liaison all made splendid marriages and were favourites of Horace. Horace's full sister, Mary, married the Earl of Cholmondeley's heir, and his illegitimate half-sister, Maria, married another bastard, Charles Churchill. So they were, in the main, disreputable and difficult, rousing mixed feelings in Horace.

His reactions to Houghton Hall were equally ambivalent. Because he was proud of his father's career and because the great house was his father's personal creation, he was constrained to value a building which was the very antithesis of his own notion of a home. Even now, when time has mellowed the majestic heap a little and when it is usual to genuflect mentally at the mere mention of 'Georgian taste', Houghton Hall very nearly merits the epithet 'vulgar'. Designed by Colen Campbell, but altered during its construction by James Gibbs, who added domes to the skyline, the house ended up neither chastely Palladian nor theatrically baroque in its exterior elevations. Its interiors are predictable in their layout and have been loaded with marble ornaments in a *nouveau riche* determination to impress rather than delight. But the new 1st Earl of Orford still had three years to live and for those years Horace played his role as dutiful and affectionate son to a fallen saviour of the British state. During summers and early autumns he attended his ailing father in rural Norfolk, drinking with dull relatives and pretending an interest in the hare coursing. 'I have been recommended to a very pretty little book, called Rider's Almanack,' he told Lincoln disdainfully, 'it teaches one when to sow parsnips, kill bees and let blood'. Such a life left him much time for writing.

That summer of 1742 he began with *A Sermon on Painting*. This was preached, not by Horace, but by Lord Orford's chaplain, to the whole household, on the text: 'They have mouths, but they speak not: Eyes have they but they see not: neither is there any Breath in their Nostrils.' It is a minor masterpiece of pastiche, heavily rhetorical, unctuously devout and quite unlike Horace's usual relaxed writing style. It catches perfectly the manner of the average contemporary public sermon with passages such as: 'Let him say, thus humble, thus resigned, looked the son of God, when he deigned to receive baptism from the hand of man; while ministering angels with holy awe beheld the wondrous office.'

Its theme is the corruption of painting to serve Roman Catholic idolatry. Bad paintings are those that persuade the ignorant to accept doctrines like the Immaculate Conception or in which 'a morose Carthusian, or bloody Dominican is invested with robes of glory'. Good paintings are those, such as Salvator Rosa's 'Prodigal', Parmigiano's 'Deposition of Christ' and Guido Reni's 'Simeon and the Child', that create true Christian devotion. After a trenchant show of Protestant prejudice the sermon concludes with a gross piece of flattery to his father. There was a Poussin of 'Moses striking the Rock' hanging in the hall at Houghton and Horace used it to compare his father to the prophet: two men who led their people 'through opposition, through plots, through enemies, to the enjoyment of peace and to the possession of a land flowing with milk and honey'. It is all writing to please, delivered with the cynical detached competence of an outsider.

Horace wrote only two brief, bored letters to Lord Lincoln in 1742, both from Houghton mocking country manners and pleading for a reply. As the new year opened he remembered the pseudo-Turkish love letter that Thomas Gray had written him from Cambridge in very similar circumstances and decided on the dangerous tactic of embarrassing Lincoln in public. A masquerade was being held in February and a party had gathered for it at the Duke of Richmond's town house. Horace appeared in Indian costume, made straight for Lord Lincoln, bowed three times and knelt at his feet, with a letter written on a long sheet of red paper, folded and wrapped in silk, balanced on his head. The Earl 'stared violently' but was persuaded to open and read the missive for the general amusement of the company.

With his usual facility, Horace had switched register from clergyman's ponderosity to Persian eroticism. It began, 'Highly favoured *among women*' and congratulated Lincoln on his recent appointment as Lord of the Bedchamber. 'Does thy admission to the bedchamber of thy Lord give thee access to his women? Or are they veiled from thy sight as ours in Persia?' it queried, and saluted

Lincoln's 'vigour' as 'nine times beyond that of our prophet' with the Earl 'more amorous than Solomon son of David'. As a mark of grace the 'Most potent Lord' was to be presented with one hundred and fifty beautiful maidens and a thousand black eunuchs 'to guard the prodigious number of women in thy seraglio'. Behind the broad humour the homosexual jealousy was strong.

The letter, supposedly written by Thamas Kouli Kan Schah Nadir of Ispahan, ended with a return to Horace's obsession with male potency and genital dimensions:

> Adieu! Happy young man! May thy days be as long as thy manhood, and may thy manhood continue more piercing than Zufager, that sword of Hali which had two points.

In modern homosexual circles Horace would be described as a 'size queen'. In one of his poems, 'The Judgement of Solomon', two women dispute before the king, not for the possession of a baby, but for a man's outsize member which Horace describes reverentially with a wealth of biblical comparisons. From remarks by Horace and his friend Sir Charles Hanbury Williams, it seems that Lord Lincoln was famous in London clubland at this time for an unusually large penis. Wilmarth Lewis bought the original Kouli Kan letter, minus its silk wrapping, and it now hangs, framed, in his Library at Farmington. At the foot of the letter Horace had drawn six Chinese, rather than Persian, characters and a Chinese couple holding hands.

It was an interesting opening to a lively year, both for Horace and for England. The star of the Whig dissident, Lord Carteret, was rising. He was urbane and intelligent and, because he spoke fluent German, had gained far more influence over King George than his superiors in the Cabinet, the Pelhams. In June he accompanied the King to the Continent where George was technically in command of the allied army that defeated the French at Dettingen. Dazzled by the victory, few people back in England noted that in the same month Lady Carteret suffered a heart attack while playing a harp in Hanover, and died. But Lady Pomfret noticed.

For much of his life, the relations between Horace and Henry

Conway were more those of two affectionate brothers than of two cousins. For long periods they would take each other for granted, but then at times of crisis strong emotions would surface. For instance, at Houghton again for the summer of 1743, Horace was in a predictable tizzy of concern about the safety of Henry in the battle. Lord Lincoln, visiting Houghton with his uncle Henry Pelham and the Duke of Grafton, brought more serious news. He was to marry his cousin, Catherine Pelham; and his two uncles, Henry and the Duke of Newcastle, had decided to make him their heir. This was an engagement from which there could be no escape. 'It will be a great joy to the whole house of Newcastle,' Horace commented tersely in a letter to Mann.

The engagement must have infuriated him because a few days later, on 22 June, in an attempt to provoke some kind of response, he wrote Lincoln a letter that came close to moral blackmail in an attempt to bring their relationship back to life. Their mutual friend, the depressed young roué the Hon. Richard Edgcumbe, was staying at Houghton as a house guest. 'If I don't express myself with as much love as I used to do,' the letter began, 'and as you know I have from you, don't wonder – Dick is here, and as he has twice perused the superscriptions of my letters, I am not sure he would not open one directed to so particular a friend of his as you are. Now, after your way of dealing with him,' Horace continued in a half-veiled threat, 'if he should find me very fond of you, God knows what he might suspect. He would at least burst the waistband of his breeches with the glee of the discovery – and, my dear Lord, I would not for the world wrong your bed – As irresistible as he is, he shall never injure you with me . . . Then he is so inquisitive.' This was clearly a bluff, as on another occasion Edgcumbe suspected that Horace might easily have had an affair with his own favourite courtesan.

'Wrong your bed' could only have been a thrust aimed at Catherine Pelham. Low as Horace's tactics undoubtedly were, they worked. Lord Lincoln replied within days, apparently with a polite enquiry as to Henry Conway's safety. In the event Conway's regiment had not been involved in the battle. Horace's response this time was a disagreeably sarcastic note congratulating Lincoln, who was of course never a soldier, on also missing Dettingen. If he enclosed a few white feathers, they are not recorded; but clearly 1743 was a summer of whetted knives.

Worse news reached Houghton in August. Henry Pelham had been appointed First Lord of the Treasury and Prime Minister on the 23rd. On the 25th Horace wrote again to Lincoln, officially to congratulate him on his uncle's new status, but in reality to warn him that all the friends who would now flock to him would be false. Only Horace would be true: 'when they fall off, I shall be very happy to take my old place again.' It is not known whether the Earl squirmed with embarrassment when the 'formal letter', as Horace described it, arrived. But this time he did not reply and Horace, who composed and wrote very quickly, settled down to an autumn of provocation. During that one stay at Houghton he wrote first, 'Patapan, or the Little White Dog', a long fairy story, part prose, part poetry, with several lightly improper passages and Lincoln as its mock-heroic central figure. Then in November he wrote 'Little Peggy', a poem in heroic couplets, crudely porno-graphic throughout and aimed directly at Lincoln. During this autumn he also found time to write the *Aedes Walpolianae,* a schol-arly and highly opinionated assessment of the great schools of European painting as represented in his father's rich collection.

The *Aedes* was aimed to please his father, to make the country aware of the cultural standing of the Walpoles and to clear his own mind of the judgements accumulated over his time in Italy and France. It is an early and important English expression of neo-Classical values in painting, perverse and paradoxical in that Horace was soon to become an arch apostle of the Gothic. The proper place for its consideration will be in chapter six on Strawberry Hill. Though written in 1743, the *Aedes* would not be published until 1747, the year Horace took the lease of his house at Twickenham. 'Patapan' and 'Little Peggy' were not published, only passed around. Both were attempts to attract attention from Lord Lincoln and to amuse a group of London friends who enjoyed the kind of light poetic pornography written by Horace's new friend, the Welsh baronet, Sir Charles Hanbury Williams. Both works combine a malicious irresponsible despair with real wit, political satire and airy humour. They are still very readable today, more so perhaps than Dryden's far more celebrated *Absalom and Achitophel* for all its superior purple passages.

'Patapan' took as its unlikely target the Speaker of the Commons, Sir Arthur Onslow, a relatively harmless, if bumbling, placeman who had clashed with Horace when, as a very junior member of Parliament with a weak voice, he attempted to raise a point of order in a parliamentary debate. Onslow is supposed in the poem to have a wife, Isabel, who gains very little sexual satisfaction from her husband. When he leaves her for his duties at Westminster, Henry, 'a young lord ... tall, well made. And his complexion of a manly brown', falls in love with her, but Isabel rejects him. At this point, as in Horace's later and more famous *The Castle of Otranto*, the plot becomes over complex and grossly dependent upon super-natural interference. Henry wanders off to Italy and saves a serpent from a peasant; the serpent turns out to be a fairy who will grant his every wish. The fairy turns herself into Patapan, a little white dog which can coin jewels from its ear. Carried back to England on a cloud, Henry and Patapan approach Isabel again and, to win a jewel-manufacturing dog, Isabel agrees to become Henry's lover.

So far so good; Horace could be reminding Lord Lincoln of past favours rendered. But then Arthur Onslow returns, discovers the infidelity and tries to have Isabel assassinated. Patapan foils this attempt and magics up a magnificent castle guarded by 'a tall, lean, dry, swarthy giant of an Ethiopian'. Onslow covets the castle and the Ethiopian tells him, 'you shall be absolute lord of it, if you will only serve me two days as a page of honour.' There follows an amusing passage of mock-heroic verse where Onslow weighs up the pros and cons of being sodomized by a black in order to gain a palace. The allegory upon Whig politics in the first half of the eighteenth century is robust and apposite:

> [I] Have taught the monarch on his throne to reign,
> Taught him to conquer France and plunder Spain:
> Shall I who have done thus, the mighty I
> Prostrate before a lech'rous Ethiop lie?
> Softened to a bardash, avert my face,
> *With robes tucked up, opprobrious to my place?*

Sand's could his dullness with his neckcloth veil;
Oh! could a neckcloth shade my injured tail!
Disgraced, abused, how shall I ever dare
To place a shameful bum in Stephen's chair?

Every prominent member of the opposition from Pitt to Pulteney receives a witty mention. The dreadful omens taken by a priest as Onslow prepares his shameful bargain are worthy of Pope in his *Dunciad*:

With madding torrents of unbounded wrath
Furious uprose the mighty Earl of Bath, [Pulteney]
Pouring the monsters of his mud along,
Sea-calves, portentous cubs, an ugly throng,
Hoopers, and Furneses, and such-like things,
Dirt-born, and warmed to life by breath of kings:
Howling they bayed the sun; and when the priest
On the reared altar placed each mystic beast,
The frightened priest the bloody knife let fall
For they were tongueless, brainless, heartless all!

When Onslow finally succumbs to temptation, Isabel and Henry catch him and his Ethiop 'in the very midst of their joys'. Isabel chides her husband in a last flurry of couplets:

Is this soft couch your *Chair,* and boasted place?
And that same swarthy instrument your mace?
Are these the *motions* that you make? Is this
The joy that you prefer to wedded bliss?

She praises in contrast the 'grace on blooming Henry shed', but then forgives Onslow. They renew their marriage vows and promise never to mention the word 'page' to the Speaker again.

'Patapan' is a good-natured invention, a private joke that reads amusingly to a public audience. Anyone wishing to understand the mind behind *The Castle of Otranto* should read it, together with the long and revealing footnotes that Horace supplied to almost every proper name. Hooper, for instance, mentioned in that passage on the omens, 'was rewarded by Lord Bath with a place of 900 a year (Paymaster of the Pensions) for one day saying his Lordship had spoke with the tongue not of a man, but an angel.' The opposition, not Lord Lincoln, was the target of 'Patapan', indeed Lincoln probably enjoyed it as much as he was meant to do. 'Little Peggy' was a different case.

In writing this verse, Horace hangs over the cradle of 'little Peggy', Lincoln's love-child by Peggy Lee, like some wicked fairy godmother willing the baby to grow up to be another whore. It is a composition of bawdy malice, designed to degrade and lower a relationship which he envies. Lincoln's own private parts feature obsessively, as in the Persian letter:

> The hour is come, by ancient dames foretold,
> E'er his small cock were yet a fortnight old,
> How with majestic vigour it should rise,
> Strong to the sense, and tow'ring to the skies!
> Women unfucked at sight of it should breed,
> And other virgins teem with heav'nly seed.

After a keenly realized tour of 'tumid dugs', 'nut-brown engines', 'goodly members' and 'titillating thighs', worthy of *Fanny Hill,* the poem ends with a twisted curse on the poor child's sexual failure and on heterosexual lust in general:

> Arise, O maid, to promised joys arise!
> Linco's sweet seed, and daughter of the skies!
> See joyous brothels shake their conscious beds!
> See glowing pricks exalt their crimson heads!
> See sportive buttocks wanton in the air!
> And bawds cantharides and punch prepare!
> The youth unbuttoned to thy arms advance,
> And feather-tickled elders lead the lech'rous dance!

Armed with these thunderbolts to amuse and dismay, Horace returned to London and wrote what he must really have been wanting to write since August: one love letter that can honestly be described as 'great'. Dated only 'Wednesday', internal references confine it to between November 1742 and late 1744, but its mood places it more precisely as written immediately after 'Little Peggy', in the winter of 1743–4. Because it compresses with resigned, stoic realism the dilemma of a homosexual in love with a bisexual, it gave its American editor Wilmarth Lewis a bad moment. Without a word of supporting evidence he dismissed it with, 'The letter is written in the character of one of Lincoln's mistresses.' It is nothing of the sort. It was written by Horace to Lincoln as a last attempt to revive their time in France, written 'To the dear man Whom folly pleases, and whose follies please'.

It opens with a bare-faced challenge, 'I have changed my mind: instead of desiring you to have done loving me, I am going to ask something much more difficult for you to comply with – pray continue to love me: I like it vastly. I could never have imagined there were half so many *agrements* in having a lover. You can't conceive how I regret the time I have lost.' Horace, who was only twenty-six at this time, has neither youth, bloom or beauty while Lincoln has 'all the tenderness, all the attentions of a lover in a romance, and all the dear indiscretion of a lover out of one'. Lincoln has exposed him to dangers but, ' 'Tis amazing how little real anger I feel.'

Then comes the astonishing paradox, the confession that in their love-making he had always been the passive partner, fascinated by another's passion but feeling none himself. 'I won't pretend that I feel vast tenderness and passion when I expect to meet you ... My satisfaction arises from your passion, not from my own. So you see, 'tis absolutely necessary you should continue to love me; for if you don't, I have no resource!'

Against all expectation, the delicately mannered and fastidious Walpole follows through the realities of physical love with a dispassionate ruthlessness worthy of John Donne or the Shakespeare of the Sonnets. If Lincoln is sexually fickle then Horace admits he will be undone: ' 'Tis no passion of my own, but yours that diverts me; and do but think how cruel it would be to deprive me of such an amusement, for to be sure, for all the little ridicules of an affair, nothing can come up to you. You have all the whims and follies that can entertain one, without any of the lamentable languishings and insipidness that consume three parts of the time of other lovers.'

Then comes the central question: if Lincoln's lust for him is what he enjoys, then how can Horace keep it; 'there is no part I won't act to keep you. Thank my stars, I have not passion enough to blind me; and if it is in the power of art to preserve your heart, it shall be mine!' At that point the letter swings superbly into a new register, from metaphysical baring of the soul to controlled eighteenth-century wit. Because he cannot accurately recall Lincoln's nature in love and all he can remember 'is, that you have loved so many and such various people', he has gone out to question those 'various people' on how 'to keep you'.

Lady Sophia replied 'without blushing' that 'beauty and sense could *not* keep you'. Fanny Macartney said 'smartness, forwardness, and half-a-dozen French songs with *double entendres* would rivet any man alive'; her sister 'with the finest circumflexion of every muscle, told me, that sentiments and a well-made naked body were perpetual chains'. Peggy Lee 'with all the naïveté of her profession', knew no way 'but by being kept oneself by some very rich one'. Moving on to another 'common woman', Lady Townshend, 'so loathsome in her person', yet with her rooms crammed with sinners, Thomas Winnington outstanding among them, 'the most inconstant, most unfeeling man alive', Horace asked her the secret, 'but she gave me so many infamous receipts, that I was charitable enough to believe that there was no more truth in this, than in all the rest she says.'

Having told Lincoln thus memorably what a squalid pack of friends he has dragged Horace down among, the letter changes register again. Horace drives to the other end of town to the Duke and Duchess of Richmond, 'both handsome enough to have been tempted to every inconstancy, but too handsome to have ever found what they would have lost by the exchange': a truly loving married couple. But when posed the usual question the Duchess knew of no art, 'she had always obeyed, been virtuous, and loved her husband; and was it strange he should return it?' Horace envied her 'for not knowing that love does not always produce love'. In short, he was melancholy. 'I could love you, only you, and you unboundedly – if I had any hopes that that would do to keep you mine – Adieu!' and this time he signed himself 'P.P.', for Percy Plunkett.

There was, apparently, no reply; and indeed, it is not easy to imagine what kind of response Lord Lincoln could have made to such a letter. Was he proud of it, as an emotional scalp to hang at his belt, embarrassed by it, or did he even respond warmly and physically to his frail and affected little friend, pushing his face down into the pillow for further sessions of lusty fun? One thing is certain: he did not tear the letter up. If it was written around December 1743, as seems likely, then there were still ten months to go before Lincoln married Catherine in October 1744. Several times in his letters to Mann of 1744, Horace mentions that he is to meet Lord Lincoln or dine with him and his friends, Dick Edgcumbe, Winnington and Lord Strafford, at their club, White's in St James's, so there had been no break.

In all these letters, Lincoln's own voice is so rarely heard. What was he really like? In Rosalba's pastel portrait the face is sensitive and refined, in William Hoare's state portrait he looks like a successful footballer in Garter robes. To King George he might be the handsomest man in England, but to Horace Mann, who gained over the years a fair impression of what had really gone on at Reggio, Lincoln was 'that strange stupid stammerer', the milord who had bored Horace Walpole all the way from Venice to Genoa.

Early in 1744, Lady Sophia struck back superbly in the sex-war. She became engaged to the fifty-four-year-old widower, Lord Carteret, the most influential man in the Cabinet, recently raised in the tables of aristocratic precedence to become the 1st Earl Granville and already the favourite of the cantankerous monarch. Lady Pomfret must have been in the seventh heaven; her daughter was only twenty-three years old. Horace was excited and, inevitably, he had a neat, spiteful epigram to meet the occasion:

> Her beauty like the scripture feast,
> To which th' invited never came,
> Deprived of its intended guest,
> Was given to the old and lame.

His true reaction was that Lady Sophia's 'beauty and cleverness' had deserved a better fate than marriage to Lincoln. Lord Carteret was a much greater prize in the matrimonial stakes. 'How graceful, how charming, and how haughtily condescending she will be! How, if Lincoln should ever hint past history, she will

> Stare upon the strange man's face
> As one she ne'er had known.'

To Horace it was like the twist in a French novel, high romance in high society. To the end of his life he kept Sophia's portrait in Strawberry Hill. Illogically for someone so conscious of male youth and good looks, he found it perfectly correct that a good-looking and intelligent woman should marry someone twice her age and a heavy drinker if that someone was a highly successful politician. As for Lord Carteret, he insisted on reading Sophia's letters out during Cabinet meetings and assured friends who warned him about Lady Pomfret that he was marrying the girl not her family. According to Horace, Lord Lincoln was 'quite indifferent and laughs'.

In March the wedding looked uncertain as Lady Sophia developed scarlet fever and her fiancé was down with the gout, but both rallied and on 14 April were married at Lord Pomfret's house overlooking Green Park. After the reception the bride went alone in a hackney chair to her husband's house, where only Carteret and the hall porter were up. The new couple mounted the back stairs without ceremony and so to bed. Horace kept his eye on them both in the months that followed, enjoying the fact that Lord Lincoln was in waiting and had to present the new Countess at Court. He appreciated the style of her dress but noted that she 'grows more short-sighted every day: she can't walk a step without leaning on one of her ancient daughters-in-law'. The marriage had made Sophia a step-grandmother.

In August that year, Horace too was beginning to feel his age, with Lincoln's marriage set for October. 'I wish I were young enough to be as thoughtless and extravagant as I used to be,' he wrote to Mann, the eternal safe, distant confidant. 'I grow older and love my follies less.' Quite what a successful front of normal sexuality he had put up to hide his true nature appears from Richard Edgcumbe's letter of the same month. Edgcumbe was hopelessly in love with a 'little whore' known as 'the Kitten' and desperate for advice from a man of feeling like Horace. He suspected that he was writing to a sexual rival, 'I know she must and will do bawdy with somebody,' he admitted, and 'I should be as little vexed to hear she had with you as anybody.' It was Edgcumbe whom Horace had pretended, the year before, might have suspicions of the affair with Lincoln.

But Horace was not collecting whores, only old master drawings, for which he had engaged the obliging John Chute as his Italian agent. 'For the Bolognese school I care not how many,' but 'I would not have above one to be sure of any of the Florentine school.' His father had virtually ceased to collect paintings, perhaps put off by the supposed Domenichino which Mann, Chute and Horace had persuaded him to buy but which turned out to be a Sassoferrato. On his own account Horace had bought, oddly in view of his dislike for the Dutch school, a Van Dyck in the manner of Teniers; also, more in keeping with his growing interest in ancestry and English art, an old picture of Lady Jane Grey's mother and stepfather. At this time Horace was based in a tiny house sandwiched next to his father's town house in Arlington Street. His growing collection, together with the approaching end to a love affair of almost three years' standing, were causing him to think of creating a more suitable home. In a letter to Mann of 18 August 1744, he wrote:

> If I had a house of my own in the country, and could live there now and then alone, or frequently changing my company, I am persuaded I should like it ... when one begins to reflect why one don't like the country, I believe one grows near liking to reflect in it.

But the country tedium of Houghton in August, where he was exiled once more, lured him not into 'reflection' but into the last two love letters of the series, the first of which, dated 25 August, was openly and scathingly jealous.

After spending many lines clumsily trying not to talk about the subject most on his mind, Horace could no longer restrain himself. He was sure that 'those reverend pastors Mr Hume and Mr Spence' would have explained Lord Lincoln's marital duties to him, but as the Earl was moving into 10 Downing Street he should be warned that his new wife's 'great youth' would 'prevent her doing the honours of your palace with half the grace of my Lady

Sandys', its last occupant. Then his sexual rage bubbled over in a flight of macabre bad taste worthy of Edgar Allan Poe. Sir Robert Walpole's mistress and second wife, Maria Skerrett, had once reigned at Number 10. 'If you have any friendship for me,' Horace blundered on, savaging himself more than Lord Lincoln, 'you will restrain the excess of your vigour . . . When you mentioned the disposition of the apartments, I observed you intended lying in the room where the last mistress of the house died – now my Lord I don't desire to see her come into play again, and I am sure your vigour if exerted, would reanimate her, though she has been dead these six years: don't shake that bed too violently!' At which point, a paragraph too late, Horace ended with: 'Adieu! do love me; I do you to excess: and am ever Yours H.W.'

Almost by return of post Lord Lincoln replied, not in outrage, but with a lost letter of 'the two most eloquent sides that were ever wrote'. Five lines of the two pages had been blotted out so thoroughly that Horace could not decipher the tantalizing concealed message, though the rest, he wrote in his reply, dated 5 September 1744, had 'sense enough and tenderness for me'.

As if to calm his nerves in his reply, Horace began with a long stilted passage in the style of a seventeenth-century French letter-writer, Vincent Voiture. Then he broke out furiously from 'this affected stuff, which makes me as sick to write as it will you to read'. What did it matter if in those blotted five lines Lincoln had 'wrote something childish and silly; you often say such things; why should you not write them? I have no patience,' he continued, exposing his own theory of style, 'with people that don't write just as they would talk: if you could say nothing simple I might admire you more, but I am not sure I should love you so well . . . Don't I even love any nonsense of yours?'

At least it had been a long letter. He had not expected it, 'but you know how to make me happy and always do'. Then, foreseeing trouble ahead, he begged, 'My dearest Lord, do make me quite well with her [Lady Lucy Clinton] and Miss Pelham: you know how devoted I am to everything that belongs to you: pray convince them of it.' That, manifestly, Lincoln failed to do because after the wedding there was no further social contact between Horace and Lincoln's family.

Reverting to his comic role as Mr Plunkett, Horace then offered a long flattering character study, or rather a eulogy, of the Comte de Guiche, one of Lincoln's pen names. Throughout the raptures certain real traits emerge: levity, a strict sense of honour, good breeding, no wit, 'because he never says an ill-natured thing', as much friendship as love for his mistresses, a fondness for teasing and a taste for all fashionable pleasures. For Horace the writing is unusually vague. There are no anecdotes, no quoted speeches, only a golden haze of affection. When Lincoln is in spirits "tis impossible not to be pleased' but then "tis impossible not to be better pleased when he is out of spirits' for then he exposes 'the goodness of his heart'. He is the man 'Whom folly pleases and whose follies please'.

In its very last lines the letter hints that Horace had been trying to match Lincoln up with his illegitimate half-sister, Lady Mary Walpole. The Pelham family would not have approved. With two sugary lines from Pope,

> Fair eyes and tempting looks which still I view,
> Long loved adored ideas, all adieu!

the last intimate letter ends, much probably to the relief of the editor Wilmarth Lewis, who wrote, 'At this point HW's friendship with Lincoln was interrupted; why is not known'. Lewis could, and should, have made some shrewd guesses.

Lord Lincoln was married to Catherine Pelham on 4 October 1744, two relatively willing lambs sacrificed on the altar of dynastic economy. Horace noted the event tersely in a letter to Mann, linking it with another wedding, that of Lord Middlesex, as if it were of no particular significance. And so there, in a sense, it ended. But if there ever was a true end to Horace Walpole's one physical love affair it is not apparent from his subsequent writings. He never broke wholly free emotionally from his Lord Lincoln. Over the years in various letters a watchful, angry devotion surfaces.

In one letter of 1752 to George Montagu, Horace reported obscurely, 'Last week Lord Downe received at the Treasury the sum of an hundred kisses from the Auditor of the Exchequer, as

being the reward for shooting at an highwayman.' Lord Downe
was Henry Pleydell Dawney, a popular young clubman about St
James's. The Auditor was Lord Lincoln. Later in the same year
Horace was repeating gossip to Mann about Lincoln's treachery in
a matter of political appointments to his 'intimate friend' at
Court, Lord Harcourt. But the Newcastle papers suggest that
Lincoln's marriage to Catherine Pelham, though arranged, was a
happy one. That 'vigorous' style of speaking which Horace had
noted, and which was originally a way of bypassing a stammer,
comes bursting through in a letter Lincoln wrote to his wife when
she was staying in London: 'I am overjoyed that our dear little boy
continues so well, pray take care of him and of yourself too, for I
hear ye town is very sickly. Good God! How immensely I love you
both!'

The Countess Catherine's death in 1760 raised hopes in
Horace that a close friendship might be renewed, though by that
time he was forty-three and Lincoln forty. Earlier he had tried to
use the Revd Spence as a go-between, asking him to 'tell my Lord
Lincoln how sorry I am that he is out of order and that I cannot
have the honour of waiting on him'. He even sent Spence a good
translation of some lines from Tibullus, as one scholar to
another; but this brought no response, written or social, from the
Earl.

Horace tried a new tack: giving presents and asking small
favours. Lincoln acknowledged in February 1762 a gift of the first
two volumes of Horace's *Anecdotes of Painting*. Then, in August
1764, Lincoln received Horace's *The Life of Edward Lord Herbert
of Cherbury*. Occasionally Horace would badger the Earl for one of
the tickets, which he controlled by right of his political office, to
witness a famous trial from his gallery at Westminster Hall. The
real purpose of this tenuous contact was revealed in a note of 1764
which opens: 'My Dear Lord, I had hoped that as you had admitted me to a renewal of our friendship, I was to have the satisfaction
of sometimes seeing you; but I begin to think you only meant to
tantalize me with the prospect of a happiness you did not intend I
should possess.' It concludes: 'It would make me seriously happy to
pass some of the remaining hours of my life with you. I will not be

troublesome ... Nobody can be more devoted to you ... You may have newer servants, but none are so attached to us as those we make when we are young.'

That last appeal brought no response or none that has survived. Where emotions were concerned, Lincoln was a realist. Horace was the romantic. It would still be interesting to know whether the Earl ended both correspondence and friendship out of a sense of marital propriety or from pressure by the Pelhams. The latter is the more likely, otherwise why should he have retained Horace's letters? The Duke of Newcastle was an affectionate, persuasive and morally upright uncle. He had eased Lady Sophia from the scene and probably eased Horace out in the same way. Horace was not, apparently, considered good company for a respectable married man. And this is where the Horace–Lincoln affair becomes rather more than just an interesting pointer to Horace's vulnerable humanity and turns into one of the most successful feats of political assassination in English historical studies.

Historians, from Thomas Babington Macaulay onwards, have always claimed to be wary of Horace's letters and memoirs as sources for his age and society. Nevertheless, they all turn to him because he was so informed, so readable, so much the detached observer. It has been almost impossible not to be influenced by his humour and his anecdotes. Those memoirs that he left in a locked chest with instructions in his will that they should only be opened at a certain time by his legal heirs have proved to be a time bomb to the reputations of his contemporaries. None, however, has been more thoroughly ridiculed and blasted than Lord Lincoln's uncle, guardian and adviser, the Duke of Newcastle. This man, who manipulated or dominated the British political scene for an unprecedented forty-two years, wheeling, dealing, surviving and resurfacing in ministry after ministry from 1724 to 1766, is dismissed by virtually every historian who covers the period as a time-serving old bumbler, the Charlie's Aunt of eighteenth-century politics; and the source of this manifest misjudgement is Horace Walpole.

The blizzard of amusing spite began to flow in 1745 when Horace remarked of the man who had separated him from Lord Lincoln, 'if one could conceive a dead body hung in chains always wanting to be hung somewhere else, one should have a comparative idea of him.' Thereafter, for twenty-one years, the attack never faltered. All Newcastle's best qualities, his energy and his warm human good nature, were turned to pantomime slapstick and folly. 'Who would not laugh at a world where so ridiculous a creature as the Duke of Newcastle can overturn ministries?' and we have all, to our shame, obediently laughed at a frustrated homosexual's clever spite.

The Duke on his way to Hanover reviews British soldiers in wartime:

> He hurried about with his glass up to his eye, crying, 'Finest troops! finest troops! greatest general!' then broke through the ranks where he spied any Sussex man, kissed him in all his accoutrements, 'My dear Tom such an one!' chattered of Lewes races; then back to the Duke of Cumberland with 'Finest troops! greatest general!' and in short was a much better show than any review!

As a damning little extra Horace added that Newcastle had dragoons out to guard his gold plate when he took it out of a pawn for a ceremonial occasion. Yet a man who had been a minister of a rich country for forty years had ruled with such integrity that he had to send his plate to the pawnbrokers!

Then again, when Newcastle, on the death of his beloved brother Henry Pelham, finally succeeded to the premiership, Horace reduced the occasion to farce:

> On Friday this august remnant of the Pelhams went to Court for the first time. At the foot of the stairs he cried and sunk down: the yeomen of the guard were forced to drag him up under the arms. When the closet-door opened, he flung himself at his length at the King's feet, sobbed and cried, 'God bless your Majesty! God preserve your Majesty!' And lay there howling and embracing the King's knees, with one foot extended, that my Lord Coventry, who was *luckily* in waiting and begged the standers-by to retire with, 'For God's sake, gentlemen, don't look at a great man in distress,'

endeavouring to shut the door, caught his Grace's foot, and made him roar out with pain.

There can hardly be an accurate word in this account, but the method is deadly: the direct speech, the telling detail of the 'King's knees', the 'one foot extended' and the mocking 'august remnant of the Pelhams'. It is the cartoonist's technique caught in prose – Gillray anticipated. What is then forgotten is that this is the man whose ministry rescued the country when Horace's father, Sir Robert, had left it floundering and unprepared in the War of the Austrian Succession. It was Newcastle who was Prime Minister in the triumphant years when, as Paymaster-General, Pitt the Elder was successfully directing the Seven Years War, a time when the first British Empire was in the fullness of its power. Yet for every schoolchild who knows that Sir Robert Walpole was our longest serving Prime Minister, how many remember that the infinitely more effective and successful Duke of Newcastle was ever Prime Minister at all? As a letter-writer, Horace Walpole was dangerously entertaining; but historians turning to him for background detail on the politics and society of the eighteenth century should be aware of his obsessively destructive bias, particularly where the Pelham family is concerned.

CHAPTER SIX

A Batty Langley poet and a Batty Langley house

As his long, emotional relationship with Lord Lincoln collapsed about him, Horace had an understandable if uncharacteristic fit of panic. In the July of 1744, before Lincoln's October marriage, he wrote a long, intense letter to Henry Conway, who was far away at that time campaigning in Germany, in an attempt to bind Conway to him in chains of gratitude that might prove more enduring than the ties of lust which had kept Lincoln. The extraordinary offer he made was to endow his cousin with the greater part of his annual income (£2000 was the sum mentioned), so that Conway would then have the financial substance to propose marriage to Lady Caroline Fitzroy, the Duke of Grafton's flighty daughter, with whom Conway had long been uneasily infatuated.

Horace claimed unconvincingly to want 'to begin acting like a man', and believed that he could not begin better 'than by taking care of my fortune for one I love'. The writing then became closer to an incoherent love letter than a generous monetary proposal:

> You have seen (I have seen you have) that I am fickle and foolishly fond of twenty new people; but I don't really love them: I have always loved you constantly: I am willing to convince you and the world, what I have always told you, that I love you better than anybody. If I ever felt much for anything, which I know may be questioned, it was certainly for my mother.

The appearance of his long-dead mother in this proposal is only one of the letter's implausibilities. How was Conway supposed to react to the idea that the whole fashionable world would be informed that his marriage to a duke's daughter had been subsidized by a bachelor cousin? Would all three live together? There was only one answer which the level-headed Henry could make. He replied politely and aptly that he had thought such goodness 'had no longer existence but in romances. But dear Horry, how very unworthy should I think myself of that goodness if I were capable of accepting it.' There followed some shrewd assessments as to just how far such a sum of money as Horace was proposing might go. His letter was dated 5 August. On 25 August the 'fickle and foolishly fond' Horace was writing again to Lincoln and ending 'do love me; I do you to excess: and am ever yours.'

If 1744 had been a difficult year, 1745 was to prove even more testing. His father died in March, Patapan died in April, Lady Sophia died in October. By December, Prince Charles the Young Pretender and his army of Scots had reached Derby. London seemed virtually unprotected and with a Stuart on the throne there would be no pensions, sinecures or places in Parliament for a junior Walpole; but Horace took it all in his stride. He had a journalist's natural pleasure in any violent event, however threatening; only emotional isolation threw him off balance.

His father's end was painful but Horace played out his part as the dutiful son in attendance. The doctors had decided to experiment, as doctors must, with the latest cure, actually a deadly corrosive 'elixir'. 'After the first four or five days, in which they gave him the bark there surmounted an explosion and discharge of thirty two pieces of stone. A constant and vast effusion of blood for five days, a fever of three weeks, a perpetual flux of water and sixty-nine years' made death a happy release. There would be no more tedious summers with bucolic relations in Norfolk, no more hunting, shooting and hare-coursing. Horace had respected his father and been hugely proud of him, but he had probably never loved him. There had been no bonding in his childhood and early adolescence.

Lord Orford had been carried off by the stone. Lady Sophia died of child-bed fever. Her honeymoon of power had been brief, less than seven months passed between her marriage and her husband's resignation from the Cabinet, squeezed out by Pelham influence. She had then to face the sterner realities of married life. Her stepson and Lord Granville's only heir had gone mad while staying with the Duke and Duchess of Bedford. He had burst in upon his host and hostess one morning with a bloodstained basket of horses' ears which he had just cropped in the Bedford stables. It became desirable, therefore, that Sophia should produce an alternative heir.

She had a careful pregnancy. Horace 'did walk one country dance with her, but the prudent signora-madre would not let her expose the young Carteret any further'. On 26 August 1745 a daughter was born and christened Sophia, but her mother could not throw off a fever. Six weeks later,

> about seven in the evening Lady Pomfret and Lady Charlotte were sitting by her, the first notice they had of her immediate danger, was her sighing and saying 'I feel death come very fast upon me!' She repeated the same words frequently; remained perfectly in her senses and calm, and died about eleven at night. Her mother and sister sat by her till she was cold.

Horace responded with appropriate feeling: 'It is very shocking for anybody so young, so handsome, so arrived at the height of happiness [she was almost forty years younger than her husband], so sensible of it, and on whom all the joy and grandeur of her family depended, to be so quickly snatched away.' He could not be so detached about his dog. 'If it would not sound ridiculous, though I assure you I am far from feeling it lightly,' he wrote to Mann, 'I would tell you of poor Patapan's death: he died about ten days ago.' None of his many later pets were to exercise quite such a hold upon his affections as that little white spaniel. The celebrated John Wootton painted its portrait; Chute and Horace wrote poems for it and when Henry Conway was reporting from the battlefield of Fontenoy, where close on 6000 British troops were slaughtered by the French cannon, he added gravely, 'but what are all deaths to poor Patapan!' Horace's friends took care to pretend to live within the known boundaries of his fantasy world.

With so many figures from his emotional past removed and with the very real possibility that a Stuart restoration would soon exile him to the shores of Lake Geneva, Horace chose that bracing time, the winter of 1745–6, to become reconciled with Thomas Gray. He seems to have decided, now love was off the agenda, that his immediate future lay in politics, in a new property and in encouraging poetry. His income was limited so all three aims would have to be pursued with caution and imagination. Printing costs were not high, poetry was prestigious, Gray was writing poetry and Horace's three close remaining friends – Chute, Conway and Mann – had all written behind his back to Gray expressing their sympathy over the Reggio incident. So it was time to recoup.

If it had been left to Horace, we would never have known the devious and shamefaced stages of that retreat back into friendship. He never even mentioned the meetings to Mann, who had grown very fond of Gray during their months in Florence. But if Horace was furtive, Gray – a very different Gray from that abject, lovesick scholar of the 1730s – relished every manoeuvre of the four-day peace talks that November and reported gleefully on them to his Cambridge friend Thomas Wharton.

An intermediary had told Gray that Horace was anxious to resume their old relations. Gray was interested in a Regius Professorship that might soon be going at Cambridge and he believed that Horace still had influence. Also, despite a show of modesty, Gray wanted to see his poetry published; Horace had the funds and the inclination. Wary as two temperamental cats, they moved towards each other.

Their first meeting was a disastrous sham. Gray called at Horace's town house and was kissed 'on both sides with all the Ease of one, who receives an Acquaintance just come out of the Country'. Horace had decided to avoid awkward apologies by behaving as if nothing had ever gone wrong. He began 'to talk of the Town & this & that & t'other, & continued with little Interruption for three Hours', then Gray took his leave, 'very indifferently pleased, but treated with wondrous Good-breeding'. The next night was much worse. In order to put on a little show of self-righteousness for his behaviour at Reggio, Horace had invited round to supper at his club that dreadful creep of Eton and Cambridge days, the fourth member of the 'Quadruple Alliance', the Revd Thomas Ashton. In an attempt to embarrass Gray, Horace confronted him with the indiscretions of one of the letters Gray had written to Ashton from Italy. Now at supper Gray found Ashton pretending to be still shocked by the ingratitude of that slight indiscretion. The situation was only saved by a jolting journey home in a shared Hackney coach which 'jumbled us into a Sort of Reconciliation'. Horace 'hammer'd out somewhat like an Excuse; & I received it very readily, because I cared not two pence'. It sounds as if both were tipsy after their dinner.

On the next day there was still no improvement. In one of his usual monologues Horace talked for hours and poured out 'abundance of Anecdotes'. But the only result of this flood of sincerity and openness was that Gray 'had still less Reason to have a good opinion of him than (if possible) I ever had before'. Only at breakfast the next morning over bread and butter does Horace seem finally to have come clean, when 'we had all the Eclaircissement I ever expected, & I left him far better satisfied, than I had been hitherto'. Both men were homosexually aware and the only truth that would have satisfied Gray would have been the truth about Lincoln. That, at least, he could have understood and that, possibly, is what he was given.

It is not likely that Horace enjoyed those four November days of talks but at least he had achieved his object. The correspondence was resumed, but on an intensely scholarly, literary level which must have frightened Horace somewhat. They often met in town and even, on one occasion in the summer of 1748, went on a country-house tour together. Horace had a great respect for scholarship, but immediately after that holiday he revealed, in a sudden flash of irritation, how much the revised friendship was costing him. Writing to lazy, easy, laid-back George Montagu, he suddenly broke from an anecdote to admit:

> I agree with you most absolutely in your opinion of Gray; he is the worst company in the world – from a melancholy turn, from living reclusively, and from a little too much dignity, he never converses

easily – all his words are measured and chosen, and formed into sentences; his writings are admirable; he himself is not agreeable.

With Gray secured, at a price, and with the Scots in retreat after their high point of success at Derby in December, Horace could at least feel secure in his pensions and places. His *annus horibilis* was over; he had his political interests and a wide circle of superficial friends, but there was an emotional void and an absence of purpose. Great letter-writers cannot afford to be mere neutral commentators. They need a dynamic of their own. It was in the new year, 1746, that the long countdown to Strawberry Hill and the fame, both instant and posthumous, which the little house would bring him, could begin.

The first step in that direction was a bad mistake. In the late summer he rented a small house, his 'little tub' as he called it, in the cloister-confusion of the lower ward of Windsor Castle. Eton College and the castle lowering above it had obsessed him from his schooldays. He had responded to the Chartreux in Paris because it had offered the same picturesque huddle of medieval complexity. His childhood had freakishly conditioned him against normal contemporary responses to classicism and classical order. Years later, in his seventies, Horace would still be referring to Windsor as 'one of my antediluvian passions . . . a Gothic chapel and an historic castle are anodynes to a torpid mind.' But in 1746 an anodyne was the last thing he needed. His 'little tub' was a foolish retreat back into the past, an attempt to recover his schooldays that led inevitably to depression because it reminded him of Lincoln. To his friends he claimed that he felt overshadowed in his new home by the near presence of the enormously fat Duke of Cumberland, now resident in Royal Lodge in the Great Park. He compared the Duke to Alexander and himself to Diogenes in his tub. But the real shadow was Eton and those golden irrecoverable days.

George Montagu took the full blast of his hopeless nostalgia in a letter of 8 August, heavy with Eton's esoteric slang. Horace had travelled up to hear the repulsive Ashton, now a Fellow of Eton, preach in the College chapel, so he was eating in The Christopher, Eton's best hotel. 'Lord! How great I used to think anybody just landed at the Christopher! But here are no boys for me to send for!' He had come back not as a proud father or even as a jolly uncle, only as a yearning bachelor and rejected lover.

> Here I am, like Noah just returned into his old world again, with all sorts of queer folks about me – By the way, the clock strikes the old cracked sound – I recollect so much, and remember so little, and want to play about, and am so afraid of my playfellows, and am ready to *shirk* Ashton and can't help *making fun* of myself, and envy a *dame* over the way that has just locked in her boarders, and is going to sit down in a little hot parlour to a very bad supper so comfortably! ... I should be *out* of all *bounds* if I was to tell you half I feel, how young again I am one minute, and how old the next ... you will think I deserve to be *flogged.*

As Gide once wrote, far too late to be any help to Horace: 'never repeat your joys'. The house in Windsor was a miscalculation. Horace was not cut out to be a brooding paedophile wandering round the playing-fields with 'no boys for me to send for'.

That autumn help, of a kind, arrived in the person of the defiantly affected old queen, John Chute, back in London from Italy and still acting as the male equivalent of a lady's companion to the stone-deaf but wealthy Francis 'Thistlethwaite' Whithed, to whom he referred as his 'other half'. Horace was delighted with the Chuteheds, as he called them. 'I am more and more with them,' he wrote to Mann that November, 'Mr Whithed is infinitely improved; and Mr Chute has absolutely more wit, knowledge and good nature, than, to their great surprises, ever met together in one man.'

Wit and knowledge Chute certainly possessed, together with an aggressive self-assurance; good nature he only assumed when it was to his advantage. His habitual manner was theatrical. There is a vignette of him in the letters, storming through a roomful of Sebastiano Riccis in a Venetian gallery, rejecting them all as rubbish, to pause reverently before a Guido Reni as 'real art'. Horace tended to be impressed by such judgements. In his next publication, the *Aedes Walpolianae*, he ranked Guido alongside Raphael and Annibale Caracci as one of the three greatest painters of all time.

As a younger son with neither profession or prospects, Chute had developed a keen eye for the main chance. While still in Florence he had kept Horace's friendship lightly on the boil, writing when there was a commission in the offing. It was he who had unloaded the large Boccapadugli stone eagle with a broken beak onto Horace and a supposed Domenichino onto Sir Robert Walpole. Chute understood the importance of humouring Horace with whimsicality better than any man. He would send compliments to Patapan, 'the little dear Knight of the Silver Fleece', and on one occasion capped Horace's scheme to have Patapan made a viscount by proposing that his own cat, Geofry, should officially adopt 'his little dear Highness' Patapan, 'settling his fortune upon him, with this only other condition, that he conform himself to the Church of England, as by law established'. Evelyn Waugh built up the persona of Sebastian Flyte's teddy bear Aloysius in exactly the same way, knowing how important a pet or a toy can become to someone reluctant to commit affection to a real person.

Both Gray and Horace assumed that the Chuteheds were devoted and inseparable, but there has to be a suspicion that Chute had dissuaded Whithed from marrying his Italian mistress, the mother of his child, and that the relationship was wearing thin now they were back in England. Chute was on bad terms with his surviving eldest brother and appears to have cultivated Horace as an alternative port in future financial storms.

What is interesting about this newly revived friendship is Horace's instant compatibility with another practitioner of what may be described as effete militancy. Horace's letter-writing talents were sexually neutral but his other two claims upon immortality – Strawberry Hill and *The Castle of Otranto* – were both instances of high-camp defiance of normal conventions. Both required some confidence and it may be that Chute supplied that confidence. He was ready to play Gothic games with Horace and Richard Bentley, Horace's new friend, artist and architectural adviser in the 'Committee of Taste' which the three men formed to design Strawberry. Later, in 1763, he devised a far more staid Gothic house, Donnington Grove in Berkshire, for an antiquary friend, but there can be no doubt that Chute's personal preference was for the Classical. This is instanced by the sumptuous and wholly inappropriate multiple staircase that he crammed into The Vyne when that Tudor house fell serendipitously into his possession. In the Committee of Taste, Horace might describe Richard Bentley as 'The Goth', but Horace himself was the only real Goth. Bentley was a Rococo artist who could turn his invention to brilliant pastiche in anything – Classical, Gothic, Jacobean or Chinese. What Chute, the crypto-classicist, supplied was confidence to rebel, and this is what makes the revival of their Florentine friendship in England in 1746 so important. There was probably never anything physical between the two men. They echoed each other's mannerisms far too closely. But for these key years of Strawberry's genesis, before Chute became a landowner and financially independent in 1754, he gave Horace the moral support to put his limited resources into brick, wood and exotic plaster. Chute was Horace's official intimate and would be mourned accordingly when he died in 1776:

> he was my council in my affairs, was my oracle in taste, the standard to whom I submitted my trifles, and the genius that presided over poor Strawberry! His sense decided me in everything, his wit and quickness illuminated everything – I saw him oftener than any man; to him in every difficulty I had recourse, and him I loved to have here, as our friendship was so entire, and we knew one another so entirely, that he alone never was the least constraint to me.

But it is possible for a detached observer to see John Chute as Horace's evil genius, hostile in subtle ways to rival friends and over tolerant of self-indulgent mannerisms.

With the Chuteheds around London, socially at a loose end, it became more urgent for Horace to have a country retreat to which he could invite friends. Windsor had been a mistake but, still essentially a London suburbanite, his next choice fell upon Twickenham. In May 1747 he took over the lease of 'Chopp'd Straw Hall' with five acres of fields leading down to the Thames.

There are rival interpretations as to the ground plan and orientation of this building. The preferred interpretation is that the house was an undistinguished little bachelor's pad with its main rooms facing east towards the river. Stylistically quite undistinguished, it was an L-shaped block some fifty years old, three storeys high, with a two-storey kitchen annexe set back to its rear. A bishop and a lord had been recent tenants, so it was not a cottage nor a working farmstead, despite Horace's description of it as 'a little farm'. It had stables and additional single-storey buildings to the west. These and the presence of a flock of four-horned Turkish sheep gave it the fashionable air of a *ferme ornée* like Philip Southcote's Woburn Farm at Chertsey. All around it were similar weekend hideaways for the gentry. There was a large pagoda in the Earl of Radnor's garden next door and Alexander Pope's celebrated villa and garden were less than a quarter of a mile away. Set on a slight rise of land above flood level, the house commanded a fine view of a long reach of the Thames down to Twickenham village.

Immediately – and this is the secret of Horace Walpole's success – he began to write up his new possession in seductive journalese, presenting a very ordinary house as a brightly jewelled artefact hung with wit. A June letter to Conway records 'enamelled meadows' and 'filigree hedges', a couplet from Pope was improved to make even the bird-life metallic:

> A small Euphrates through the piece is roll'd
> And little finches [eagles in the original] wave their wings in gold.

Barges are as 'solemn as Barons', dowagers 'as plenty as flounders', no ambience was perfect for Horace without titled old ladies. From those earliest months, the new home comes across as bright, bustling and cheerful. There were prosperous neighbours, the river was alive with boats, the roads with carriages, Twickenham village closed a main vista like a little seaport at the bend in the river. There were no dark woods or Salvator Rosa rocks and its only ghost was Pope's, 'just now skimming under my window by a most poetic moonlight'.

This was the beginning of Horace's most successful paradox: he sold the Gothic Revival, hitherto largely an experimental style of the suburbs, to high society as the proper setting for the Rococo *fête champetre*, for pastoral idylls conducted in Claudean surroundings. Claude's paintings had always featured a ruin or two, a castle or temple; now Horace, a natural francophile, gave a delicate tilt to the Rococo world of Watteau and Fragonard, anglicizing it with stage props that evoked, very lightly, the ruins of the English Middle Ages. His Strawberry Hill Gothic was the reverse of intimidating. From the start of his occupancy it was accessible, frivolous and brightly coloured. There was some inherent quality to that reach of the river, now quite lost. Even the melancholy Gray sensed it: 'I do not know a more *laughing* scene', he wrote to Wharton, and Horace used exactly the same term, but, being Horace, had to put *'riant'*, in French. Remembering the later associations which were to gather around the Gothic, it is important to grasp that Strawberry Hill was chosen for its cheerfulness. It was a scene 'without the least air of melancholy: I should hate it if it was dashed with that.'

By the June of the following year, 1748, his mind was made up. 'I like to be there better than I have liked being anywhere since I came to England,' he told Mann. He had escaped from past associations with Lord Lincoln, the ugly little house was not a 'villa' in any accepted sense of that word, nor did it remotely suggest that picturesque mediaeval confusion which Horace always found satisfying. But it was a blank canvas; it had possibilities. So he bought it for £1,356.10.0, securing a private Act of Parliament to clear up a previous shared ownership and establish his freehold. 'Chopp'd Straw Hall' was not euphonious. For a few months it was called 'Kyk in de Pot' from a Dutch fort briefly in the news; but then Horace discovered from the title deeds that the land had been known as 'Strawberry Hill Shot', so Strawberry Hill it became and he promptly spent £381 on improvements.

Years later, in his *Description of Strawberry Hill*, Horace dismissed this building work of summer 1748 as unimportant, as 'designed by Mr W Robinson of the Board of Works before there was any farther improvements to the house'. This was because Robinson's addition to the east-facing, riverfront of the house was pure Batty

Langley and Horace had come by that time, rather foolishly, to regard Batty Langley as a name of shame. Originally a Twickenham landscape and nursery gardener, Langley had established a line for himself in pattern books of Gothick and classical designs suitable for journeyman builders and architectural amateurs. His most popular Gothick pattern book, *Ancient Architecture Restored and Improved,* had appeared in parts between 1741 and 1742 and was reisssued as a single volume in 1747 with the more fashionable title of *Gothic Architecture.*

Langley's Gothic designs were perfect for suburban extroverts wanting to extend an existing modest house with a startling new wing or to build a summerhouse which would set the neighbours talking. Novelty was in the air, and provided the expense was not too great, it was stimulating to experiment with any number of exotic styles – Gothic, Chinese or Turkish. Another suburbanite, Dickie Bateman, a friend of Horace living in Old Windsor, began his villa additions in Chinese style but then converted to the Gothic and that was typical. There was still something reassuringly English about a Gothic house, and if builders were honest no one knew much at first-hand about Chinese design apart from what could be learnt from their tea-cups.

Robinson's clumsy, Langley-inspired improvisations set the tone for Strawberry's later most appealing elevations. By commissioning them, Horace had committed himself to the Gothic rather than to the Chinese when his stylistic options were still entirely open, when he was actually planning an Indo-Chinese drawing-room at Mistley Hall in Essex for his friend Richard Rigby and when the vista from his new Gothic bay centred upon Lord Radnor's Gothic summerhouse and Chinese pagoda.

Robinson had created a first-floor Breakfast Room, 'where we all live', enlarged by a canted bay with three Langley-style ogee windows conventionally paned. This 'charming bow window', where Horace liked to sit enjoying the view east across his new terrace and lawns to the river, was crudely projected out upon two posts to form a porch to what then appears to have been the main entrance. It would be hard to design anything more remote from 'the true rust of the Barons' Wars', as Horace described a contemporary sham castle at Hagley in Worcestershire by Sanderson Miller, but it was a likeable, amateurish start. Most of it still survives, squeezed between later additions. Horace enjoyed the outlook so much that in 1755 he built himself a bedroom over the Breakfast Room, giving it a large, vaguely Tudor, mullioned window to catch the morning sun. A dotty crow-stepped gable and a cross then topped the composition. The porch was filled in much later.

Horace was eager to dissociate himself from a petty bourgeois figure like Batty Langley. The immediate inspiration for those ogee windows and that canted bay had been the villa at Esher which William Kent had designed in 1729 for Henry Pelham, now the Prime Minister and Lord Lincoln's uncle–father-in-law. Horace had visited Esher twice that summer, once in the company of Gray. 'I prefer it to all villas,' he wrote, and Gray was of the same mind: 'it is my other favourite place' was his verdict. It has, however, to be said that what the pedestrian Robinson roughed out at Horace's bidding savoured more of Langley than of Kent. Esher had the advantage of a genuine gatehouse of about 1480 as its centrepiece and two spreading wings alive with multiple ogees and quatrefoils, each extended by two five-sided, canted bays.

Both Gray and Horace were perfectly aware of the origins and nature of this popular 'Gothick' vernacular that was being created around them, though Horace never spelt his Gothic with a 'k'. Gray commented disparagingly that Kent 'had not read the Gothic Classics with taste or attention. He introduced a mix'd style, wch now goes by the name of the Batty Langley Manner. He [Langley] is an architect that has publish'd a book of bad designs.' So this Kentian way of handling the Gothic was at one and the same time bad design yet, at Esher, highly covetable. The two men's instinctive approval was aesthetically sound, their disparagement was no more than antiquaries' snobbery. An authentic new style was evolving: the Middle Ages approached through classical schemata. It was functional and nationalistic, a welcome escape from the predictabilities of the Palladian. Critics who damn it as a back-garden phenomenon have to explain Esher, a large villa built for a powerful politician of the Whig old guard, a Prime Minister and the brother of a duke. Even so, it has to be admitted that Esher is topographically suburban and Pelham's villa, for all its size, seems to have had a relaxed air of amateur improvisation on every front. This Gothick played symmetrically with those feminine trefoils and ogees characteristic of the Decorated Gothic that had flourished in England between 1298 and 1345, around the reign of Edward II. Horace saw it as 'the florid Gothic' which 'owes its beautiful improvements to England alone': a sure sign that he was beginning to take it all a little too seriously.

Architectural historians explain this eighteenth-century enthusiasm for medieval forms as either Gothic Survival, due to the conservatism of High Church clergy and university common rooms, or as a deliberate revival of the past by newly ennobled gentry and merchants anxious to impress the baronial origins of their families. Gothic did also acquire a spurious political significance. It was seen – wrongly, of course – as being the architecture of England's liberty-loving Saxon ancestors and, therefore, the right style for those who supported a parliamentary democracy rather than royal absolutism. Batty Langley may have believed that the Anglo Saxons built delicate Gothic *'ombrellos'* but Horace was far too sophisticated to suppose that the Witanagemot had ever met under curvaceous Gothic arches.

One other association of this eighteenth-century revival of Gothic, an aspect very relevant to Horace Walpole, deserves a cautious consideration. This is that the style, with its sinuous forms and conscious rebellion against orthodox classicism, may have had a particular attraction for homosexuals. While there was no covert conspiracy to subvert wholesome classical design, the following facts and half-facts should be noted.

Horace and his homosexual clique of Chute, Gray and Montagu were all bachelors. Thomas Wright of Durham designed mock castles, Gothick arbours and ruined grottoes. He was another bachelor and so was his patron Norborne Berkeley for whom he redesigned Stoke Park in Gloucestershire in castellated form with Rococo interiors. Sir Richard Hill of Hawkstone was a bachelor responsible for an influential and much visited landscape park in Shropshire with Gothic features. Two bachelor architects, James Gibbs and Robert Adam, both designed striking and original Gothic buildings. Gibbs usually worked somewhere between the Baroque and the Palladian, but his Temple of Liberty at Stowe was among the earliest (1741–4) and most spatially brilliant of Gothic inventions. Horace 'adored' it as 'pure and beautiful and venerable'. Robert Adam is rightly associated with a delicately feminine version of the neo-Classical, but his lost reshaping of Alnwick Castle for the Northumberlands was, in its time, the most dazzling of all major Gothicizations. His Brizlee Tower survives in the park at Alnwick to prove the quality of the castle.

John Carter, the antiquary who recorded Strawberry's rooms, was a bachelor who went around on his sketching expeditions with a young female servant 'dressed in boy's clothes,' and Thomas Pitt, Lord Camelford, who succeeded Bentley on Strawberry's Committee of Taste, was 'outed' by that early queer-basher Mrs Thrale. He did, however, make a late marriage and produced a son. William Kent, whom Horace always saw as his arch rival in Gothic invention, behaved all his life like a jolly camp comedian, never married, but is reputed to have had a mistress. Sir Richard Newdigate of Arbury was a lifelong Goth of great achievements who used Sanderson Miller, the Hiorns, Henry Keene and Henry Couchman to devise a house of intense Gothic and Gothick complexity. He married twice but had no children. Lastly there was William Beckford, married and with children, but disgraced for sexual romps with the young Earl of Devon and left to express his emotional drives in the tremendous towered fabric of Fonthill Abbey, the Gothic ultimate. All this could be no more than statistically explained coincidence but certainly leaves Horace the aesthete in good company.

This is not, of course, to suggest that the parliamentary committee which decided upon Barry's designs for the Palace of Westminster or the Manchester aldermen who backed Waterhouse's pinnacled project for their new town hall were two gangs of secret homosexuals. By the nineteenth century, the Gothick had become Gothic and lost all its engaging connotations of protest and deviant aesthetics. To confuse the psychological implications of stylistic choice a little further, Horace had published, just a year before he built his 'charming' Gothic bow window, a trenchantly neo-Classical critique of European painting in his *Aedes Walpolianae*. He had written this back in the idle, bucolic summer of 1743, but by 1747 with the 2nd Earl of Orford in frail health and hopeless debts mounting, the collection was in danger and Horace was anxious to alert the nation to its importance. In the event he failed and the paintings were snapped up by the Russians for the Hermitage, where they joined that very mixed collection of art bought in bulk. The *Aedes* did, however, give Horace the flattering notion that he might be a serious scholar and that publication was a route to fame.

Given that in art criticism there is always a tendency for subjective opinions to appear as objective truths, the *Aedes* is consistently and impressively written, often anticipating by several decades Sir Joshua Reynolds on 'the Ideal'. It opens with a populist assault on fellow critics worthy of the best tabloid journalism:

> No science has had so much jargon introduced into it as painting: the bombast expression of the Italians, the prejudices and affections of the French, joined to the vanity of the professors, and the interested mysteriousness of the picture-merchants, have altogether compiled a new language. 'Tis almost easier to distinguish the hands of the masters than to decypher the cant of the virtuosi. Nor is there any science whose productions are of so capricious and uncertain a value.

Because he was personally always competitive, Horace had to have a league table, a ranking order of artists, so he followed up with the bald statement that the three greatest painters were Raphael, Guido Reni and Annibale Caracci. Much of the *Aedes* is a justification of that opening. The three artists were great because they painted, not reality, but ideal beauty, nature improved by the study of antique sculpture. In the next decade the Abbé Winckelmann would be hyping the same notion. Horace was a deist with leanings towards Plato's theory of realities; 'I cannot help believing,' he told one lady admirer, 'that the Great Author of all things had types or standards of sublimity, beauty, grace, harmony and proportion in his mind'. Sublimity can become a very personal concept. Just as Winckelmann would become fixated upon the Greek sculptors' handling of their models' testicles,

Horace believed that the surest guide to a great artist was his handling of draperies. They had to be bold and simple in their folds, nothing fussy or naturalistic. He looked for a quality of ideal generalization in a painter and for that reason wrote of 'the great Salvator Rosa ... and his masterly management of horror and distress'; his 'Prodigal' at Houghton was 'not foul and burlesque' like a Caravaggio, nor 'minute circumstantial and laborious like Dutch painters'. His pictures like Shakespearean characters 'contain the true genius and sense of satire', which was to be credible. Compositions should be clear and subjects should be morally improving. Though he was a deist, Horace could switch roles easily and take the New Testament accounts of Christ's life very seriously. Dark colouring was best in a painting, but dark and clear, not dark and Rembrandt. The Dutch school was given a generally low rating because of its realistic representation of 'earthen pots and brass kettles' and, though he had spent a year in Florence, Horace had no time at all for the Florentine painters. Their drawing was 'hard', their colouring was 'gaudy and gothic'. This last point is valuable as it proves that Horace associated things 'gothic' with bright, light colours. Meanings of words shift treacherously over the centuries. Strawberry Hill was 'gothic', so Strawberry Hill was bright, not, as we have come to expect, dark and gloomy. On another occasion Horace used the word 'Gothicisms' synonymously with vulgarities.

The *Aedes* makes a strange background to Horace's building ventures, but the book does explain his drive to become, like his father, a collector and, unlike his father, to educate people of his own class by offering them, free of access charge, a gallery of paintings, objects of virtue and curiosities to enjoy and discuss. Horace would become in 1753 one of the first trustees of the British Museum and his Strawberry was itself a miniature and egocentric British museum: a measure of compensation for the loss of his father's collection, kidnapped by the Tsarina and now in the Hermitage.

In 1748 what was wanting was a theme, a framework, in one sense a gimmick, to direct the next development, the way ahead. Horace needed an artist, a designer to whom he could relate affectionately, yet still control and direct. This is why it is so frustrating that we have no clear record of when Richard Bentley came into his life. Horace was familiar with the Bentleys as early as November 1748, when he mentioned the scandalous behaviour of 'Madame Bentley' in a letter to Mann. By June 1750 Bentley had already been staying at Strawberry Hill for some time as a guest and familiar friend 'whom I adore'.

There are suggestions, in a remarkable letter to George Montagu, that it was in September 1749 that the idea, not only of a brave, bright new Strawberry, but even the first hint of *The Castle of Otranto*, was beginning to take shape in Horace's quirky and convoluted mind. Montagu, Conway, Chute perhaps, and possibly Bentley were involved. Montagu had, in a rare fit of activity, been visiting tombs at Bisham Abbey, writing to Horace about them and questioning the authenticity of a portrait of Henry VI's son, thereby rousing Horace's competitive interest. Chute had been deep in genealogies all summer, constructing an impressive ancestry for Horace Mann, who was being snubbed as a parvenu by the snobbish aristocracy of Florence. Horace was back at Strawberry, gardening – 'I dig and plant till it is dark' – but he was recently returned from another country house crawl with Henry Conway, this time in Buckinghamshire where a half-ruined seat of the Russell family – Chenies – had captured his fancy to a quite unusual degree:

> There are but piteous fragments of the house remaining, now a farm, built round three sides of a court. It is dropping down, in several places without a roof, but in half the windows are beautiful arms in painted glass. As these are so totally neglected, I propose making a push and begging them of the Duke of Bedford: they would be magnificent for Strawberry Castle.

If there was one single obsession behind the building of Strawberry, now shifting in concept from 'villa' to 'castle', it was to create a frame in which to hang 'painted glass'. Horace loved old portraits but, more than anything, he adored stained glass. He applied the term 'painted' indiscriminately to true stained glass and modern painted imitations. Light filtering into a room through colour was his anticipation of Paradise. His enthusiasm repeatedly comes through in his letters to Bentley: 'the Bishop of Worcester's chapel of painted glass' at Hartlebury, 'the profusion of painted glass' at Oxford which was 'entertainment enough' for him. But now, at Chenies, all that glass was going begging. The resolution to build followed naturally in the next sentence. 'Did I tell you,' he asked Montagu, 'that I have found a text in Deuteronomy, to authorize my future battlements?' So 'future battlements' were already proposed, extensions to that strip of token castellation which Robinson had already set up over the rickety new porch. The biblical encouragement was based on a mistranslation: 'When thou buildest a new house, then shalt thou make a battlement for thy roof, that thou bring not blood upon thy house, if any man fall from thence.' But that was still not the end to this flow of prescient and prophetic writing. Six lines later came a change in focus from building to hero: 'In the church at Cheneys, Mr Conway put on an old helmet we found there; you can't imagine how it suited him, how antique and handsome he looked, you would have taken him for Rinaldo' – the knight in Tasso's romantic epic.

The Castle of Otranto, Horace's Gothic romance, was to be written in a burst of a few weeks of inspired writing in 1764, just as a plot to project Henry Conway into political power was coming under strain. By Horace's own account, he began to write it after a dream of seeing a monstrous mailed hand on the stairs at Strawberry. In fact, the novel opens not with a huge hand but with a gigantic helmet falling from heaven into the courtyard of a castle with such thrilling military violence that the castle's heir, Conrad, is crushed to death beneath it. The unravelling of symbols is an inconclusive literary game, but helmets, castles, handsome men and violence do seem to be linked here in Horace's consciousness.

His remarkable letter to Montagu of 28 September 1749 ends on a note of high enthusiasm, 'all my works are revived and proceeding'. In January 1750 Horace was begging Mann to 'pick me up any fragments of old painted glass, or anything' for 'a little Gothic castle'. Two letters to Montagu later, Horace was chatting excitedly about the next man in his life, Richard Bentley: 'He has more sense, judgement and wit, more taste and more misfortunes than sure ever met in any man.' Horace always overrated the talents of his friends; a positive and generous side to his nature and one curiously contrary to his generally destructive commentary upon social life and political motivations. In this instance his mixed assessment of Bentley was fair, but missed out the quality that really drew the two men together for the ten years of their friendship: Bentley's malicious and mocking sense of fun.

Although it involves moving ahead a little, to 1751, nothing illustrates the interaction of the two better than Bentley's illustration for Thomas Gray's doom-laden and apprehensive 'Ode on a Distant Prospect of Eton College'. Horace had been encouraging and publishing Gray's poems for years; indeed, it is no exaggeration to say that without Horace's interventions half of Gray's poems might never have been written and the other half would never have been published. Now, with Bentley's dazzling talent as an illustrator at his disposal, Horace hit upon the idea of a finely produced limited edition, six 'Odes' all illustrated by Bentley with various head and tail pieces. As usual Gray cavilled and fussed but allowed himself to be projected, protesting, toward immortality.

Horace's reward was Bentley's illustration to the 'Eton' ode. This poem, it will be remembered, is a serious affair. The Thames is mentioned, the boys' games are allowed one verse, but the emphasis falls upon the miseries awaiting the schoolboys when they go out into the world: 'These shall the fury Passions tear, The vulturs of the mind, Disdainful Anger, pallid Fear, And Shame that sculks behind', and so on. Bentley transformed all this angst into a paedophile's vision of bliss. Father Thames, a nude and bearded old gentleman crowned with rushes, lolls watchfully while a typical group of Etonians, all stark naked and well fleshed, enjoy the famous playing-fields. Five release a linnet and flaunt their bottoms at Father Thames, one bowls a hoop, while two swim in the river, one swimmer looking lustfully at the other swimmer's bum, which Bentley has raised out of the water at an impossibly provocative angle. Overhead, between two half-naked herms, a depressed man and a lunatic woman, whose symbolism hardly needs to be stressed, the Furies, all naked of course, are impending over the boys and one male fury is doing something actionable to a female who is bending over a cloud – 'Shame that sculks behind', no doubt. It is easy to imagine Horace and Bentley in helpless fits of giggles over this lewd yet comical interpretation of Gray's melancholy posturing. In the light of these irreverent designs for the six Odes, the easy interaction of the two new friends begins to make sense. 'You,' Horace once wrote to him, 'have always laughed at me in a good humoured way'.

Both Bentley and Horace were physically small, though Bentley had winsome and defiant good looks; and both were the sons of famous and admired fathers; Bentley's had been Master of Trinity College, Cambridge for more than thirty years and was a classical scholar of considerable stature. Where the two differed in their responses to life's handicaps was that Bentley mocked his father's world while Walpole struggled gallantly with Sir Robert's world of serious politics and also struck out on scholarly and artistic lines that were purely his own. It was the difference, in short, between negative and positive spirits. Bentley made a hobby of procrastination, Horace was compulsively busy and occupied.

Richard Bentley had begun as a child genius and never thrown off either the child or the genius. He had matriculated, inevitably at his father's college, when he was only eleven; he took his BA degree at fifteen, was Keeper of the King's Libraries at nineteen and a Fellow of Trinity three years later. So much for his 'sense, judgement and wit'. Then came his 'misfortunes'. Part of the Cottonian and King's Libraries at Ashburnham House were destroyed in a fire when Bentley was in residence. He was blamed and obliged to resign. He married his first wife soon after and got into such hopeless monetary troubles that his father disinherited him. He then fled to France for three years to escape his creditors and lost his Trinity fellowship. The Archbishop of Armagh once entertained Montagu for an entire afternoon with amusing stories of Bentley's exploits and Lord Granville considered him a delightful joke, so there were clearly other misadventures now forgotten and Bentley had a national reputation as a scamp and ne'er-do-well.

By 1748 he was back in England again and, like John Chute,

always alert for promising openings, he met Horace. For his part Horace loved Bentley, forgave, humoured and coaxed him in the face of wilful contrariety and disappointments past counting. Bentley was the prodigal son whom Horace could never sire and yet – a point rarely noticed as Horace cajoled and bullied Bentley like a father with a spoilt but brilliant child – Bentley, born in 1708, was nine years older than Horace. In terms of years their relationship was back to front.

Bentley was to act as Horace's visual interpreter, almost as if Horace, when he went on a tour, took photographs and needed Bentley to develop them. From a wild jaunt in Sussex with Chute, Horace wrote back to Bentley at delightful length and added 'by the way, we bring you a thousand sketches, that you may show us what we have seen'. Simply by using his eyes and pencil, Bentley had far more appreciation and understanding of a Gothic vault than had most contemporary antiquaries.

As Bentley entered his inner circle of friends, Horace's letters took on a new register of humour and shared critical reactions. In August 1752, while the south front of Strawberry was being remodelled, Horace was writing excitedly to Bentley about 'a beautiful tomb, all in our trefoil taste ['our', not 'my'], varied into a thousand little canopies and patterns'. It was the same letter in which he joked about the idea of Chute having to share a double bed in a low alehouse with a smuggler, then went on to debate the rival merits of the Palladian, the 'pert bad apartment' in Leeds Castle and the 'ancient magnificence' of Knole. In all his wide correspondence there are no equivalents to these relaxed and discursive journal-letters which his friendship with Bentley encouraged.

Apparently Bentley's letters were written in the same mood, but Horace allowed nothing except three brief business notes to survive. It is unlikely that Horace ever entertained a sexual relationship with a man nine years older than himself and with a wife and six children living nearby in Teddington. His new friend-ship was warmly possessive rather than physical. He was prepared to spend considerable sums to bring Bentley back from a second debtor's exile, this time in Jersey, between late 1753 and 1756.

The exact terms of the financial settlement were never made public, but where Horace spent money there was usually a strong emotional undercurrent. That the relationship was close, even romantic, is clear from some of the letters. Writing to Bentley from Southampton, where he was visiting Netley Abbey with Chute, Horace related: 'We walked long by moonlight on the terrace along the beach – Guess, if we talked of and wished for you!' Bentley was resolutely heterosexual but where Horace was concerned that would have been an added attraction, and it was jealousy of Bentley's socially ambitious wife that would eventually contribute to their separation.

Timing is important in relationships and Bentley gained an ascendancy of a kind over Horace at a time when Chute was becoming something of a liability. Francis Whithed had died early in 1751 and, to ingratiate himself with Horace, Chute attempted to direct the young heiress whom Whithed had been about to marry, a girl called Margaret Nicholl, worth £150,000, towards Horace's scatter-brained and ultimately mad nephew, the penurious 3rd Earl of Orford. Thus, at a stroke, the Walpole fortunes would be restored and Sir Robert's picture collection saved for the nation. That was the plan but Horace, eagerly in favour, appealed to his uncle 'Old' Horace for family support. 'Old' Horace decided that Miss Nicholl would make an admirable catch for his own second son and scuppered everything. A major family disaster resulted, with a plot that reads not so much like Richardson's *Pamela* as Fielding's *Shamela*. In a final dreadful scene Chute attempted to bully the Nicholl girl into his choice of a new guardian. During 'three hours all but ten minutes' of histrionics, he knelt, implored, flew around the room in a rage and three times lost his temper, leaving Miss Nicholl in 'the greatest fright and disorder'. All to no avail. She married neither Lord Orford nor 'Old' Horace's son, but the Marquess of Carnarvon. It was not Chute's year. Horace supported him in all his unscrupulous behaviour, sitting with him in court when the case came before the Master of the Records to decide who was Miss Nicholl's true guardian, and acting, according to 'Old' Horace's legal spy, 'with more impudence during the attendance than I am capable of informing you

... they were making faces and affronting all the time'. This, it must be admitted, sounds very much like Horace in one of his high camp fits.

Horace's schemes for turning Gray into a major British poet were going more smoothly. By leaking copies of Gray's 'Elegy written in a Country Church-yard' all over London, he had manoeuvred his neurotic friend into doing what he had wanted in the first place, namely to commission his publisher, Dodsley, to bring out a quick official edition of the text. Gray was even beginning to enjoy fame a little. He rose to the bait of a collected edition of all his poetry illustrated by Bentley and produced two new 'Odes' for it; one of them, 'A Long Story', being exceptionally tedious. Originally the volume was to be entitled *Poems by Thomas Gray, with Designs by Richard Bentley*, but Gray panicked at the notion of so straightforward a title and insisted on a change to *Designs by Mr R. Bentley for Six Poems by Mr T. Gray*. Horace considered the new version to be vulgar – 'Mr is one of the Gothicisms I abominate' – but he endured it and calmed Gray when a second crisis arose as Gray discovered that his portrait was to be included among the other 'designs'. (The portrait was removed.)

As his frontispiece to the *Designs*, Bentley drew himself as a naughty monkey painting Gray as an effete nude youth holding a lyre. He excelled himself with the design for the 'Church-yard' elegy: an elegantly emaciated Gothic archway and vault of tense linear precision. For 'A Long Story', he changed register and went Gray-baiting again, showing the poet trapped in his garden by two half-naked women, one of whom is twitching her enormous skirt up over the terrified poet's head, forcing him to inspect what he obviously has no wish to see. Bentley's excuse for this mild pornography was a line in the poem, perfectly inoffensive in itself, describing how the Muses had rescued Gray from some predatory women and 'Convey'd him underneath their hoops To a small closet in the garden'. The artist has translated this hint into a parody of Fragonard's *The Swing*, where a gentleman lolling on the grass attempts a discreet glimpse up the ankle of the lady on the swing.

In order to plump the desperately slim volume out a little, Horace had decided to include an occasional poem which Gray had sent him as a joke back in 1747, after one of Horace's cats had suffered a fatal accident in a tub of goldfish. To describe this as an 'Ode' was to parody a serious poetic form, but then Horace's delight in the light-hearted mockery of serious forms was his great artistic strength, the source of his populism. For every reader who knows Gray's Odes 'On the Distant Prospect of Eton', 'On Spring' and 'On Adversity', there are a hundred who can quote from his 'Ode on the Death of a Favourite Cat'. Gray stood in the same relationship to serious poetry that Strawberry Hill did to original Gothic architecture. Both his poetry and Horace's architecture charmed a wide and influential public by a quality of cheeky detachment, a popular updating of earlier forms. That was precisely what Batty Langley had offered to prospective designers: an unserious but immediately pleasing version of something hitherto inaccessible.

Bentley's illustration for the Cat poem was a masterly projection of its spirit, with mice gleefully celebrating, the cat, Selima, tilting perilously towards the brink, and a marvellous group of mandarin cats presiding from the roofs and cornices of Chinoiserie pavilions. If only Bentley's sketches could have been worked up into illustrations for Gray's later poems: 'The Bard', 'The Fatal Sisters' and 'The Descent of Odin', the poems would have enjoyed the same popular success as Selima. Their pastiche, Langleyesque medievalism, should have been sold to the reading public by Bentley's presentational skills. 'The Bard' was to be, in 1757, the first publication of the Strawberry Hill Press at a time when it was far too amateur an operation to attempt such illustration.

While Bentley was drawing his meticulously detailed designs for Gray's six poems, the Committee of Taste – Horace, Bentley and Chute – was preparing over the winter of 1751–2 for the building season which would begin with the fine weather. There was to be an obvious spin-off from Bentley's Gothic vaults for the forthcoming book and the lean, elegant Gothic forms, Pugin with anorexia, that the Committee contrived for the dramatic centrepiece of Horace's villa-castle. This was the central entrance hall, far and away the most spatially complex and theatrically successful interior of Strawberry Hill's first building phase. Bentley's inspiration had been neither Tudor nor the earlier Decorated Gothic, but the emaciated forms of Early English as found, for instance, in the Lady Chapel of Salisbury Cathedral. Horace reported to Mann: 'my house is so monastic that I have a little hall decked with long saints in lean arched windows and with taper columns, which we call the Paraclete, in memory of Eloisa's cloister.' It would be the visual shock of the Paraclete – dim shadows, brilliant lights from the 'long saints' in the painted glass windows, attenuated columns supporting acutely pointed arches, the complexities of trefoil and quatrefoil forms in the banisters, every surface of the walls elaborated with the panelled decoration of Prince Arthur's chantry chapel at Worcester – that made Strawberry famous. This was the initial stylistic assault of the house which would make visitors catch their breath and report excitedly to their friends.

There would, by the early summer of 1753, be other delightful rooms: a parlour with Venetian prints hung on Gothic paper, a Red Bedroom for Mr Chute, and a Green Closet. This last was, until the Library was fitted up in the 'Great Tower' after 1756, Horace's favourite room. It had two windows, one to the garden, the other to the beautiful prospect, and the top of each was 'glutted with the richest painted glass of the arms of England, crimson roses and twenty other pieces of green, purple, and historic bits': old Flemish glass bought as a job lot. Next to this was the Breakfast Room, 'where we always live'. This was the room which Robinson had created in 1748 and that was now 'hung with a blue and white paper in stripes adorned with festoons'. Its original Langley-style bow window was 'gloomed with limes' and 'darkened with painted glass in chiaroscuro, set in deep blue glass'. After all the extensions to Strawberry in subsequent years, this small, first-floor room probably remained the real heart of the house. Under it was 'a cool little hall' where, until the Great Parlour was added, 'we generally dine'.

Characterful and atmospheric as these little apartments must have been, they were unremarkable when compared with the

Paraclete and 'Armoury', as Horace called the spaces at the foot and landing of his Gothic stairs. All the other little rooms, bright and amusing as they might be, hung with paintings and curiosities, were relatively commonplace. The Paraclete–Armoury was unique, innovative and memorable, and it was wholly Richard Bentley's concept and achievement. If its stylistic links with Bentley's 'Designs' for Gray were not evidence enough, there is Bentley's ink and wash 'View of the Hall and Staircase' in the Lewis Walpole Library at Farmington to prove its designer. 'I cannot leave my workmen,' Horace wrote in June 1753, 'especially as we have a painter who paints the paper on the staircase under Mr Bentley's direction. The armoury bespeaks the ancient chivalry of the lords of the castle and I have filled Mr Bentley's Gothic lanthorn with painted glass which casts a most venerable gloom on the stairs that was ever seen since the days of Abelard.'

Everything else about this first major building phase at Strawberry, that part of the house which went up in the building season of 1752 and was being fitted up then and in the spring and summer of 1753, is predictable, charming, but no more than that. The entrance hall was the stunner that brought aristocratic and royal visitors flocking for the privilege of a viewing and founded the legendary reputation of the house.

By combining the evidence of Horace's letters with the existing structure of Strawberry Hill, it is clear that the Committee of Taste planned in 1751–2, and built in 1752–3, a remodelling of the south or garden front. This involved the creation of the Paraclete on the north side of the house; the service buildings – stable, cow-shed, laundry – at the back and to the west of the original main block were left to confuse later, post-1758, building works. This first major building operation would give Strawberry an impressive five-bay elevation to the south with a central canted bay projecting boldly to give views in three directions. Such a front was fashionable in 1751. The canted bay had been borrowed from William Kent, so there was nothing particularly original in the form, though Strawberry Hill preceded all Robert Taylor's Thames-side villas with canted bays. What was so striking about the

Committee's elevation was the fenestration. Horace always loved a trefoil. The form is not, strictly speaking, English Gothic; but more, in fact, Venetian. Yet all the windows of Strawberry's new south front were trefoil-headed. Obviously pleased by their sinuosity, Horace was to insist, in the next (1753–4) building phase, on cinquefoil-headed windows – five cusps instead of three. Trefoil and cinquefoil-headed arches feature prominently in Langley's beautifully produced second edition of *Gothic Architecture*.

John Chute is often described as being the architect of Strawberry Hill, but in the vital first phase when the house was so influential, its architects were the committee of three, with Chute as its least active member. He favoured the linear 'collegiate' or Tudor Gothic which he used when he designed Donnington Grove as a favour for a neighbour. He was a gentleman amateur, not a professional architect. Two drawings for Strawberry's new south front which Wilmarth Lewis attributed to Chute are not in anything remotely like his fussy drawing-hand of over-ruled pencil lines or spluttering Indian ink. A careful presentation drawing to charm a client and a much larger working drawing, they must be by Robinson, who supervised its construction. But the trefoils will have been the choice of Horace and Bentley. It was the more exotic and not always native Gothic forms which Horace enjoyed. Bentley favoured the Early English but skilfully combined the two with Rococo details to make this initial phase of Strawberry Hill both original and acceptable.

Quite how original and immediately famous can be seen from its guest list. Horace did not make his castle-villa or villa-castle open to the public on a ticket system until 1763, by which time a whole sequence of gallery, cloisters, tribune and new bedrooms had been added to display his collections. But already on 2 March 1754, before the 'Great Tower' with the Great Parlour below and the Library above had been completed, the corpulent Duke of Cumberland, the King's favourite son and the nation's military hero, had arrived to inspect the 'castle'. Horace wrote in triumph to Bentley, exiled in Jersey:

Nolkejumskoi [the Duke] has been to see it, and liked the windows and staircase. I can't conceive how he entered it. I should have figured him like Gulliver cutting down some of the largest oaks in Windsor Forest to make jointstools, in order to straddle over the battlements and peep in at the windows of Lilliput.

By July that year, the Duke of Bedford, who had still not seen the house, was talking of Strawberry as if it were some marvelous prodigy too expensive for him to afford to copy. In March 1755, with the Great Parlour complete and Strawberry ready for serious entertainment, Horace dined the Duke of Grafton, Lord and Lady Hertford, Henry Conway and his wife Lady Ailesbury, Lord Orford and the Churchills. A month later, there was a breakfast for the Duke and Duchess of Bedford, their children, Lord and Lady Gower, the Ladies Egerton, Waldegrave and Coke, William Pitt's sister and Sir John Sebright. Less than a month passed before the King's sister, Princess Amelia Sophia, was around poking into every corner of the house and in 1759 Horace had the Duchesses of Hamilton and Richmond and Lady Ailesbury all sitting together in Bentley's shell-shaped garden seat. All this before Strawberry was ten years old.

His account of the Bedfords' breakfast, written to Bentley again, for all Horace's best and happiest letters of the 1750s were directed to Bentley, gives some feeling of how his 'castle' was functioning:

> The first thing I asked Harry [his footman] was, 'Does the sun shine?' It did, and Strawberry was all gold and all green. I am not apt to think people really like it, that is understand it, but I think the flattery of yesterday was sincere; I judge by the notice the Duchess took of your drawings. Oh! How you will think the shades of Strawberry extended! Do you observe the tone of satisfaction with which I say this, as thinking it near? Mrs Pitt brought her French horns: we placed them in the corner of the wood, and it was delightful.

That was probably the occasion which set Horace's mind towards raising an echoing cloister for further outdoor performances of music. At that time Strawberry was still virtually all Bentley's ideas realized. At its spiritual heart was his mood-creating set-piece of the Paraclete and Armoury and there were his chimneypieces, all enchanting frivolities pitched between Gothick and Rococo and usually the only substantial decorative features in their rooms; the rest of the illusion was paper and paint.

But Horace's obsession with scholarly correctness directed by the dull hand of Chute, a devotee of panelled Perpendicular, was already beginning to settle upon a Strawberry of its essence sun-filled and architecturally incorrect. Richard Bentley, or 'poor Cliquetis' as Horace and George Montagu usually referred to him from his habit of a dry cough, had fled, late in 1753, to Jersey to escape his creditors. From the island he sent perhaps his most exquisite design, his second for the interior of the Library. His first had been a charming gimcrack affair of intersecting arches which Horace must have rejected out of hand. For this second design he had played on the theme of the nodding ogees, as in the Lady Chapel of Ely Cathedral, fusing them with a section of a screen from Old St Paul's Cathedral as drawn by Hollar. Horace had urged the attention to Hollar's drawing, but Bentley still managed to make the conflation appear light-hearted and elegant rather than dull and scholarly. In typical Bentley fashion, he included a sketch of Horace with gangly legs reaching up for a book from one of the bookshelves. Had it been realized, it would have been one of Strawberry's most poetic interiors. But, taking advantage of the favourite's absence, Chute had roughed out an inferior alternative based far more closely on a repetition of the St Paul's screen arch, which he persuaded the fickle Horace to adopt. Horace wrote rudely back to Bentley: 'For the library, it cannot have the Strawberry imprimatur: the double arches and double pinnacles are most ungraceful: and the doors below the bookcases in Mr Chute's design had a conventual look, which yours totally wants. For this time, we shall put your genius in commission, and, like some other regents, execute our own plan without minding our sovereign.' Fatally, pretentious scholarship had taken the place of inspired invention – Gothick was giving way to the Gothic Revival.

CHAPTER SEVEN

A failure in human relations

Richard Bentley's sixteen-month exile on the island of Jersey produced one of the most human and revealing of Horace's letter sequences, but it also set up tensions of loyalty and gratitude between the two friends that would bring about their permanent separation in 1760. Because Horace destroyed all Bentley's letters, despite finding them 'more and more entertaining', we have only one side of the events leading up to the final quarrel, but George Montagu played a negative role in it all as Horace's confidant. Between them, the two selfish, ageing bachelors seem to have regarded Bentley as their special discovery, an amusing cultural toy to divert them in matters artistic. Neither Horace nor Montagu took the wives of their friends seriously, and Horace in particular seems to have resented the very existence of Bentley's second wife, referring to her always by such disparaging nicknames as Hecate (queen of the witches), Cleopatra, Tisiphone (leader of the Fates or hounds of hell), a 'bunter' (rag-picker), and even on one occasion a 'whore'. She appears at one time to have been Bentley's mistress and Horace never accepted her as a respectable domestic figure. There was a baffled bewilderment in his account of visiting the Bentleys' Teddington home once and finding 'Mr Bentley sitting in his chimney corner with *five* girls', his daughters; and there was also a son.

When Bentley first fled to Jersey to escape incarceration in the Fleet prison, Horace tried hard to hide the destination from his wife. 'We don't talk about his abode,' he wrote conspiratorially to Montagu, 'for the Hecate his wife endeavours to discover it.' Bentley was 'where he was, and now and then makes me as happy as I can be having lost him, with a charming drawing.' Despite his own real sense of loss, he seemed unable to appreciate that Bentley could love his wife and need her with him.

Still half-dependent upon Bentley for inspiration in design, Horace clamoured for new drawings. Bentley, desperate for money and piqued at the rejection of his inspired Library scheme, bombarded Horace with absurd get-rich-quick projects. One was for Horace to rent a granite quarry on Jersey and produce everlasting garden ornaments. In another Horace, the ever abstemious, was to import cheap French wines by a customs fiddle. Gifts were exchanged and demanded. Bentley developed a lust for goldfish from Horace's round pond, Po Yang, a relic of his Chinese period, and for bantam fowl, probably because there was a quick sale for them on Jersey. Horace reluctantly supplied both. In return, Bentley sent Jersey Lily bulbs and pickled partridges, but these last only irritated Horace because they reminded him of Mrs Bentley, who must have pickled them. Her husband had soon told her where he was exiled and she had joined him out on the island. An oil painting which Bentley sent as a present to Horace tactlessly emphasized the reunion by showing Bentley and his Mrs Hecate standing on a wild sea-shore.

Horace's letters to Bentley, despite some acid remarks about the oil painting, were unusually wide in their emotional range. While so many of his chosen correspondents were the most appalling old blimps, Bentley was the eighteenth-century equivalent of a trendy left-winger, irreverent and critical. Writing to him, Horace could sound sincerely disturbed about the Society for the Propagation of the Gospel's involvement with the slave trade, and it is clear that in one of the lost letters Bentley had taken him to task for his amoral enthusiasm for another war. 'To be sure,' Horace fluttered back, 'war is a dreadful calamity! But then it is a very comfortable commodity for writing letters and writing history . . . why there is no harm in being a little amused with looking on': a confession at the very heart of Horace's existence and one which should have been engraved on his tombstone.

Their exchanges come to be increasingly concerned with the launch of a rescue from Bentley's financial problems. For Horace, careful over money matters, to allow himself to become involved in such details is proof of his real affection for Bentley and his equally real need for Bentley's stylistic advice. 'Your poor Cliquetis,' he wrote to Montagu, as if referring to a shared responsibility, 'is still a banished man. I have a scheme for bringing him back, but can get Mrs Tisiphone into no kind of terms; and without tying her up from running him into debts, it is vain to recover him.'

The strains began to tell. One day Horace would be the earnest friend, concerned and encouraging:

> When every day I see Greek, and Roman, and Italian, and Chinese, and Gothic architecture embroidered and inlaid upon one another, or called by each other's names, I can't help thinking that the grace and simplicity and truth of your taste, in whichever you undertake, is real taste. I go farther: I wish you would know in what you excel, and not be hunting after twenty things unworthy of your genius. If flattery is my turn, believe this to be so.

On another day, he would lecture like a schoolmaster as Bentley pressed him to mount a rescue from the debt problems:

> If I treat you as a child, consider you have been so. I know I am in the right – more delicacy would appear kinder, without being so kind. As I wish and intend to restore your happiness, I shall go thoroughly to work. You don't want an apothecary, but a surgeon – but I shall give you over at once, if you are either froward or relapse.

Such a passage explains why Bentley's playwright nephew, Richard Cumberland, described his uncle's relations with Walpole as 'of a sickly kind, and had too much of the bitter of dependence'. But Horace kept up his reports on the progress of building, praising Bentley's 'chimney with the two dropping points' now installed in the Blue Bedchamber, demanding designs for Gothic chairs with traceried backs and sending a sketch for the Library ceiling 'which you must adjust and dimension'.

It was to solve such needs that Bentley, generously but unwisely, sent Horace a live present on two legs. This was the morose German-Swiss, Johann Heinrich Müntz, an ex-engineer officer of the French army whom Bentley had discovered, penniless, in Jersey. Horace had expressed an interest in him but had not expected him to arrive in June 1755 with a ten-guinea bill to pay for his travel expenses: 'My good Sir,' he wrote to Bentley, 'is this the sample you give me of the prudence and providence you have learned?' Nevertheless Walpole kept Müntz on for the next four years with board and lodging at Strawberry and a salary of £100 a year. Müntz was a meticulous draughtsman and a soulless artist with the ability to make Perpendicular Gothic buildings look as if they had been built of cast-iron. Horace enjoyed this precision, used Müntz to design for himself, Chute and Montagu and also to copy any paintings that took his fancy. What he never quite appreciated was that, behind the barricade of his severely broken English, Müntz considered himself to be a gentleman first and an artist second.

Müntz had almost a year to settle in at Strawberry before Richard Bentley could rejoin the Committee of Taste. Exactly how generous Horace had been over his resettlement is never made clear. Horace reported testily that Bentley 'waits the conclusion of the session before he can come among us again. Everything has passed with great secrecy: one would think the devil was being tried for his own life!' That was written in May 1756, by which time Müntz had become an alternative to Bentley as a source of inspiration in the creation of Strawberry, though he remained permanently bemused by English living standards and more interested in the foreign news columns of the *Gazette* than in turning out art-works for Horace. He had, however, been coaxed into painting convolvulus over trellis-work on the walls of the China Closet.

The year 1756 marked a pause in Horace's building drive. In Bentley's absence, the so-called 'Great Tower' had been completed. On the outside there was no attempt at an archaic finish, it gleamed in white painted render, a boldly asymmetrical addition to an already asymmetrical east front. Within, on the first floor, was the Library. It was there that Horace posed to be painted by Müntz, seated in an armchair with books littered about him on the floor and a shapeless black dog of indeterminate breed waiting for attention. But it is the detail of the room that steals the picture: the window with its cinquefoil head alive with saints and coats of arms, more stained glass in the quatrefoils above, and on each side of the window the pinnacles and foliated ogees of Chute's book-cases, compressions of the choir screen in Old St Paul's. These lined the room in an overwhelming rhythm broken only by the responding ogee curves of the chimneypiece, a copy of a tomb illustrated in Dart's *Westminster*. What Müntz's painting does not show is the brilliant display of Walpole ancestral coats on the ceiling, their subjects chosen by Horace, scaled by Bentley and painted by Andien de Clermont. Downstairs the Great Parlour was, in contrast, surprisingly plain, dominated by Bentley's finest chimneypiece, a Gothic sedilia which its designer had mischievously set into a pinnacled dance of cinquefoils and pierced quatrefoils around the actual grate.

Over the last two years, 1755 and 1756, Horace had been concentrating on practical problems of domesticity, like bedrooms. Over the Breakfast Room he had created a fine new bedroom for himself, with the Plaid Room next to it, for guests. Various quatrefoils and dormers in the roofs lit servants' rooms. 1757 was to prove a tense and testing time politically, with grave worries over Henry Conway's military career, but Horace still found time to launch an eccentric venture of doubtful value, his own private Strawberry Hill printing-press, lodged initially in an ex-farm building immediately behind the house.

This press has given much pleasure to bibliophiles by its often very limited editions – only six copies, for instance, of *Hieroglyphic Tales* in 1785 – but it was principally self-indulgence. The world was no richer for *An Account of Russia* by Lord Whitworth of 1758, 700 copies; *Poems* by Countess Temple of 1764, 100 copies; or *Vestial* by Cornelie Henault of 1768, 200 copies. Really valuable contributions to the art-history world, like the four volumes of

Anecdotes of Painting in England – a joint venture: George Vertue's notes skilfully edited by Horace – would have been handled more efficiently by a professional publisher; while influential works like *The Castle of Otranto* of 1765 and *Historic Doubts on the Life and Reign of King Richard the Third* of 1768 were, in any case, published professionally in London.

In 1758, Strawberry's next building phase opened with a lurch in design towards the north-west service area of the house. Modern analysis of Strawberry's building history has been obscured by a failure to identify the site of the original kitchen, crucial to its subsequent growth. Wilmarth Lewis admitted to being baffled by the problem and guessed that it might have been in a windowless cellar. No one has been more responsible for this vexatious problem than Horace. But since it lies at the root of all Strawberry's subsequent development it needs to be faced. Being the foremost Walpole scholar, Lewis was more aware than any other expert of how wildly inaccurate Horace could be on the history of his own creation. In his 1774 *Description* of the villa, Horace, as Lewis pointed out, gave incorrect dates for the construction of every new room in the house except for the small Beauclerc Tower. So when he made a casual remark to Mann in a letter of 1755 about converting the 'old kitchen' into a 'china-room', what he meant was that he was indeed converting the 'old kitchen' at the rear of the original house, but converting it into the 'pantry' where silver and crockery would be stored, hence a china room of sorts.

The room referred to on the plans of the ground floor in Horace's time as the 'China Closet' – a display place for rare porcelain – is a small cramped room at Strawberry's south-east angle, one of the few that still recalls the meagre dimensions of Chopp'd Straw Hall. On Horace's rough sketch of the house as he bought it, this room is captioned 'best parlour'. It lay immediately to the left of what was then the main entrance facing east. As Peter Guillery's admirably thorough survey for the Royal Commission on Historical Monuments points out, this could never have held a kitchen range with a wide flue, only a small chimneypiece for a parlour. Indeed it is so small that it has now been turned into a lavatory. Once this misunderstanding has been grasped, the development of the house from its first, narrow, east–west axis becomes crystal clear. In reality the kitchens and service area were always to the rear and west of the house, adjoining the stables, cowshed and small farmyard.

As his next major extension, in 1755, Horace decided to build a new bedchamber, the Holbein Chamber, over this 'old kitchen', now the pantry. But because the Holbein Chamber was to be much larger than its supporting structure it had to be propped up on one side by a little three-arched cloister and under its canted bay by two posts. This compromise produced a romantic, cloistered approach to the main entrance and a refrigerated guest room chilled by the north wind blowing on three outside walls and through the open Gothic arches.

The interior of the Holbein Chamber was as dysfunctional as its exterior. First came a shadowy bed alcove cut off from any light source by a three-arched tracery screen. This improbable structure was a copy of French Rococo–Gothic work of almost contemporary date, 1732, in Rouen Cathedral, and Bentley has to bear the responsibility for it. As a gesture towards warmth, he also designed a huge chimneypiece, part Rouen, part Archbishop Warham's tomb from Canterbury Cathedral. Müntz designed the papier mâché ceiling of six-petalled flowers. The wallpaper was purple. There has to be a suspicion that Horace kept this room for susceptible guests. Gray, sinking now into melancholy depressions, described it as 'the best of anything he has yet done'. The Holbein Chamber should be considered as the first in a series of set-piece Gothic extravaganzas intended more to astonish a visitor than to extend the living accommodation. When Chute added in 1762 a little 'Oratory' under its propped-up bay, Strawberry Hill had gone over the top aesthetically into high-camp posturing.

Horace warned Mann what he was plotting next in a letter of 9 September 1758: 'A day may come that will produce a gallery, a round tower, a larger cloister, and a cabinet, in the manner of a little chapel – but I am too poor for these ambitious designs yet, and I have so many ways of dispersing my money that I don't know when I shall be richer'. He went on to boast of 'my friend Mr

Bentley' – 'such a treasure of taste and drawing' – and Müntz, who had 'all the industry and patience of a German'. Yet in 1759 he sacked Müntz, with angry recriminations, and in 1760 he lost Bentley's friendship for ever.

What was happening to Horace over these years could be politely described as a midlife crisis of identity. He was becoming difficult to live with, over-sensitive about his own feelings, insensitive to other people's, and above all, arrogant. In defence, it should be said that from 1755 onwards he began to suffer severely from gout and what he described vaguely as 'nervous fevers'. In 1757 political pressure, which will be explored later in a Westminster context, became intense. When in trouble he was far too reliant for advice and sympathy on George Montagu, his mirror image, a self-centred bachelor like himself, but with none of Horace's redeeming energy and creativity. In extending his house, writing memoirs and scholarly studies of art, following an active political career and running a private printing-press, he was taking on too much.

In September 1759 the Holbein Chamber was complete and fitted up. Horace promptly decided to write and publish a *Catalogue* of its fifty-eight paintings and drawings. When he looked around for help from Müntz, he learned he was in London. His instant response was that Müntz was with some 'Hannah', his private term for a kept woman. In the old days such lusty activity would not have worried him; now he had grown possessive and moral. It had always been his intention to use Müntz as a source of landscapes, with the possibility that he could be leased out to other art fanciers for a period of years, as Canaletto had been by Consul Smith. This arrangement may not have been made clear to Müntz. On his return from London, there was a dreadful row, its details glossed over by Horace: 'the substance was, most extreme impertinence to me, concluded by an abusive letter against Mr Bentley, who sent him from starving on seven pictures for a guinea, to £100 a year, my house, table and utmost countenance.'

Obviously gratitude, most dangerous of emotions, had been involved and Horace told Montagu to expect no more landscapes: 'I turned his head and was forced to turn him out of doors.'

Horace realized, thinking back to Reggio, that friends like Gray would consider him to blame, but rage trapped him into aristocratic hauteur at its most contemptible: 'Poets and painters imagine *they* confer the honour when they are protected – and set down impertinence to the article of their own virtue, when you dare to begin to think that an ode or a picture is not a pattern for all manner of insolence.' Montagu wrote back soothingly, 'I have long seen the Muntz was filling up his vessel of impertinence . . . I know nobody but Mr Horace Walpole the younger would have borne it so long.' Müntz, however, wrote a defiant but honourable letter. Horace kept it to be amusing about a foolish foreigner's broken English, but it tells against him. 'Protection I never wanted, to purchase it at the rate I did for these last fifteen months past. Protection of the house of comons [*sic*] I never stood in need of. I dare to go tete Levee every wheres', he stormed. Then, in a thrust at Horace the moral inquisitor, he wrote, 'I was prepared for all this, this good while ago, if you thought me so little acquainted with mankind and their different passions it is not mi fault.' Courteously acknowledging that Horace had now paid him what he was owed, sixty guineas, he left Strawberry for ever, with the contemptuous promise that if a jointly held lottery ticket should come up lucky, Horace could have it all.

Another factor behind this confrontation and separation had been the book which Müntz, a considerable scholar in his own right, had been hoping to publish. In his usual thoughtless way, Horace had supposed that he was doing Müntz a favour by bringing it out on his own amateur toy press without remunerating the author. Once away from Strawberry, Müntz published it himself, early in 1760: *Encaustic, or Count Caylus's Method of Painting in the Manner of the Ancients.* It caused no great stir and Müntz left for the Continent where he took up service with the King of Poland.

Meanwhile Richard Bentley was preparing to make a similar break for independence, social consequence and a new career. He was not making enough money and Horace was beginning to ignore his designs for extensions to Strawberry. Bentley was one of those multi-talented individuals who can turn their skills to most kinds of creativity. This time he fancied his chances as a poet–play-wright. He had already written a play – *The Wishes or Harlequin's mouth opened* – his nephew Richard Cumberland was urging him to try his luck on the London stage and his wife, a socially ambitious, but tactless woman, had been snubbed by Horace when she attempted to move in on his carefully selected gatherings of refined society. Horace's world of male companions was beginning to look vulnerable.

What probably decided Bentley was Horace's rejection of his designs for the Gallery and the Cabinet in the proposed western extension of Strawberry. The ground for this was being cleared in 1759, and in that year the Holbein wing had been completed, not with the flowing curvilinear window tracery which Bentley had designed to match his internal screen, but with Chute's drab sash windows. For the Gallery, which Bentley conceived as essentially a space in which to hang pictures, not the dazzling whore's boudoir of red velvet, mirrors and gilt-work which was actually built, he drew a dignified and functional room. Brilliantly lit from the south, it had a shallow tunnel vault springing from well above the three rich canopies on the north wall. These last, chosen by Horace from book illustrations as usual, were details from Archbishop Bourchier's tomb at Canterbury. For the Cabinet, Bentley devised an exquisite vaulted room of needle-sharp pointed arches and pure linear forms, the refined essence of an Early English chapter house which the Middle Ages had never built.

Neither design satisfied Horace's mood of Gothic excess. With the Library and the Holbein Chamber achieved, his confidence was growing. From his Cambridge past he recalled the roof of King's College chapel; from his recent travels he remembered the fan-vaulted cloisters of Gloucester Cathedral. These, he had told Bentley, were 'the very thing that you would build when you had extracted all the quintessence of trefoils, arches and lightness'. Yet now, when the opportunity arose for Bentley to build it and sur-pass the earlier plaster fan vaulting at Welbeck Abbey which Horace had admired, Bentley was phased out of the design team. When, after a year of delays, the interior fitting up went ahead, Horace brought in a new Twickenham neighbour, Thomas Pitt, to

1. Lord Lincoln's preferred image of Horace Walpole – a portrait of 1745 by Jonathan Richardson which was once in the possession of Lincoln at Clumber Park

2. Sir Robert Walpole and his first wife Catherine with Houghton Hall in the background. The profusion of small dogs and *objets d'art* may indicate the origin of Horace's own future enthusiasms

3. Eton College as Horace Walpole knew it, homely in scale and confused in profile

4. The poet Thomas Gray as a young man. Richard Bentley's portrait of him,
nude and playing a lyre, drawn to illustrate Gray's six 'Odes',
suggests that this may have been a fair likeness

5. A print of Henry Conway, after the portrait by
Eccardt, which Horace kept in his bedroom

Prosp: de l'Eglise de R.P. Chartreux

6. The Carthusian house in Paris – its gloomy halls, chapel and civilized bachelor living
quarters captured Horace's imagination as an ideal setting for his own life-style

7. Henry Fiennes-Clinton, 9th Earl of Lincoln and later 2nd Duke of Newcastle-under-Lyme – one of a matching pair of portraits by Rosalba Carriera drawn when Lincoln and Horace were in Venice together

8. Horace Walpole by Rosalba Carriera, designed to face her portrait
of Lord Lincoln. The two young men are wearing the same coat
as a gesture of intimacy

9. John Chute, Horace's closest bachelor friend, holding the pince-nez which he was inclined to flaunt in camp oratory

10. This 1756 engraving of the Thames at Twickenham indicates how much Strawberry Hill was stylistically indebted to the Earl of Radnor's house next door with its Gothick and Chinese garden buildings

12. Lord Lincoln as a pillar of the establishment, painted about 1755 in his garter robes and now a happily married man and the father of a family

11. Thomas Pelham-Holles, 1st Duke of Newcastle-under-Lyme. As the uncle of Lord Lincoln, the Duke earned Horace's lasting and potent enmity. He has never been given his due as one of the greatest Prime Ministers of the eighteenth century

13. Bentley's frontispiece of 1751, drawn for Walpole's
devastating *Memoirs of the Reign of George II*, proves that the
east front of Strawberry Hill was intended to be
asymmetrical from its first conception

14. Richard Bentley in Van
Dyck costume – his
exquisitely irreverent
illustrations helped to
project Thomas Gray into
fame as a poet and he,
rather than John Chute,
inspired the first building
stages of Strawberry Hill

15. Strawberry Hill, the east front in 1758.
Horace's bedroom under the crow-stepped gable was an afterthought imposed
upon Bentley's 1751 scheme. On the left is the symmetrical south front built to command
the garden, on the right is the 'Great Tower' with its first-floor Library

16. The playing fields of Eton as envisaged by Richard Bentley in his mocking headpiece
to Thomas Gray's melancholy 'Ode on a Distant Prospect of Eton College'.
This pederast's fantasy was part of Horace and Bentley's light-hearted conspiracy
to popularize Gray's poems

17. Bentley's headpiece to Gray's 'Elegy written in a Country Church-yard'. Wilful asymmetry, emaciated forms and scholarly observation characterize the design which was a spin-off from Bentley's conception of the staircase hall at Strawberry Hill

18. The Armoury at Strawberry Hill – Richard Bentley favoured this attenuated Early English Gothic in the first building period of the house. The door into Horace's Library is open, the other door is a symmetrical sham to an asymmetrical wing of the house

19. Bentley's first design for the Gallery at Strawberry Hill with a plain barrel vault and three, not five, canopied niches. If it had been built this would have proved more functional as a picture gallery

20. The Gallery at Strawberry Hill as executed, crammed with an eclectic confusion of paintings and sculpture. The papier mâché fan vaulting, realized by Thomas Bromwich, was the joint concept of Horace and Chute after Bentley's dismissal

21. An illustration by Bertie Greathead for
The Castle of Otranto showing Manfred's
comic servants being terrified by the
ghost's gigantic foot

22. The ghost destroys Manfred's castle at
the end of the Gothic novel – another
Bertie Greathead illustration

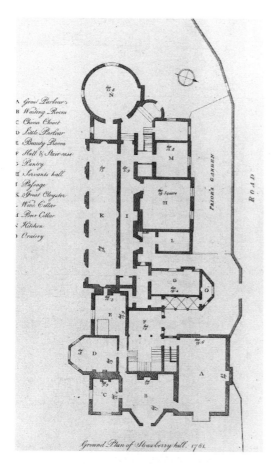

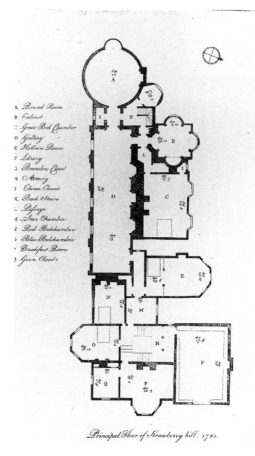

23. A ground plan of Strawberry Hill from the 1781 edition of the *Description*. There is no internal connection between the later, western, half of the house and the original villa at this floor level. Food from the Kitchen was taken out from the Little Cloister and in through the front door to the Great Parlour

24. A first-floor plan of Strawberry Hill which makes clear the division between the private rooms of the villa and those of the show house for visitors

25. Horace Walpole
in old age, drawn by
George Dance

26. This drawing of Strawberry Hill's north front and Prior's Garden shows,
from left to right, the Oratory under the Holbein Chamber, the Great North
Bedchamber and the Beauclerc Tower projecting from the Round Tower

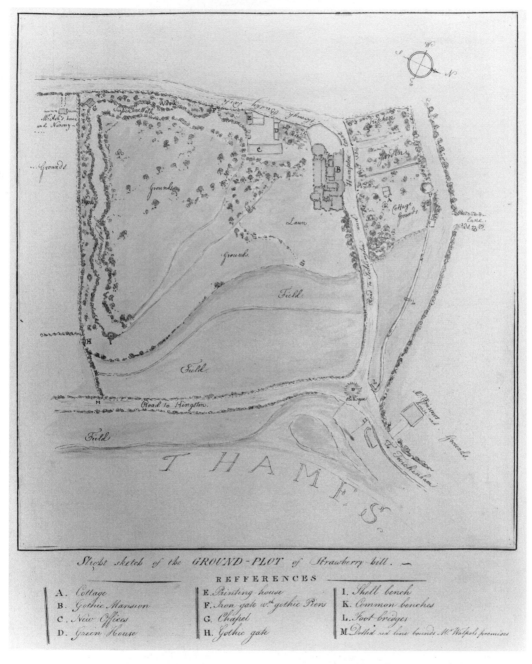

27. This map of the grounds of Strawberry Hill in their mature prime illustrates the Serpentine Walk, the concentration of ornamental features at the lower left of the map on the route to Little Strawberry Hill, and the practical Kitchen Garden across the road from the main house

advise him and Chute. For the gallery, they commissioned a papier mâché expert, Thomas Bromwich, to copy a riotous fan vault with pendants in an aisle of Henry VII's Chapel at Westminster Abbey. Those three Bourchier canopies were increased to five with the fans springing awkwardly from behind them. Doors copied from one of Müntz's paintings commanded the axis of the room; velvet, mirrors and gilding did the rest. The space created was and remains an eye opener, a preparation for the excesses of the Regency. It was undoubtedly influential; whether that influence was benign is a matter of opinion.

Much the same happened in the Cabinet. Chute devised a curvaceous, fussy rendering of York Minster's chapter house with an overlay of Decorated tracery from one of York's windows. Once again, the space has a real impact. It almost brought the visiting French ambassador to his knees. Indeed, the Duc de Nivernais went so far as to remove his hat before retrieving it with an irritated '*Ce n'est pas une chapelle pourtant.*' If Horace was aiming only to surprise and deceive he had half succeeded. By rejecting Bentley he achieved unique interiors. Whether either room deserves to be called elegant, tasteful or imitable, is doubtful. But they set precedents of a kind. Together with the stylistic jumble of objects which Horace stuffed into them over the next forty years, these two rooms in particular gave not only the Regency but the Victorians the aesthetic courage to confuse.

A flood, a fire scare and a workman's strike delayed the works on this western limb of the house. The shell of the walls, including the three-storey round tower, was up in 1761, but the Gallery was not fitted out until well into 1763 while the tower's upper storeys remained empty until 1771. The kitchens of Strawberry had moved into the ground floor of the round tower as early as 1761. Horace could not wait to keep his domestics at a good distance from his private rooms. An Edwards illustration of the north entrance, drawn in 1774, shows a servant carrying a tray out of the main door on his way back to the kitchen, still a fair distance away, through the front cloister. There was, incredible as it may seem, no way from the kitchen to the Great Parlour on the ground floor without going out into the open air and back again; yet it would have been the easiest thing in the world to have cut a way through into the Red Hall of the Paraclete. For someone with a talent for publicity, Horace had an illogical need for personal privacy.

Horace had finished behaving badly to Müntz in 1759. Soon he was to begin behaving badly to Bentley. In between, following the death of George II on 26 October 1760, he had the time and was in the mood to write a short masterpiece: his letter to Montagu describing the funeral of the old king at Westminster Abbey. It is worth dwelling on this because it depends for its literary power on its writer's vices as much as his virtues. It is snobbish, theatrical in its aesthetic appreciation, unkind, malicious and alive. This letter, every bit as much as the Gallery at Strawberry Hill, explains why that often detached and hypercritical little man still matters two centuries later.

'Nay, I walked as a rag of quality', he began in casual, near-Shakespearean compression. Partnered by George Grenville, Secretary to the Navy, soon to be Prime Minister and a mortal enemy, Horace marched in the midnight procession to Westminster Abbey revelling in the Gothic richness of the show, the foot guards lining the route, 'every seventh man bearing a torch', the purple velvet and 'six vast chandeliers of silver on the catafalque . . . the drums muffled, the fifes, bells tolling and minute guns, all this was very solemn'. In addition there were the kind of incongruities for which he was always alert: the ambassador from Tripoli and his son in oriental robes both being carried to the church.

Then, in a transformation scene, came the Abbey interior, lit by torches, 'the tombs, long aisles, and fretted roof all appearing distinctly, and with the happiest chiaroscuro. There wanted nothing but incense, and little chapels here and there with priests saying mass for the repose of the defunct.' Horace the superior deist was in full imaginative flight of aesthetic Catholicism. How the Oxford Movement would have delighted him sixty years later.

After dignity came the human scrimmage and folly that pleased him even more: 'When we came to the chapel of Henry VII all solemnity and decorum ceased – no order was observed, people sat or stood where they could or would, the yeomen of the guard were crying out for help, oppressed by the immense weight of the coffin, the Bishop read sadly, and blundered in the prayers.' There followed the malicious vignettes, 'the figure of the Duke of Cumberland, heightened by a thousand melancholy circumstances. He had a full, dark-brown Adonis wig, and a cloak of black cloth with a train of five yards. Attending the funeral of a father, how little reason soever he had to love him, could not be pleasant. His leg extremely bad, yet forced to stand upon it near two hours, his face bloated and distorted with his late paralytic stroke, which has affected too one of his eyes', not a physical failing of the poor man was missed out, 'and placed over the mouth of the vault, into which in all probability he must himself soon descend – think how unpleasant a situation.' But how enjoyable for Horace.

Then, inevitably in such company, he closed in on the real enemy: 'the burlesque Duke of Newcastle' must not escape whips:

> He fell into a fit of crying the moment he came into the chapel and flung himself back in a stall, the Archbishop hovering over him with a smelling bottle – but in two minutes his curiosity got the better of his hypocrisy and he ran about the chapel with his glass to spy who was or was not here, spying with one hand and mopping his eyes with t'other. Then returned the fear of catching cold, and the Duke of Cumberland, who was sinking with heat, felt himself weighed down, and turning round, found it was the Duke of Newcastle standing upon his train to avoid the chill of the marble.

It is the conflict between solemn, ritual pretensions and laughable, human realities which gives such an absurd yet moving beauty to the writing. In the middle of it all – shadows, confusion and the gaping grave – is Horace, an outsider on the inside of the English establishment.

Müntz had been shown the door and told never to return, not even to claim a lottery prize. Bentley, on the other hand, was implored to remain and his departure, predictably, blamed upon his wife. In February 1760 Horace appealed, vainly of course, for help from the complacent Montagu:

The Teddington history is grown woefully bad. Marc Antony [Bentley], though no boy, persists in losing the world two or three times over for every gipsy, that he takes for Cleopatra.

Mark Antony's Cleopatra, or Mrs Bentley, had six children to provide for, four of them by Bentley's first wife. Consequently she was casting around for more reliable sources of income than the occasional £5 notes that condescending bachelors like Montagu dropped in her husband's direction after several days of professional advice on interior decoration. Without asking his permission, she had appointed Montagu as godfather to her second child and, from Horace's later gossip to his antiquary friend William Cole, she had been bursting uninvited into Horace's élite house parties to try to pick up a few useful patrons for her husband. How little she needed to rely on Horace's support was soon to appear.

Bentley decided to take the plunge, quit his Teddington cottage, leave Horace's employment and try his fortune in London. In the October following the old king's death, Horace wrote again to Montagu, his fellow Bentley-fancier, desperate for sympathy and advice:

> I have laughed, been cool, scolded, represented, begged, and at last spoke very roundly – all with equal success – at present we do not meet – I must convince him of ill usage, before I can make good usage of any service to him. All I have done is forgot, because I will not be enamoured of Hannah Cleopatra too ... They are going to London, that she may visit and be visited; while he puts on his red velvet and ermine, and goes begging in robes!

As usual, Montagu was sympathetic and unhelpful: 'it would not have been in my power to prevent his journey to London though I should have endeavoured at it.' So Bentley settled in London to try the power of flattering verse upon the influential. Either his inside information was accurate or he was exceptionally fortunate. He and his nephew directed their attentions upon Lord Bute, the ex-tutor and close friend of the Prince of Wales, only a few days before George II died. Both Horace and Montagu kept their eyes firmly and uncharitably on their ex-protégé. On 19 October Horace was predicting that Mrs Bentley's 'McAnthony' would get a service of silver plate as a reward for a poem he had written. He got much more than that, but it took some months for the rewards to feed through the system.

In January 1761, the Strawberry Hill press published Bentley's father's edition of Lucan's *Pharsalia*. This was Bentley's property, had Bentley's introduction and Bentley's head- and tailpieces as illustrations. Horace owed his friend £100 for the rights, but kept the money. Then, quite suddenly, Bentley was almost a celebrity. His *Epistle to Lord Melcomb* had pleased its recipient in an age notably susceptible to flattery in competent verse. Melcomb had worked upon Lord Bute, and Bentley's play *The Wishes* been shown to Bute along with 'a recommendatory copy of verses, containing more incense to the King and my Lord Bute, than the Magi brought in their portmanteaus to Jerusalem'. The King was young and given to impulsive gestures and even Horace admitted that 'there is a great deal of wit in the piece'. A bank note for £200 was sent from the Treasury with an order that *The Wishes* should be put on by the summer company at Drury Lane that July. In addition, Bentley's drawings were shown to the King, himself an amateur draughtsman.

Hopelessly outpointed, Horace was reduced to reporting that Bentley, 'the *comely young* author' (he was fifty-two years old) 'appears every night in the Mall in a milk-white coat with a blue cape, disclaims any benefit, and says he has done with the play now it is out of his own hands, and that Mrs Hannah Clio alias Bentley writ the best scenes in it. He is going to write a tragedy and she, I suppose, is going to court.' If it was a bitter moment for Horace, it is impossible to feel a scrap of sympathy for him.

The Wishes played for five nights at Drury Lane to mixed receptions. Horace was there at the first night, 28 July 1761, 'What do you think in a house crowded was the first thing I saw! Mr and Madam Bentley perked up in the front boxes and acting audience at his own play – no, all the impudence of false patriotism never came up to it! Did one ever hear of an author that had courage to see his own first night in public?' But Lady Bute, Lord Halifax and Lord Melcomb were there in support.

Bentley had opened his play with a generous compliment to

Thomas Gray. As the curtain rose it revealed the God of poetry lying fast asleep beside the Helicon. Various lines by contemporary poets were called out to him but he slept on peacefully. Then the first line of Gray's 'The Bard', the poem Bentley should have illustrated, was declaimed:

RUIN seize thee, ruthless King!

and instantly the God awoke and smiled. It was a pity that Gray could not have been there to savour the moment. Horace praised the second, third and fifth acts, the fifth being the funniest in the play. It was written as a parody of the conventions of Greek drama, with a gloomy chorus which sees a murder about to be perpetrated but then wastes five minutes on declamatory verse instead of calling for help. The ending of the play strained a conventional audience too far and it was hissed. Harlequin, the hero, had been given three magical wishes which would all be granted. After using the first two, he forgot himself and cried out 'Well, I'll be hanged!' whereupon he was. In its perverse irony and sophisticated whimsicality, the play was pure Bentley and a reminder of what Horace had lost by his inability to treat intellectual equals as social equals.

Just as he never forgot to follow the fortunes of Lord Lincoln, whose wife died at about this time, so Horace, helped by Montagu, kept himself informed of Bentley's new literary career. As Bentley went on, if not from strength to strength, at least to a creditable burst of middle-aged creativity – a tragedy, *Philostrate*, satirical poems and the libretto to a light opera – Horace and Montagu followed his progress with something close to dismay. 'He says it is only in his old age he began to write verses,' Montagu reported, and quoted maliciously Nero's dying words, '*Quontus artifex pereo*' – what an artist thus perishes! 'He should always give his wit to someone else to make up,' was Horace's possessive verdict; but he added, 'If any of his things are printed in Dublin, let me have them. I have no quarrel to his wits.' Only, he might have added, to his wife.

So Horace lost the irreverent and versatile friend who might have eased him through the emotional traumas of the next few years.

With Bentley gone, Horace moved quickly from a time of self-indulgent building and decorating into a serious political phase where Henry Conway became once again the emotional centre of his life. For a few years, from 1760 to 1765, Horace would be not merely the cold-eyed commentator on his age, but an actual political mover at Westminster. Had he kept Bentley by his side, he might have been happier, but he is most unlikely ever to have shaken a government or written *The Castle of Otranto*. He let it be known discreetly through William Cole and George Hardinge that he had forgiven his old friend and brought him into the way of a comfortable minor sinecure. This may be so. Certainly Bentley was rewarded with a Post Office sinecure in 1764 worth £160 a year, but that was for a mock-heroic poem in five cantos, 'Patriotism', which pleased the King and the government.

In 1766 Montagu reported that Mrs Bentley was carrying on with a Scottish officer, 'said Mr Bentley is much chagrined'; and in the same year 'the General met Mr Bentley, very dirty, very poor, and very old.' Yet in 1780, fourteen years later, Hardinge wrote to Horace to tell him, 'At Sir John Griffin's the other day I met *your* Bentley, whom I was glad to see, a very singular genius. I discovered by an accident, that you are still generous to him.' Precisely how generous Hardinge did not know. In 1761 Horace had put the £100 he owed his friend for *Pharsalia* in the 'funds', to accumulate, claiming that Bentley would waste it if he got his hands on it. Bentley lived on quietly in Westminster and died in 1782. By that time, the £100 had become £200. Horace distributed this sum among Bentley's children, the five girls, 'the sickly Infantas', as he called them, and the son: a thoughtful and provident gesture for the children, if not for poor Bentley.

CHAPTER EIGHT

The casualties of war

To appreciate the concerns and distractions which may have caused Horace to mismanage his relations with Müntz and Bentley so crudely, it is necessary to return to his public problems during the first campaigns of the Seven Years War.

A decision taken at a council of war held on board the *Ramillies* off Minorca on 24 May 1756 proved, literally, fatal to the presiding admiral, John Byng. In a chain of consequences, it also threw shadows of blame across Henry Conway, and across Horace himself. On 20 May, Byng's fleet of thirteen ships of the line had fought an inconclusive four-hour battle against a French fleet of twelve ships under the Marquis de la Galissonnières. Two English ships had been badly damaged with virtually no loss to the enemy, but the British had remained in possession of the sea area where they had fought. At stake had been the naval base on nearby Minorca where General Blakeney was besieged in Fort St Philip by an army of 15,000 French under the Duc de Richelieu, that 'genteel but wrinkled old Adonis', as Horace admiringly described him.

If Byng's council of war had decided to remain off Minorca, blockading the island and waiting for the reinforcement of five ships of the line at that time approaching Gibraltar, one of two things could have happened. Admiral Galissonnières might have returned to the attack and destroyed the entire British fleet in the Mediterranean: an unlikely event as the French ships had already shown a tendency to sheer away from sustained ship-to-ship broadsides. If, on the other hand, the French had kept their distance until the five reinforcing British ships had arrived, Richelieu and his army would have been forced into a humiliating surrender and Byng would have been made a viscount.

Byng need never have called the council of war. He could have made his own bold decision to remain on station and carry out his orders to relieve Fort St Philip. But if only to confirm his own irresolution Byng did call it and the council agreed unanimously to return to Gibraltar on the grounds that the Rock had also been within their remit to secure. The dividing line between cowardice and politic indecision is a fine one. When he sailed into Gibraltar, Byng found himself relieved of his command and he was hurried back to Portsmouth to face a furious government and an angry nation. A court martial cleared him of cowardice but found him guilty of not doing his utmost to take, seize and destroy the ships of the French king and of not assisting those of his ships in the front of his battleline which it was his duty to have assisted. Under the Twelfth Article of War, an Act of Parliament passed in 1737, the penalty for this offence was the mandatory one of death by shooting. Horace, with his feeling for natural justice and his delight in harassing any government in which a Pelham held office, was fascinated by the Byng case and managed to put off Byng's day of execution for a fortnight by various agitations in and around the Palace of Westminster. The court martial's members had unanimously recommended mercy but the royal family and most of the cabinet were intent on an execution. Horace, being one of the select band regularly invited to play loo with Princess Amelia and the Duke of Cumberland, was able, much later, to quiz the Princess on her apparent blood-lust for the unfortunate Byng.

It transpired that, during the fortnight Byng's life lay in the balance, the Duchess of Newcastle, the Prime Minister's wife, a lady whom Horace often mocked for her tendency to grow a beard, had sent Lady Egerton to the Princess to ask her to press for the execution. Without it, Lord Anson, whom Horace had also mocked, even more often, for his supposed impotence and sexual partiality for sailors, would have found his position as First Lord of the Admiralty untenable. 'Indeed,' the Princess told Horace, 'I was already for it, the officers would never have fought if he had not been executed.' So Voltaire, with his famous quip about the British shooting one admiral, *'pour encourager les autres'*, was only stating what was already accepted in Britain's governing circles.

It was an intriguingly German rather than English moment in British history. Byng had been sent off with an inadequate force as a result of the years of peacetime underspending on the navy. So while Newcastle, Henry Fox and Lord Hardwicke fretted to cover up their own inefficiency in handling the war, the three Hanoverians – King, Princess and Duke of Cumberland – made a firm stand for discipline by terror. It worked. Byng conducted his own slaughter with half the fleet watching; Britain won the Seven Years War hands down, raising the first and very short-lived British Empire to its peak of wealth and consequence. Around the world, in India, Africa, America and on the high seas, British generals and admirals remembered the ignominy of Byng, took chances, often, like Wolfe at Quebec, unreasonable chances – and won battle after battle.

There were, however, a few exceptions to this parade of nervous heroes. One, with dramatic irony, was the Duke of Cumberland himself. Defeated at Hastenbeck, he was given secret orders by his father, King George, to save Hanover from the ravages of war, whatever the price. Cumberland obediently signed, in September 1757, the Convention of Klostezeven, neutralizing most of his army and abandoning the greater part of Hanover to French occupation under the command of the very successful Duc de Richelieu. Cumberland could hardly be shot on Horse Guards Parade on his return, but his father did interrupt a game of cards to greet him with, 'Here is my son, who has ruined me and disgraced himself.' The Duke was an example of well-protected but unheroic common sense, a quality that loses wars. Another example, not quite so well protected, was Henry Conway who was involved, soon after Cumberland's return, in a raid on Rochefort and in a second indecisive council of war.

It is easy to sit at a desk and write about combined operations, weighing up the odds and pointing out the missed opportunities. The realities of winds, tides, sandbanks and dubious pilots, and above all the lack of information as to the strength and disposition of the enemy, are almost impossible to reconstruct and sympathetically appraise. Nevertheless it does seem to have been extraordinarily courageous, if not foolhardy, of a second council of war, meeting again on board a ship, this time a few miles off the French coast, the estuary of the Charente and the port of Rochefort, to have decided to do nothing: not to attack Rochefort, not to attack the Île d'Oléron, not to attack the Île de Ré, not even to make an attempt on the little fort of Fouras, but simply to go home and suggest that the whole of William Pitt's plan had been misconceived from the start.

This inspired pusillanimity took pace in the late September and early October of 1757, mere months after the exemplary execution of Byng on 14 March that year. With that horrid instance so fresh in their minds, this second council of war still decided to do nothing more than return home. Princess Amelia was both right and wrong. Perhaps the general in command, Sir John Mordaunt, his second in command, Conway, and the other army officers – Cornwallis, Howard and Wolfe – thought that only naval officers were liable to suffer the extreme penalty for indecision; and if they did think this then they were right. Only Mordaunt was court martialled and even he was acquitted with honour. Horace probably took the Rochefort débâcle more grievously than its actual participants, but for some time Horace had been losing touch with realities, political even more than military.

His disastrous misjudgements seem to date back to 6 March 1754 when he wrote a disgraceful letter to the exiled Bentley, gloating over the death of Henry Pelham. The letter contained much foolish sarcasm but never a single line to explain why the death of a notable peacetime Prime Minister should be an occasion for national rejoicing. Hate tends to destroy judgement and Horace had been trapped in hatred for the Pelham brothers ever since he was separated from Lord Lincoln in 1742; but he appeared to find Newcastle an even more infuriating target than his brother Henry. The Walpole family interests still controlled several seats in the Commons, most of them in East Anglia. All through the 1740s Horace had had two good friends in politics:

Richard Rigby and Henry Fox. Rigby was not a Whig of great influence, but Henry Fox was a risen star, a key man. To control the Commons, Newcastle had to favour either Fox or Pitt. The King disliked Pitt because Pitt despised Hanover. Newcastle sensed that Fox was a safer colleague, being more interested in the prestige of office than in rocking the boat of state with dynamic new policies. Horace, for all his private rant about freedom and good government, was basically a negative and disruptive force. On his own admission he loved faction for its own sake, 'leaned most to a man in opposition', and did his utmost to persuade his friend Fox 'that he would be betrayed, mortified, disgraced' if he accepted office under Newcastle. Fox decided to take that risk and became in 1755 Secretary of State for the south and Leader of the House.

In his political memoirs, Horace claimed that he 'had uniformly persisted in detaching himself from Fox, from the moment the latter had entered into engagements with Newcastle'. That is untrue. Horace as a politician was as devious and unprincipled as any in the House of Commons. When Fox accepted office, Horace wrote him an ingratiating letter, 'I must entreat you that you will leave me your commands. Let me but know how you wish me to act and vote, and I shall obey it.' What he actually did over the next five years, without any open breach with Fox, was to scurry around passing backstairs information and raising little cabals in an attempt to frustrate anything that Fox was trying to do. Usually Horace failed, but when he allowed his nephew, the 3rd Earl of Orford, to accept a rich sinecure from Fox without changing his own hostile tactics or persuading his nephew to support the government in the Lords, his friendship with Fox and all the influence which he could have exerted through that relationship finished. Rigby too had come to the end of the road. He, as Horace admitted with engaging frankness, 'was grown weary of Walpole's ardour for factious intrigues'; Rigby pledged his loyalty to the Duke of Bedford and prospered accordingly.

*

Anyone who has enjoyed the Horace Walpole of the letters: relaxed, unpretentious, even homely – 'all the morning I play with my workmen or animals, go regularly every evening to the meadows with Mrs Clive, or sit with Lady Suffolk, and at night scribble my painters' – should read a chapter or two of the *Memoirs* of both George II and George III to absorb an entirely different persona. He called these volumes 'Memoirs' yet wrote dispassionately of himself in the third person. They are histories in all but name, hugely impressive in their confidence.

> A century had now passed, since reason had begun to attain that ascendant in the affairs of the world, to conduct which it had been granted to man six thousand years ago. If religions and governments were still domineered by prejudices, if creeds that contradict logic, or tyrannies that enslave multitudes to the caprice of one, were not yet exploded, novel absurdities at least were not broached; or if propagated, produced neither persecutors nor martyrs. Methodism made fools, but they did not arrive to be saints.

This is wonderful nonsense from a wise sage, poised upon his pinnacle of rational history. But the narratives which follow such claims are equally impressive, detailed, informed of every back-parlour intrigue, analytical, balanced and, when necessary, suitably aphoristic. Poor Fox, for instance, is convincingly dismissed:

> His natural bent was the love of power, with a soul generous and profuse; but growing a fond father, he became a provident father – and from a provident father to a rapacious man, the transition was but too easy!

Exit from the pages of history Henry Fox, Leader of the House of Commons; enter Henry, Lord Holland, the greedy Paymaster-General of the Forces from 1757 to 1765, a man who 'had neither the patriotism which forms a virtuous character, nor the love of fame which often supplies the place of the other'. This was lofty. Horace the outsider, the arbiter of eternity, the writer of many registers, had made judgement.

When a real moral crisis, that of Byng's death sentence, came up, Horace did feel called upon to act; whether out of principle, for justice and mercy, or merely to irritate the Duke of Newcastle and Henry Fox, it is not easy to say. But having alienated his influential friends by years of petty intrigue and double dealing, he proved impotent. On the Friday when he decided to act, Byng was to be shot on the following Monday. By bad luck (or was it a fortunate detachment from responsibility?) Horace was temporarily not an MP. He had resigned from his very rotten borough of Castle Rising and was about to stand for the most important 'Walpole' borough of King's Lynn, with an electoral roll of roughly 2000. Because he could not act himself, he appealed to Fox and predictably got nowhere. Eventually Sir Francis Dashwood responded to Horace's personal appeal and successfully proposed a motion that the House should sit on the Saturday when it voted to delay Byng's execution for two weeks. This gave Lord Hardwicke a chance to bully most of the original members of the court martial into retracting their merciful tendencies and Byng was shot anyway. Horace told Chute he had only been able 'to add a fortnight to the poor man's misery'.

His next response was far more effective and may well have been what saved Henry Conway when Conway fell, a few months later, into a situation at Rochefort very similar to that of Byng. Horace wrote in one day, 12 May, or so he claimed, one of his two best political pamphlets, *A Letter from Xo Ho, a Chinese philosopher at London, to his friend Lien Chi at Peking*. The piece is pure Voltaire, punchy, amusing and popular. It went quickly through five editions and must have done much to shame not only the public but members of the government, out of their previous gut reactions to the Byng case. The chinoiserie of *Xo Ho* is not overdone. It is written in a tone of bland incomprehension at the follies of the English, the *faux naïf* carried to a fine pitch. Xo Ho's opening attack on the character of the nation remains disturbingly relevant today:

> Here one is told something every day: the people demand to be told something, no matter what. If a politician, a minister, a member of their assembly, was mysterious, and refused to import something to an enquirer, he would make an enemy: if he tells a lie, it is no offence; he is communicative; that is sufficient to a *free* people: all they ask is news; a falsehood is as much news as truth.

Passing quickly on to the Byng affair, Xo Ho ignores the admiral's fate and concentrates on the equally guilty ministers, namely Anson, Hardwicke, Newcastle and Fox; the ministers who had sent Byng out with a weak, ill-trained force and then failed to rescue him from the decrees of the court martial:

> ... the imprisoned admiral was tried, acquitted, condemned and put to death. The trials of the others were delayed. At last they were tried – not as I expected, whether they were guilty, but whether they should be ministers again or not. If the executed admiral had lived, he too might be a minister!

And of course, with a few changes of post, they were all still in government. Xo Ho then turns to entertain, with general observations on England from a Chinese viewpoint:

> England is not China. – Hear, and I will tell thee briefly, the English have no sun, no summer as we have, at least their sun does not scorch like ours. They content themselves with names: at a certain time of the year they leave the capital, and that makes 'summer'; they go out of the city and that makes the 'country'.

He describes the king's progress to Kensington Palace. He 'goes along a gravel walk, crosses one of the chief roads, is driven by the side of a canal between two rows of lamps, at the end of which he has a small house, and then he is supposed to be in the country, then all the men and women said *it was hot*. If thou wilt believe me I am now writing to thee before a fire!' After a few rhetorical questions: 'Will those who value royal authority, not regret the annihilation of it? Will those who think the ancient ministers guilty, not be affected if they are again employed?' – Xo Ho ends, 'My friend Lien Chi, I tell thee things as they are; I pretend not to account for the conduct of Englishmen; I told thee before, they are *incomprehensible.*'

Most political pamphlets of the eighteenth century are unreadable and much too long. *Xo Ho*, like Horace's later *An Account of the Giants lately discovered*, is both brief and amusing. The jokes about the weather and Kensington by simple association imprint the culpability of Newcastle, Fox and company. By its very mildness, the pamphlet shamed the nation out of its recent mood of vengeful militancy. Cabinets as well as admirals are involved in sea fights and when a civilized country laughs it does not mount firing squads so readily. To have put that lesson of decency over in five entertaining pages was not a small achievement.

Xo Ho had two practical impacts. It muted any mood of punitive anger that might have arisen in the following October when Mordaunt, Conway and their ignominious crew returned from a feeble performance before Rochefort. But it had a second result which Horace could not have foreseen. After *Xo Ho* no future government would underrate Horace's satiric stature and threat. Men who can make a nation laugh thoughtfully are dangerous. When he next took up his pen as a political pamphleteer, in 1764, this time directly to defend Henry Conway, he would be taken seriously enough for someone in the government – possibly the Prime Minister, George Grenville himself, more probably Henry Fox – to instruct a scribbling hack writer to go for Horace's jugular of vulnerability: first imply that the man is a sodomite and only then deal with his arguments.

All that was for the future. Now, in the summer of 1757, Henry Conway was preparing to go to war. In April he had been made a Groom of the King's Bedchamber, a political appointment. Already a major-general and the colonel of an élite regiment of dragoon guards, he might have hoped for an independent command but his military record was undistinguished. He had arrived too late for Dettingen and had had to be rescued at Lauffeldt. At that battle in 1747, he had been pulled off his horse backwards and taken prisoner when the prisoner whom he was escorting had jumped up and grabbed him by the hair. This was not a creditable incident, but pure Conway: he had been trying to shield his captive from friendly fire. So when Pitt persuaded the Cabinet in July to mount a major raid on a French port, to relieve the pressure on the King of Prussia's armies on the eastern front, King George insisted that the experienced Sir John Mordaunt should be in command with Conway only as second.

It was to be a surprise, secret operation; but after the soldiers had drilled for almost two months in Dorset and on the Isle of Wight, that element was lost. Rather ominously for military morale, the naval forces were to be under Sir Edward Hawke, who had relieved Admiral Byng of his command. Horace was in his usual tizzy of apprehension – 'Sure no wife could be more concerned for you than I' – but Conway, equally in character, was cool: 'This island is a most delightful spot', and they had not discovered and hanged a French spy, despite the rumours that had reached Horace.

On 7 September they were off, and when Conway wrote next on 26 September the expedition had already failed. The navy had battered a small island fort off the mouth of the Charente into submission, but on the 25th the military had decided that a frontal assault on Rochefort was impractical. Recent French research suggests that the town would probably have fallen quite easily. 'I doubt our operations are likely to end here,' Conway wrote to Horace, 'though I am grieved to go back without doing some little matter to talk of.' Sir Edward reported at the later inquiry that before they even sighted the French coast the military commanders had decided that to take Rochefort would be impossible.

For several days the officers debated alternative attacks on any of the neighbouring islands. Conway was all for an attack on the small mainland fort of Fouras, and in a ridiculous *pas de deux* Mordaunt threatened to serve on such an assault if Conway, his second, took the responsibility. Conway refused. One night they all got into the ship's boats but 'an easterly wind blowing a little fresh has saved us or the French, probably, from pretty serious accidents,' Conway limply reported to an increasingly worried but always loyal Horace. 'I gave my opinion' he continued 'against an undertaking I thought impracticable, *as then proposed*. I have ever since been labouring to prevent the disgrace of coming away so poorly as I think we shall.' And as, of course, they did.

Horace was immediately supportive. He hurried back to town to learn the worst. 'How can you ask me such a question, as do I think you are come too safe?' he demanded. 'Is this a time of day to question your spirit?' But he warned that he had been taking soundings in London and found 'there is a scheme of distinguishing between the land and the sea'. The naval officers, from Hawke downwards, had behaved faultlessly, but junior army officers like James Wolfe were telling the truth about their seniors. Pitt and the King were enraged. In future Pitt would rely more upon the Duke of Newcastle's underrated organizing abilities to carry his bold schemes into action. In later surprise assaults there would be adequate forces, better equipped and better supplied. The King snatched his hand away when Mordaunt tried to kiss it, but there was not quite the degree of national anger that had greeted Byng in 1756.

Horace embarked on a skilful exercise in damage limitation. There was to be a Report of the General Officers into the débâcle. 'I am neither acquainted with, nor care a straw about, Sir John Mordaunt,' Horace told his depressed friend, 'but as it is known that you differed with him, it will do you the greatest honour to vindicate him, instead of disculpating yourself.' It was wise advice. Only Mordaunt was court-martialled and, with Conway's backing, came off with at least the appearance of honour. Horace then advised a course of mildness and compliments to the old Commander-in-Chief, Lord Ligonier, and no fighting back against Pitt. Conway followed his direction faithfully. Next June he was at home with his wife and child at Park Place, overlooking the Thames near Henley. Another expedition was soon to sail against the French, with St Malo the principal objective this time. Only Cherbourg was taken, but a number of ships in St Malo harbour were destroyed or taken as prizes. With his record at Rochefort, Conway had not been invited to serve. 'I think I seem condemned to home service for the present at least', he told Horace; his mind was easily distracted by domestic pleasures: 'our double flowering syringa has blown', he reported, 'but very single.'

For a professional soldier, and he would end up, it should be remembered, as a field marshal, Conway was a refreshingly complex figure. The giggling cross-dresser of masquerades in the 1730s had already come a long way. He had married a widow, Lady Ailesbury, always referred to by her title, and they had one child, a girl, Anne, whom Horace sometimes cared for when the parents were abroad on military postings. She would grow up to become a lesbian sculptress of some ability, inheriting Strawberry Hill, for her lifetime, in Horace's highly complicated will and testament. The biggest gap in our knowledge of Horace at his most domestic and affectionate was created when she, by that time the widowed Mrs Anne Damer, burnt all his letters to her.

Ingeniously Conway had contrived to get married without forfeiting Horace's regard. He had written at a sensitive moment in 1753 just after his marriage:

> I want to see Strawberry when you'll let me, and I want you to see Park Place, that is, I want to see you there very much. In all and every part of this you'll please to understand Lady Ailesbury and me is one, though I have so impertinently spoke in the first person; we go together, return together and think entirely so in what relates to you.

Handled with such caution, Horace responded well. He liked women when he could be confident that there would be no sexual involvement. Commenting on the Conways, Lady Caroline Fox had marvelled 'how Conway and she ever could produce a child with such icy dispositions, but to speak seriously, I do think there is in mother and daughter as much insensibility and want of that sort of cordial unreserved affection in their nature which I can't describe'.

Whatever the realities, Lady Ailesbury and Horace performed a stately social dance around each other. She visited Strawberry without her husband and created needlework panels to decorate the house. Horace often wrote impersonal but polite letters to her at times of stress when Henry Conway was away campaigning on the Continent. But every now and then Conway would express odd flashes of nostalgic regret and something close to an emotional possessiveness for Horace. He had written, for instance, frantically, when there was no news for months as Horace journeyed up from Italy to Paris with Lord Lincoln. Then in 1759, after he had been trying to persuade Horace to Park Place:

> They were good old times when cousins used to come with bag and baggage and cram for months together. But now everybody is so fond of their own place they never think of anybody else's; all ones

friends come to see one's place once at least, that's of course, and then leave each couple like Adam and Eve in their respective Paradises to converse with the beasts and the serpents.

He was describing accurately how men are separated by marriage if they play fair by the institution. Horace in his letters never hid the fact that he loved Conway. More surprisingly he noted it in his *Memoirs.* But it does seem that, in his reserved fashion, Conway loved Horace, writing angry cold letters that began 'Dear Sir' if Horace had failed to write for a time and appeared to be neglecting him.

The year of victories, 1759, was particularly hard for Conway, trapped in Kent, waiting for a French invasion that would never be launched, while other officers gathered the laurels of victory all around the world. Partisan as ever, Horace was delighted when Lord George Sackville, who had served on the committee of inquiry into the Rochefort expedition, was disgraced for failing to bring up the Hanoverian cavalry at Minden. Then, when Wolfe, a critical underling at Rochefort, met death and glory at Quebec, Horace twisted that triumph into a total vindication of Conway's actions off the French coast. He wrote Conway an ingenious paraphrase of Wolfe's last report:

> Quebec is impregnable; it is flinging away the lives of brave men to attempt it. I am in the situation of Conway at Rochefort; but having blamed him I must do what I now see he was in the right to see was wrong, and yet what he would have done; and as I am the commander, which he was not, I have the melancholy power of doing what he was prevented doing. Poor man! his life has paid the price of his injustice.

It is one of the strangest eulogies ever written for a dead hero. At least Horace was being loyal to the living, but it would be surprising if Conway took much comfort from it.

In 1760 Conway was posted to Germany where he befriended the allied commander Prince Ferdinand of Brunswick who, nevertheless, called him away from the Siege of Marburg just when he seemed about to take the town and claim at least one success in seven years of war. Back home, Horace was living quietly and writing hard. In 1758 he had bought from George Vertue's widow all her husband's chaotic notes, and now in 1760 he set them into order and wrote the first two volumes of his *Anecdotes of Painting*, a foundation study of British artists, intended to be accessible and popular, 'to try', as he said, 'if I could not redeem antiquarian works from the deserved imputation of being the worst books that are written'. The first two volumes would not come out on the Strawberry Hill Press until 1762. There were delays also on his building works. The Cabinet would not be finished until September 1762 and the Gallery not until August 1763. For relaxation he would stroll over in an evening to Little Strawberry Hill, a small but genteel house that was a part of his modest forty-acre estate. There the cheerful, red-faced actress Kitty Clive was installed, with her brother Mr Rafter to keep their sessions of card-playing respectable.

Mrs Clive was the perfect instance of Horace's preference, in social matters, for the company of women rather than men. A celebrated comedienne in her time, she was, at forty-three, just past the peak of her acting career when she accepted Horace's offer of Little Strawberry Hill as a weekend home and eventual place of retirement. On an average day, when he was resident at Strawberry, Horace would write in his library in the morning, visit another old lady, the Countess of Suffolk, at Marble Hill on the other side of Twickenham, and then, after an early dinner, spend an evening of cards and gossip with Mrs Clive. He preferred his women friends to be worldly wise, to have led interesting lives and to be entirely unthreatening in any sexual sense. It was, nevertheless, rumoured in Twickenham that Mrs Clive was his mistress. That might well have been his intention, as it would have given him a healthy reputation for sexual normality. 'I am an old gouty man that live in my armchair, and can't tell how the world passes,' Horace told Conway's elder brother, Lord Hertford, 'I have done with it.'

He was, in fact, just poised on the brink of some of the most dangerous and productive years of his life. In October of that same year, 1760, when Horace declared his resignation from life, the old king died and George III was proclaimed to a hopeful and victorious nation. 'The young King, you may trust me who am not apt to be enamoured with royalty, gives all the indication imaginable of being amiable.' Horace reported to Mann. 'His person is tall and full of dignity; his countenance florid and good natured; his manner is graceful and obliging: he expresses no warmth, nor resentment against anybody; at most, coldness.' So the most politically incompetent monarch ever to sit on the English throne (if James II is excepted) began his sixty-year reign, and Westminster would never be the same again.

For a time Horace seems not to have appreciated the change. He still ranged around his gossips to find irrelevant ways of mocking his old enemy, Newcastle. Central to his account of the splendid proceedings in the Abbey at the coronation was the anecdote of the new young Queen retiring to a special 'convenience', set up behind the high altar, 'what found she but – the Duke of Newcastle perked up and in the very act upon the anointed velvet close-stool'. Soon, that ridiculed, humane and remarkably forgiving Duke would be kissing Horace on both cheeks and being received politely as a guest at Strawberry.

A sinisterly suggestive letter that Horace wrote to Conway in February 1763 is the first real warning of how his mind had begun to work, of his reckless intentions and of a change in political pace. Newcastle had resigned as Prime Minister in May 1762, the true ending to an era, to be succeeded by Bute, a Scot and a creature of the King and of the dowager Princess of Wales. For almost a year the Duke of Bedford laboured at the peace negotiations until, on 10 February 1763, the Treaty of Paris was signed and the long war was ended. Horace had sensed correctly that Lord Bute's tenure of office was also nearing its end. The English still found it unnatural for a Scot to be a first minister under the Crown. Now Henry Conway was returning without a future to an ungrateful government and an unappreciative country. Bute had written him the 'driest' letter about his prospects that Conway had ever seen. 'You must not expect much,' Horace told him severely, and continued, like Lady Macbeth working on her malleable husband, 'Your mind was not formed to float on the surface of a mercenary world. My prayer (and my belief) is, that you may always prefer your integrity to success.'

After that grim opening, Horace ranted on about the unspecified 'attacks and malice of faction' which he had suffered. Princess Amelia had been rude to him at one of her 'wonderfully select and dignified' loo parties. But Horace would soon show them all; 'my mind does not reproach me' he wrote, still in Shakespearean mood. He would prove that he still had some virtue, 'and it will not be proved', he added dramatically, 'in the way they probably expect'. Not for Horace 'the tattered ensigns of patriotism'. By this time Conway must have become both bemused and nervous. 'But this and a thousand other things I shall reserve for our meeting,' Horace promised, and just managed to hold back from concluding with the equivalent of Lady Macbeth's 'But screw your courage to the sticking point and we'll not fail.'

The end result of all this pressurizing was not recorded, but 1763 was the year of Wilkes and of his scurrilous, anti-establishment journal, the *North Briton*. Horace had chosen his time for serious trouble-stirring very intelligently. Conway had missed his chances, through all those years of war, to create a military reputation. Now he was in the mood for desperate measures in Parliament, to create a reputation as a defender of English liberties. As the old party certainties began to crumble, a failed general like Conway might, with Horace's skilled and unscrupulous direction, reach the top of the political pyramid. Wilkes gave Horace and Conway a perfect opportunity to pose as martyrs, to speak out for integrity against an uncertain establishment. Bute had given way, thankfully, to George Grenville, who had walked side by side with Horace in the crocodile of nobility at George II's funeral. By nature a decent, reasonable man, Grenville was made tetchy by power. Not sensing the mood of aimless popular dissent that was sweeping the country, he determined to crush Wilkes and kill off his *North Briton* in order to silence its irreverent flow of criticism of himself and the increasingly corrupt Henry Fox. Issue number forty-five of the journal had dared to suggest that the King had been tricked by his ministers into telling lies.

That did it. In an action more Stuart than Hanoverian, forty-nine 'authors, printers and publishers' of the *North Briton* were arrested for seditious libel on the legally unsound device of a general warrant. Wilkes himself was flung into the Tower, then got himself released by a writ of habeas corpus and his imprisonment declared illegal as a breach of parliamentary privilege. The sequel is well known but none the less intoxicating: riots in the streets, £4000 damages for Wilkes, more riots and more damages, but this time to windows and chariots; Wilkes 'the blasphemer of his God and the libeller of his king', was expelled from Parliament. These were tremendous months, as the nation, naturally conservative and disinclined to political idealism, sensed the potential strength of the people when they rallied to protect their traditional rights.

What is fascinating is to observe Horace in the midst of this turmoil while Grenville flailed about, trying to defend general warrants, though few intellectual lawyers thought them defensible. That Lady Macbeth-style letter to Henry Conway was written early in the year, on 28 February, before the Wilkes storm broke. Horace's instincts, as an outsider in a society he secretly enjoyed, had independently alerted Conway to the possibilities of trouble-making now that the old style Whigs were collapsing and obstinacy incarnate occupied the throne.

In one almost impenetrably devious episode, Horace had alerted Wilkes anonymously to the fact that he, Horace, had once written a false and flattering eulogy of Henry Fox's character and published it back in 1748. How about, the suggestion went, reminding readers of the sketch and ridiculing it? Wilkes promptly took up the idea, made Fox look foolish, but refrained from mocking Horace. This incident illustrates admirably the complexity of Horace's political manoeuvring.

In all this, Conway is the mystery. If he wrote letters to Horace, as he seems likely to have done, then Horace destroyed most of them. Were they plaintive and protesting, as his salary and his security were threatened, or were he and Horace in courageous alliance to set Conway up as the next Prime Minister but one? Conway came so close to control of the state by following Horace's advice that it seems almost certain that the two men were, at this early stage in the game, deliberately playing for the highest stakes.

Whatever pressures Horace may have exerted on his friend, they both voted, on 15 and 24 November 1763, with the minority of 111 against the government's 300 on the question of general warrants. George III, not unreasonably, according to precedent, wanted no grooms in his bedchamber who failed to support his ministers. So he told Grenville to sack Conway from his post. That was in December. Grenville demurred and tried persuasion, three hours of it in Horace's case, giving him clear warnings as to what might happen to Conway if he continued to rebel. Horace's Twickenham friend Thomas Pitt, designer of the chimneypiece in Strawberry's Gallery, was also employed to suggest that now was the time when all good men should come to the aid of the party. Both Horace and Conway stood firm, Horace becoming unconvincingly strident because Grenville had hinted that those who opposed ministers in Parliament might be unfit to serve their country in the armed forces. High rank and promotion in the army and the navy had always been tied to politics, so Horace was being tactically self-righteous.

Throughout these tense months, Horace had deliberately chosen to step up the length and frequency of his letters to his cousin, Conway's brother Lord Hertford. Horace and Hertford had always been reasonably close, but when Hertford, a career aristocrat who had already served in Ireland, became the British ambassador to Paris in October 1763, Horace began writing him a regular and very well-informed newsletter. The aim of this correspondence was to enlist Hertford's support for his brother. Horace told Hertford quite bluntly that he ought to resign as ambassador to register a protest.

Like most Britons appointed to that post, Hertford had been bowled over by the refinement, snobbery and condescension of the French establishment. His wife spent weeks preparing her ensemble before she was presented at Court. Hertford proudly related his own reception to Horace: 'the King of France was most particularly gracious to me . . . he kept me half an hour in the Closet talking to me upon different subjects, and was pleased to tell me that the King my master could not in his Court have chosen a person to

represent him more agreeable to him than myself ... His Majesty
is observed to talk to me with ease, which is the greatest compliment he can pay; in return I have been twice a-hunting, once in
my coach and once on horseback.' He thought he had scored extra
points by being quite close when Louis shot a boar at Compiègne.
Presumably on that occasion he had got out of his coach.

Most of his brood of thirteen children had been scattered strate-
gically around France in order to improve their accents, and the
ambassador himself was looking forward to an oleaginous three
years in post. He was, consequently, horrified to receive the news
from Horace that his own brother had defied both King and
Prime Minister. 'You know,' Horace declaimed absurdly, 'that I
would die in the House for its privileges and the liberty of the
press. But come, don't be alarmed: this will have no consequences.' Hertford was alarmed and the consequences for Conway
and Horace would be dire in the short term. A nervous reply came
back from Paris:

> your own and my brother's conduct on the opening of Parliament
> does not make me happy ... I cannot discover a member of
> Parliament should be more at liberty to write a seditious libel than
> another man ... though I am a friend to liberty I am against the
> use of it in profligate hands.

The ministry, as a first sign of disapproval, had made 'a kind of
refusal' to pay Hertford's travel expenses for the move to Paris and
the exiled Wilkes was soon to be signing the visitor's book at the
Paris embassy, so Hertford was right to be nervous. But Horace
was still riding high. He had just won £500 on the national lottery
and at the Duke of Cumberland's levee he had allowed the Duke
of Newcastle to embrace him and hope he 'could come and eat a
bit of Sussex mutton with me. I had such difficulty to avoid laughing in his face that I got from him as fast as I could. Do you think
me very likely to forget that I have been laughing at him these last
twenty years?'

At such times it is fair to accept that Horace Walpole was ungra-
cious, even hypocritical. It was in these years, 1763 and 1764, that
he was making those few, pitiful and unsuccessful, attempts to

revive his lost relationship with Lord Lincoln. It will be recalled that one of his humble little notes urged that, 'It would make me seriously happy to pass some of the remaining hours of my life with you. I will not be troublesome, and you may get rid of me whenever you please, as you may command me whenever you will accept of me.' Significantly, Lincoln's wife had just died.

In April 1764 realism closed in. Grenville could no longer defend Conway from the King's anger; he was dismissed not only from the bedchamber but from his regiment. For three days Horace could not believe the news. Ingeniously the Treasury had chosen the day of Conway's dismissal to pay punctiliously every penny owing to Horace from his various sinecures. 'Is it possible,' Horace raged, 'that they could mean to make any distinction between us?' It was very possible. After *Xo Ho*, any government was likely to treat Horace with caution. His first response was to offer Conway the £6000 he had in funds and to alter his will, leaving everything to his ruined friend. This was the second time that he had made such a gesture. Naturally, Conway refused the £6000 and took it all with his usual cool composure. What he made of Horace's windy rhetoric – 'Ask yourself – is there a man in England with whom you would change character? – is there a man in England who would not change with you? Then think how little they have taken away!' – is not recorded.

Grenville had written to Hertford assuring him of the continued 'approbation of his Majesty'. In answer to Horace's appeal for him to resign, Hertford wrote back that the state and circumstances of his family had settled him in Paris. 'If I was a *garçon* I could retire to my woods in Warwickshire and be indifferent to the folly and madness of England's ministers'; but since he was a married man he intended to sit tight. There was to be no gesture of brotherly solidarity. 'The hotel I have taken here is charming', he added. 'I hope you will see it soon. The best compliments of the family attend you. I am, dear Horry, Always most affectionately yours, Hertford.' 'Dear Horry' quite understood: 'when a younger brother has taken a part disagreeable to his elder, and totally oppo-site, even without consulting him', there was no obligation for the elder brother to change his opinions. 'I have loved you both unalterably' he assured Lord Hertford, 'and without the smallest cloud between us from children.'

That reply was written on 27 May 1764. There followed the five most traumatic and productive months in Horace's life: traumatic because a government-sponsored tract published in August suggested at some length that he was a decadent homosexual who had been in love with Major-General Henry Conway, MP for the last twenty years; productive because somewhere between June and October Horace wrote *The Castle of Otranto*, his best known and most influential writing.

CHAPTER NINE

Otranto and the 'outing'

Horace Walpole had never, in twentieth-century terms, ventured out of the 'closet'. He was a confirmed bachelor, had a number of effeminate friends and walked with an affected delicacy; but he dressed with simple good taste, mocked known homosexuals like Lord George Sackville and the Archbishop of Armagh, and enjoyed the company of women at least as much as, and probably rather more than, that of men. Lord Lincoln had kept a mistress during his affair with Horace. Both Richard Bentley and Henry Conway were married men and the fastidious Horace was never tempted into London's homosexual underworld of 'Molly Houses'. There had, however, been one sordid court case back in 1751 when he had been a witness for the prosecution in a matter of blackmail and alleged sodomy.

This had centred around Horace's brother, Edward Walpole. He had been staying with a friend, Lord Boyne, in Ireland and had unwisely offered to take into service a young man, John Cather, if he ever came over to London looking for employment. Cather appeared at Edward's London town house but was turned away as unsuitable and fell into bad company. Soon afterwards he and three other men, Adam Nixon, Patrick Cane and a rogue lawyer, Daniel Alexander, began to threaten Edward Walpole with a prosecution for 'that detestable and sodomitical Sin (not to be named amongst Christians) called *Buggery*' unless he paid up a substantial sum. Edward asked Horace for help and Horace contrived to be present, taking notes, when Alexander repeated his threats. With such a prestigious witness, Edward accused the four of attempting 'to extort a large Sum of Money under the Pretence of an Assault, with an Intent to commit *Buggery* on the Body of the said *John Cather*'. They were found guilty as charged, all four were sentenced to prison and Cather stood in the pillory at Charing Cross, Chancery Lane and the Royal Exchange. Officially the Walpole honour had been cleared, but Horace had managed to combine the roles of detective, *agent provocateur* and witness in faintly suspect circumstances. A tract, *The whole Proceedings on the wicked Conspiracy carried on against the Hon. Edward Walpole Esq.* made the case known to a fairly wide public, and pitch tends to stick.

That was all; but it was enough. Horace had already proved himself a formidable opponent in his *Xo Ho* pamphlet. If he were to write again in more personal circumstances, not only would he be noticed and feared but he would be vulnerable to counter-attack.

The first of a chain of political pamphlets on Conway's dismissal was published in May: a government defence of the action, written by William Guthrie, entitled *Address to the Public on the late Dismissal of a General Officer*. It was a serious, closely reasoned, but rather dull, rehearsal of the precedents for linking positions at Court and senior rank in the army with supportive behaviour towards the government in Commons' votes. While neither vulgar nor suggestive, the pamphlet did say that Conway had not been a notably distinguished officer and it did mention the deadly word 'Rochefort'. Horace's reply, the *Counter Address*, written between 29 May and 12 June 1754, was as tightly reasoned and repetitive as Guthrie's initial blast and, it has to be admitted, equally dull. Reasonably enough, it praised Conway's personal moral qualities at some length and Horace no doubt felt that he had done what was required and faced up to the implication that Conway was a less than successful officer:

> How shall Defamation be fastened? How asperse one of the most
> spotless characters this or any country has produced? His virtues as
> a man, a husband, a father, a subject, a senator, are unquestionable.
> We will drop the word 'Rochefort'. Will not Ministers be justified
> in breaking a man in the year 1764, who might have taken
> Rochefort in 1757?

This was fair enough, though in the relaxed moral climate of 1764 it was asking for trouble to stress the purity of a hero with quite such rhetorical insistence. What seems to have provoked the government and caused Guthrie to reply with scurrilous personal abuse was not so much Horace's text as its epigraph, a few lines from Voltaire's *Henriade*, about greedy and corrupt ministers who profit in both peace and war:

> *Henri voit près des rois leurs insolens ministres:*
> *Il remarque sur tout ces conseillers sinistres,*
> *Qui des moeurs et des lois avares corrupteurs,*
> *De Themis et de Mars ont vendu les honneurs:*
> *Qui mirent les premiers a d'indignes enchères,*
> *L'inestimable prix des virtues de nos pères.*

[Henry saw the kings with their arrogant ministers gathered around them. He found these evil advisers everywhere: rapacious men who corrupt our laws and morality, sell off the civil and military honours of the state and are the first to auction shamelessly our priceless inheritance of ancestral integrity.]

Henry Fox, who was coining a small fortune each year by manipulating his powers as Paymaster General, may well have considered those lines as a thrust below the belt, and Fox had been a personal friend of Horace for many years, fully aware of his sexual nature.

At the very end of August the thunderbolt fell. Guthrie replied to Horace's *Counter Address* to his *Address* with the unimaginatively titled but venomous *Reply to the Counter Address*. It was in this that Horace was well and truly 'outed' as being, 'by nature muleish, by disposition female, so halting between the two that it would very much puzzle a common observer to assign to him his true sex'. There was a good deal more on Horace's style of writing:

> there is a weakness and an effeminacy in it which seems to burlesque even calumny itself. The complexion of the malice, the feeble tone of the expression, and the passionate fondness with which the *personal* qualities of the officer in question are continually dwelt on, would tempt one to imagine, that this arrow came forth from a female quiver.

Horace's person recalled 'the hermaphrodite horse which is just brought to town and may, perhaps, not inaptly represent him. He possesseth all the characters of both sexes, but the odd situation and transposition of the parts, appear as it were, the sport of nature.' To make quite clear to even a dim reader exactly who was the target of this abuse, Guthrie slipped in, quite gratuitously, a quotation from *Hamlet* – 'Thou art a scholar, speak to it, Horatio' – and in a most wounding shaft at Horace's 'regard' for Conway reported that 'One of the *beaux esprits* of the present times, has christened this regard, calling it, with a feigned concern, "an unsuccessful passion during the course of twenty years" '.

As a first response, Horace's letter to Conway of 1 September was relatively muted, even defiant:

> It is the lowest of all Grub Street, and I hear is treated so. They have nothing better to say that I am in love with you, have been so these twenty years, and am no giant. I am a very constant old swain: they might have made the years above thirty; it is so long I have had the same unalterable friendship for you.

Inevitably Horace made a ritual gesture to share all his fortune with a ruined Conway, and inevitably the ruined Conway ritually declined it.

The Conways closed ranks loyally. Lady Ailesbury sent Horace a landscape worked in wool as a token of family solidarity. Alarmed at the idea of hanging this object on the walls of Strawberry, Horace wrote back equivocally, 'I shall have more satisfaction at seeing it at Park Place; where, in spite of the worst kind of malice, I shall persist in saying my heart is fixed. They may ruin me, but no calumny shall make me desert you.' Although there is a hint of hysteria here, everyone was, so far, behaving well under pressure. Lord Hertford's response was rather more evasive and diplomatic: 'The press,' he wrote, 'must be at liberty, to avoid a greater evil, but I abhor the abuses of it and despise those who encourage it.'

But then Horace seems to have wilted under the pressure of polite sympathy and knowing sneers. The letter which he wrote to Henry Conway on 5 October, a month after Guthrie's onslaught, shows signs of the classic homosexual reaction to a public accusation. 'It is over with us,' the letter opened melodramatically, 'everything fights against this country! You see I write in despair ... We cannot combat. We shall be left almost alone ... For the rest, come what may, I am perfectly prepared.' He then demonstrated that the only thing he was 'perfectly prepared' for was a headlong, ignominious flight to the Continent: 'and while there is a free spot of earth upon the globe that shall be my country.' The parliamentary campaign that he and Conway had contrived to wage was now hopeless and 'since we have no longer any plan of operations to settle, we will look back over the map of Europe, and fix upon a pleasant corner for our exile – for take notice, I do not design to fall upon my dagger.' This was mere histrionics; Horace would never have considered suicide. Instinctively he projected himself in heroic literary terms: a second Mark Antony, perhaps. He picked up a quotation, not from Shakespeare's *Antony and Cleopatra*, but from Dryden's version of the play, *All for Love, or The World well Lost*: 'They tell me 'tis my birthday', he quoted, but then rejected the implication of suicide as the only way out: 'I'll not go on with Antony and say "I'll keep it with double pomp of sadness".' Not for Horace the bloody complexities of a dagger in the guts, he preferred the posture as a noble hero, laughing in the face of disaster:

> No, when they can smile, who ruin a great country, sure those who would have saved it may indulge themselves in that cheerfulness which conscious integrity bestows.

What had initially provoked this storm of curiously mingled patriotism and invaded privacy was Horace's belief, falsely grounded as it was to turn out, that their two principal supporters in Parliament had been lost. He had been told that the Duke of Cumberland was dead and that the Duke of Devonshire was dying. Cumberland was not dead. He had merely suffered yet another apoplexy and would soldier on for more than a year, still a potent force in Westminster politics. Devonshire, on the other hand, was really dying but his death saved Henry Conway from financial problems because the Duke generously left him £5000 in his will.

These developments were excellent for Conway who had served as Cumberland's aide-de-camp during the War of the Austrian Succession. There was now no question of dependence on Horace's money and Cumberland was still there, firmly supporting an old officer of past campaigns. But it left Horace traumatized. Through the next twelve months he was in two minds: one was dedicated to Westminster and the thrills of intrigue, one brooded bitterly on the 'outing', on the invasion of his private affections and on the need to escape abroad from a parliamentary game which had lost its savour. Not only for the next twelve months, but for two years Horace Walpole endured a peculiarly literary nervous breakdown, writing himself through his letters into one emotional scenario with one set of friends – Montagu and Mann – and into another completely contradictory scenario with another set – the Conways and women correspondents like Lady Hervey, Anne Pitt and Lady Suffolk.

It is impossible to say which was the true Horace of this split personality, because for a year or two, under the shock of Guthrie's 'outing', he was, if not quite mad, gently distraught and the first result of this distraction was the writing of *Otranto*. The book was first published on 24 December of that year, 1764. According to the often unreliable but in this instance suspiciously exact, dates given by Horace in his 'Short Notes on the Life of Horace Walpole', *Otranto* was begun immediately after he had completed his *Counter Address* on 12 June and was finished by 6 August. This would mean that the whole novel had taken between seven and eight weeks to write and that it could have had no psychological connection with Guthrie's 'outing', which would not be published until 28 August.

This dating, imposed by Horace long after the events, is suspect. He made no mention in any of his letters of June, July and August 1764 that he was writing his most influential and exciting book. The celebrated letter describing its inspiration and composition was written to William Cole a year later, on 9 March 1765. In that Horace claimed:

I waked one morning in the beginning of last June from a dream, of which all I could recover was, that I had thought myself in an ancient castle (a very natural dream for a head filled like mine with Gothic story) and that on the uppermost bannister of a great staircase I saw a gigantic hand in armour. In the evening I sat down and began to write, without knowing in the least what I intended to say or relate.

This explanation of such an inexplicable work of fiction is so picturesque and romantically satisfying that it has always been accepted despite the plain fact that the concluding events of *Otranto* are clearly anticipated on the first page of the novel, implying an element of deliberate plot development. Then there is the matter of the date of composition. Would someone desperately concerned for the fortunes of a good friend whom he had just ruined by bad political advice, sit down immediately after writing a serious defence of that friend and of parliamentary liberties and scribble a sensational novelette?

It is necessary, for those not familiar with the plot of *Otranto*, to sketch in the outline of its fantastic incidents, although a brief précis is impossible. In an Italian castle Manfred, Prince of Otranto, is preparing for the wedding of his only son Conrad to Isabella, daughter of the Marquis of Vicenza. Manfred has a wife, Hippolita, and a daughter, Matilda. Without warning, a huge helmet crashes down into the castle courtyard and kills Conrad. Manfred immediately decides to divorce Hippolita and marry Isabella in order to produce a new heir. His family has only owned Otranto for three generations and there is a prophecy that they will lose the castle when its real owner grows too large for it. When Theodore, a young man in the crowd of onlookers, remarks that the helmet on the tomb of Alfonso the Good in the nearby church has disappeared, Manfred, in a nervous rage, orders him to be imprisoned under the helmet. Manfred then presses his suit upon a terrified Isabella, who is only saved when the figure of a portrait of his grandfather on the wall steps out of its frame, sighs and marches out of the room.

Isabella escapes down into the castle's dungeons, where she meets Theodore who has entered through a hole in the pavement of the courtyard. Together they open a trapdoor into a secret passage leading to the local church. Isabella flees down this but

Theodore is recaptured. A gigantic leg appears and disappears in a gallery of the castle, an episode which Horace treats in comic Shakespearean pastiche.

The plot-line then switches to Matilda and Hippolita. They are visited by Friar Jerome who tells them that Isabella is safe in the church. Theodore is revealed as Jerome's son and of a noble Sicilian house. The Marquis of Vicenza and his party arrive, carrying a gigantic sabre which joins the huge helmet in the courtyard. Isabella flees from the church and in the confusion, as Manfred sets off in pursuit, Matilda releases Theodore from prison. The two young people fall in love, but Theodore has to take refuge in the woods near the castle. He meets Isabella, hiding in a cave, then fights a stranger knight whom he confronts at the cave entrance, wounding him seriously. Unfortunately the wounded knight turns out to be Isabella's father, the Marquis of Vicenza, who was trying to rescue his daughter. Theodore escorts Vicenza back to the castle for medical treatment, and this allows Vicenza to relate his history to Matilda, telling her how he had discovered the giant sabre in the Holy Land. Manfred returns and a general reconciliation seems to be approaching.

Isabella and Matilda have a long, tearful discussion in which Isabella manages to persuade Matilda that Theodore loves Matilda and not, as Matilda had feared, Isabella. The problem here is that Manfred is proposing to marry Matilda off to Vicenza provided that Vicenza allows his daughter Isabella to marry Manfred, once Hippolita has been divorced. Matilda is so upset that she hurries off to church to pray.

After another comic dialogue with Bianca, Matilda's maidservant, there is a reported appearance of a giant hand which causes much alarm. Vicenza sees a skeleton which warns him not to try to marry Matilda and as a consequence Vicenza snubs Manfred. Angered by this affront, Manfred learns that Theodore is talking to a woman in the church. Believing the woman to be Isabella, Manfred rushes into the darkened church and stabs her, only to find that he has killed his own daughter Matilda. This tragedy is the sign for the gigantic ghost or spectre, parts of which have been appearing throughout the action, to manifest itself entire, ruining the whole castle as it does so. It declares itself to be the ancient

Lord of Otranto, Alfonso the Good, and ascends into heaven where it is received by St Nicholas.

Friar Jerome then explains that Alfonso had been poisoned in the Holy Land by Manfred's wicked grandfather, but that before his death he had married a Sicilian lady and she had born a daughter. He, Jerome, had married that daughter and Theodore is their child and Alfonso's grandson. Manfred and Hippolita both retreat to convents to expiate their sins and Theodore becomes Lord of Otranto and what little remains of the castle, with the prospect of eventually marrying Isabella, in whose company 'he could forever indulge the melancholy that had taken possession of his soul'.

Before dismissing this as a compendium of Gothic self-indulgence, certain facts have to be absorbed. Ridiculous as the action may appear, for more than two hundred years the book has never been out of print and it has been translated into fourteen languages. It must, therefore, touch upon certain archetypal themes and attract adult readers in the same way as Oscar Wilde's *Portrait of Dorian Gray*, despite thin style and improbable narrative. *Otranto* is easily ridiculed but dangerous to ignore. Written quickly in a state of high excitement by a man too disturbed to notice its incongruities, *Otranto* appears to reflect Horace Walpole's state of mind, but his state of mind after 28 August and the 'outing', not before.

The underlying theme of *Otranto*, as the précis reveals, is one of the guilty past catching up with the present, of sudden disastrous manifestations that have their causes in past evils. An entire castle and an established way of life is ripped apart by a monstrous 'ghost'. A lustful man is exposed and obliged to give up everything, his castle in particular, and retire to hide his shame. There are undoubted echoes here of that letter of 5 October which Horace wrote to Conway – all is over; we are discovered; let us flee together. The parallels should not be pressed too hard but, unless Horace's dating to June and July is discounted, we are left with the implausible coincidence that Walpole wrote a tortured and improbable masterpiece three weeks before being traumatized by a cruel public exposure and ridicule of his inmost sexuality and his most valued emotional relationship.

What is far more likely is that he wrote *Otranto* after 28 August, probably over September and October, in a state of febrile excitement, a first stage of the nervous collapse that was to afflict him for at least the next two years. He might well have considered it expedient, after being described as a hermaphrodite, to bring out a rip-roaring, red-blooded romance that included threats of rape in gloomy cellars and portrayed normally sexed young men falling in love, normally, with beautiful high-born maidens in distress. *Otranto* would have functioned in its time at two levels. It would have established its author as a regular sexual tearaway and it would allow him privately to express his alarm at the sudden destructive force which Guthrie had brought into his life. Insecurity and sexual menace are the essence of *Otranto*.

At another level, the book is hauntingly similar to his creation of Strawberry Hill. Neither the book nor the house are, strictly speaking, originals; yet both, by a quality of naïve directness and clever presentational skills, have come to be accepted as true innovators, the one of the Gothic novel, the other of the Gothic Revival. In both cases, Horace the public relations expert has bemused posterity into accepting him for what he was not, and in each case the illusion created has been so strong as to become virtual reality. Strawberry Hill did not begin its transformation until 1752. Long before that, there had been other middle-sized neo-Gothic houses: Clearwell Castle in the Forest of Dean of 1727–8, Esher Place (1733), Stout's Hill, Uley, Gloucestershire (1743) and Radway Grange, Warwickshire of 1744–6. There had been a superb fan-vaulted Gothic great hall created within Welbeck Abbey, Nottinghamshire in 1748–51. Yet not one of these had the inventive bijoux charm of Horace's villa and not one of them was publicized as assiduously as Strawberry, with the upper and most influential aristocracy in its first decade, and then with the bourgeoisie and gentry by ticket admission in Horace's later years.

It has not always been remarked that while young men in the eighteenth century tended to pick up their architectural ideas in Italy, young women, debarred by their sex from the Grand Tour, picked up their notions on style and decoration from a known circuit of visitable houses and villas. Prominent on that circuit was Strawberry, converting the brides of the future and young married women to the propriety of Gothic for their new houses and interior refittings.

As with Strawberry, so with *The Castle of Otranto*. By its merciful brevity, it was accessible. Many faint readers may have given up half-way through *The Mysteries of Udolpho* or *The Italian* and turned in revulsion from *The Monk*, but most would get to the end of *Otranto*, in which so much happens so soon. Horace had no time for introspective *longueurs*. His book is essentially a play with links to the various dialogues and scenes. But its vignettes were destined to become the classical clichés of the genre – the chivalric procession approaching a castle gate with trumpets sounding, the cowled and kneeling figure that turns to reveal a grinning death's head, the trapdoor leading to stone stairs down into 'a vault totally dark', and above all the young girl fleeing from a predatory male, yet still allowed 'a kind of momentary joy to perceive an imperfect ray of clouded moonshine gleam from the roof of the vault'.

It is an intoxicating mix of themes for all the crudity of its contrivance; and even its gaucherie escapes real criticism because Horace, following Shakespeare faithfully, intersperses the horrors with the slapstick comedy of cheeky Bianca and the prevarications of Jacquez and Diego, which reduce the frightful Manfred to spluttering incoherence. But it is no more innovative than Strawberry; even less so if anything. Two years before *Otranto*, Thomas Leland had published *Longsword, Earl of Salisbury*, 'an Historical Romance', a more convincing performance in precisely the same vein, handsomely illustrated with a Gothic interior. *Longsword* has Reginald, a wicked monk, a countess threatened with a forced marriage and a crusader earl returning in the nick of time to effect her rescue; who now has even heard of it? But long before either of these two books were published, the French had invented and developed Gothic romance. The genre was copied by Leland and Walpole, not pioneered by them.

Thirty years before Horace wrote *Otranto*, the Abbe Prévost and his followers, writers like Madame de Tencin, had established the

popularity of novels with gloomy Gothic backgrounds, ruined castles, dark caverns and forced marriages. Second-generation writers
in this school, Baculard d'Arnaud in particular, had made a special-
ity of novels with a religious background of monks, nuns, cloisters
and all the neuroticisms attendant upon Catholic vows of chastity
when they conflict with romantic passions. D'Arnaud's *Coligni*,
published in 1741, was so outrageously anti-clerical that he ended
up with a brief spell in prison. *Les Époux malheureux* came out in
1752, but his best-known production was a play, not acted in his
lifetime, *Le Comte de Comminge*, which was published in the same
year as Horace's *Otranto*. Baculard d'Arnaud's *Comminge* is only a
dramatized version of Madame de Tencin's novel *Mémoires du
Comte de Comminge*, published in 1749 and readily accessible to
the English by Charlotte Ramsay's translation of 1756.
Comminge's lover disguises herself as a monk in order to live near
her beloved in the monastery to which he has retired. He only discovers the deception as she is on her deathbed, whereupon he
throws himself into the grave already prepared for her.

This is the kind of *'darnauderie'*, as the French called it, at which
Horace was aiming when he had Manfred stab his daughter to
death in a church, leaving Matilda plenty of time to forgive her
father in a storm of tears: pity and terror combined. Edmund
Burke would have approved. His *Philosophical Inquiry into the
Origin of our Ideas of the Sublime and the Beautiful*, had explored
these concepts and effects as long ago as 1757. Interestingly,
Horace never mentions Burke's seminal study of these Romantic
emotions, though he followed Burke's political career with interest
and approval. But Horace was never notably generous about his
sources.

Perhaps Horace's *Otranto* is best seen as a typical production of the
1760s, a decade of innovative, eclectic fakes and foreign introductions. James Macpherson's *Fingal* was coming out in parts between
1760 and 1764. Horace instantly detected it as a bogus Scottish
attempt to rival Homer. Bishop Percy published a translation
(from the Portuguese) of a Chinese novel in 1761 and his carefully
'edited' *Reliques of Ancient English Poetry* in 1765. Salomon

Gessner's *Death of Abel* appeared in Mary Collyer's translation (from the French of Huber, not the original German Swiss) in 1761. Klopstock's *The Messiah* and *The Death of Adam* reached English readers in 1763. Thomas Chatterton began to deceive the gullible, though not Horace, with his fifteenth-century poet-monk, Thomas Rowley, from 1769 onwards.

Read in the context of these emotional writings, *Otranto* comes to be seen as, if not commonplace, at least appropriate to its time. Unnoticed by Horace and by most of his contemporaries, John Henry Fuseli had arrived in England in 1761. He had been sent on a deliberate cultural embassy by reputable Swiss pedagogues and writers from Zurich, men like Bodmer and Sulzer, to attempt a stealthy conversion of the British to a mild Swiss version of '*Sturm und Drang*' and establish the prestige of Swiss literature in a country which they admired. Horace Walpole's Manfred, Prince of Otranto, a figure motivated at all times by fury and lust, and a man still spiritually unresolved in the novel's final episodes, should have been a perfect '*Sturm und Drang*' creation. But even as Horace was creating Manfred, to express his own personal anger and dismay at being 'outed', he was unable to resist the comic potential of such a character and left him exposed to the foolery of grooms and pert maidservants. Even the ghost of his grandfather treats Manfred with something less than perfect respect, beckoning him to follow, but then rudely slamming a door in his face. *Otranto* has survived because not only does it pack all the horrors and clichés of the Gothic novel into a hundred pages, but it adds a subtext of laughter which ridicules the entire convention. Horace the outsider had even contrived to stand outside himself and find his own intense creations more than a little ridiculous.

CHAPTER TEN

Trauma, triumph and a retreat to France

Henry Conway made no written reply to that disturbed letter from Horace of 5 October 1764, beginning 'It is over with us!' and urging flight to the Continent. Horace was at Park Place a few days later, soothed to a calmer and more optimistic political perspective and for the whole of the next embattled twelve months there were no more letters exchanged between the two friends because they were meeting regularly to plot their parliamentary campaign. Instead, Horace switched his attention to Henry's elder brother, Lord Hertford, sending him long, informative, weekly newsletters with positive, persuasive accounts of the changing alliances at Westminster. In return he received grateful and warmly affectionate letters from Hertford who knew, or thought he knew, via Horace, that Henry Fox coveted his job as ambassador to France. Hertford was anxious to make the right moves, to be loyal to his brother Henry, who might be a rising power, and yet not offend the Prime Minister, George Grenville, who could dismiss him at any time if he was prepared to forfeit the Hertford interest in the Commons.

All through these months, from September 1764 to September 1765 when he eventually crossed the Channel, Horace was claiming to be disenchanted with the political power-game and eager for a season of sophisticated shopping in Paris with the Hertfords as his social base. The protestations came thick and fast: 'The first moment I can quit party with honour I shall seize. It neither suits my inclination nor the years I have lived in the world, I am heartily sick of its commerce.' A little later, 'I will own to you fairly, that I think I shall soon have it in my power to come to you on the foot I wish, I mean, having done with politics, which I have told you all along, and with great truth, are as much my abhorence as yours.'

Lord Hertford must have been bewildered, and eventually a little irritated, by the prevarications. The Hertfords had prepared their absent son's apartment for their guest, who wrote again in November, 'I am preparing, in earnest, to make you a visit – not next week, but seriously in February'. Horace would wait only until Parliament met in January and then, unless Grenville's majority was only a matter of one or two votes, he would be in Paris among friends. 'I am so sick of politics, which I have long detested, that I must bid adieu to them. I have acted the part by your brother that I thought right. He approves what I have done, and what I mean to do.' This last point is important. Horace had discussed his future retirement from politics with Henry Conway so there could have been no question of his being offered a position in some future Conway-controlled administration. Letters to William Cole, Horace's new correspondent on matters historical tell exactly the same story of determination to quit Westminster and enjoy Paris. Inevitably with Horace, there was also a health angle: 'I have a return of those nightly fevers and pains in my breast ... change of air and a better climate are certainly necessary to me in winter', and Lord Hertford was, perhaps optimistically, describing Paris as a health resort.

While Horace was all politeness and sensitive tact in letters to cousin Hertford, George Montagu caught his friend in a completely different mood, one of neurotic tension not all that remote from a nervous breakdown. Content in rural Northamptonshire, Montagu had allowed two months to pass without writing to Horace and with no show of bachelor solidarity over the Guthrie 'outing'. Then Horace wrote him an impassioned letter dated 16 December 1764, to declare savagely, 'I hate you for being so indifferent to me ... I live in the world and yet love nothing, care a straw for nothing, but two or three old friends, [by implication including Montagu] that I have loved these thirty years. You have buried yourself,' Horace accused him, 'with half a dozen parsons and squires, and yet never cast a thought upon those you have always lived with.' His own mid-life crisis of aims and values came pouring out upon inoffensive, self-centred and basically indifferent George:

> I don't want you to like the world; I like it no more than you; but I stay a while in it, because while one sees it, one laughs at it, but when you give it up, one grows angry with it, and I hold it much wiser to laugh than to be out of humour.

But there was no obvious laughter in his nihilistic conclusion: 'I used to say to myself, "Lord! This person is so bad, that person is so bad, I hate them" – I have now found out that they are all pretty much alike, and I hate nobody'; except, on his initial admission, George Montagu. He signed off with the warning that he would be in Paris in February next and that George had better start writing long letters.

Montagu did in fact reply quite briskly, to report that he, in Northamptonshire, 'was never so lively, because freed from the mortal vexations of these horrid times', to have to deal, like Horace, with 'the hateful junto would exceed my patience'. Tactfully he did not remind his friend that two prime movers in 'the hateful junto', Lords Halifax and Sandwich, both up for the Garter, were members of the Montagu clan and his own cousins. Endearingly bland, he concluded:

> by the by, I wish you would buy me a muff; it must be grave and warm, for I and my brother pass many evenings alone, I grow cold by my fireside with reading, for we never play above two hours at cards together, and I find reading troublesome by candlelight.

Such were the realities of country house life in the eighteenth century. Horace sent him his muff; it was the soft answer that had turned away wrath. In February he was not, as promised, in Paris, but still agonizing to Montagu from Arlington Street:

> I am not old yet [he was forty-seven], and have an excellent, though delicate constitution, I may promise myself some agreeable years, if

I could detach myself from all connections, but with a very few persons that I value. Oh! With what joy I could bid adieu to loving and hating! To crowds, public places, great dinners, visits – and above all to the House of Commons!

He had a very bad cold and was taking James's powder.

By this time Hertford, at least, had seen the truth. 'There is no tempting you from the House of Commons,' he wrote on 9 February, 'though you hate and despise it'. Paris was postponed yet again and, at the very moment when he was proclaiming his contempt for the Commons, Horace plunged eagerly into the most intense political five months of his life. Britain's mid-century politics were inextricably internecine, but group antagonisms were Horace's forte. Because he made arrogant claims to influence and power at this time in his *Memoirs*, some historians have tended to play down his real importance. But there is a case for saying that if Horace had not intrigued, persuaded, rallied and interposed again and again behind the scenes, though not on the floor of the House, then Henry Conway would never have become joint Secretary of State with the Duke of Grafton under the new Prime Minister, the Marquis of Rockingham, as he did in June. It was a remarkable leap for one cold and not particularly distinguished Major-General to move in one year from a disgraced and dismissed figure with little parliamentary background to one of the greatest offices of state and subsequently to become so popular across the Atlantic that the American colonists named several small towns 'Conway' in his honour.

What Horace had done over those spring months, with a sly word here and a warning there, was so to rally the scattered opposition (which could, in February, only raise 185 votes to the administration's 224) that it became a potent near-majority, humiliating Grenville in every debate of consequence. Conway's role was to remind the House at each opportunity about the scandalous misuse of general warrants in the Wilkes case and the injustice of his own dismissal from the army. That, however, would not in itself have been enough. On two matters both government and opposition were agreed. They disliked Lord Bute, the 'favourite' of the King and the Princess Dowager, and they disliked the Scots.

Horace manipulated these foolish prejudices to lure the administration into a disastrously wrong decision. George III had already
begun to show signs of mental confusion and was, indeed, thought
unlikely to live out the year as his symptoms shifted from his head
to his chest and some doctors whispered of consumption, so there
was a pressing need for a Regency Bill. One natural candidate for a
Regency council was the Princess Dowager; but she was believed,
with some truth, to be under the influence of Lord Bute. Rumours
even went about that Bute himself might be one of the Regents.
After days of argument in May, the government finally proposed a
council in which virtually all potential candidates, the Queen, the
royal brothers and the royal uncles, were included, and only the
Princess Dowager was excluded. The King was furious at the
implied insult.

Foolishly, Henry Conway wished to support such a move and
Horace had a desperate struggle to stop him from fatally and permanently alienating the King by declaring that his beloved mother
was unfit for the Regency. He succeeded, but only just; and even
then, when an issue had arisen over which the opposition members
could show their loyalty to the King, several of them allowed their
hatred of Bute to carry them in the wrong direction. Horace raged
frustratedly to Lord Hertford:

> Could I, who have at least some experience and knowledge of the
> world, have directed, our party had not been in the contemptible
> and ridiculous position it is. Had I more weight, things still more
> agreeable to you had happened.

By this last remark, Horace meant that with Henry Conway in
power Hertford would have mounted the final step in his career
ladder and become Lord Lieutenant of Ireland, the Viceroy.
Fortunately for the divided opposition, the government displayed
their death-wish. The ministers had alienated the King, who
immediately forced them to think again about excluding the
Princess Dowager, but they still not only proposed but appointed
as Viceroy the least appropriate candidate available – Lord
Weymouth – young, inexperienced and 'an inconsiderable
debauched young man', to use the King's words.

George III was recovering his health and complaining of Grenville that 'when he has wearied me for two hours, he looks at his watch to see if he may not tire me for an hour more'. He told his uncle Cumberland to set up a new administration for him. Conway was Cumberland's favourite and his moment had almost arrived. Only the great William Pitt stood in his way. Cumberland offered Pitt the office of Prime Minister. Ravaged by the gout, Pitt raised impossible conditions and was turned down. Next on Cumberland's list was the young and untried Marquis of Rockingham. He offered to lead an artificial combination of various opposition figures; Lord Bute was not among them. The Duke of Newcastle was slipped in as Lord Privy Seal, but second only to Rockingham was Henry Conway as Secretary of State for the south. This meant, in modern terms, that he was not only Foreign Secretary, but also Home Secretary for the southern half of the country. The Duke of Grafton took the lesser secretaryship for the north.

In mid-June, just when he should have been most active with his advice and intrigues, Horace was incapacitated, confined to his room and, for a day or two, to his bed, by his favourite complaint, 'the flying gout'. This was a combination of real gout with every other ailment of the head and stomach that Horace was suffering. To the gout we owe an enchantingly bizarre letter to Henry Conway, dated 3 July, which can only have been composed when the pain-racked Horace was flying miles high on some hallucinogenic drug, probably opium, prescribed for him by his apothecary, David Graham. In a junkie style almost reminiscent of the 1960s, the letter opened with an impenetrable burst of gnomic significance, Horace describing himself as 'sitting on my bed and wishing to forget how brightly the sun shines'. This was followed by reference to 'a bushel of roses and a new scarlet nightingale which does *not* sing "Nancy Dawson" from morning to night'. He informed Conway, with dreamy and detached superiority, 'You are ignorant what provocation the gout is, and what charms it can bestow on a moment's amusement. Oh! It beats all the refinements of a Roman sensualist!' Rapturous over the significance of trivia, he claimed, 'it has made even my watch a darling plaything'. He was apparently chiming his repeater-watch every few minutes and prolonging his dreams of Rococo sensuality into a half-waking state. In one he had visited Madame de Bentheim, a friend of George Selwyn, in Paris where she had 'the prettiest little palace in the world built like a pavilion of yellow laced with blue'. Even more improbably he had made love to her daughter, Mademoiselle Bleu et Jaune, 'and thought it very clever'. Finally Mr Pitt had been introduced to Madame de Bentheim where 'he granted all her demands' despite being crippled, like Horace, with the gout.

Even if Horace had not many times confirmed his determination to quit politics, Conway would have hesitated to introduce such an unstable figure into the new Cabinet. But contrary to what he wrote later in the *Memoirs*, Horace seems to have been thoroughly satisfied with the new administration at the time it was formed. Montagu, usually the recipient of his friend's gloomiest prognostications and most scandalous revelations, learned that 'the great and happy change, happy I hope for this country, is actually begun,' and would bring 'regulation of general warrants and undoing of at least some of the mischiefs these wretches have been committing.' Proudly Horace noted that Lord Hertford had been offered the viceregency of Ireland 'from his brother's office'. Only a few years later, with the advantage of hindsight, he was to describe the hopeful Rockingham as 'a preposterous figure', and his Cabinet as 'young and inexperienced men, unknown to the nation, and great by nothing but their rank and fortunes'.

Any depression which he may have suffered in these July days stemmed not, as he was to claim later, and his biographers have accepted, from any ingratitude on Conway's part, but from the shattering impact of disease upon one of England's greatest, and most enduring, valetudinarians. 'To enter into old age through the gate of infirmity' was, he complained to Montagu, 'most disheartening. This confession explains the mortification I feel ... I have had so many years heaped upon me within this month, that I have not the conscience to trouble young people, when I can no longer be as juvenile as they are.' More, perhaps, than a heterosexual, a homosexual clings to the illusion of youth. 'I am convinced,'

Horace told Montagu as he prepared to leave for France at long last, 'that nothing is charming but what appeared important in one's youth.' 'Christ!' he exclaimed with uncharacteristic profanity, 'can I ever stoop to the regimen of old age ... nobody can have truly enjoyed the advantages of youth, health and spirits who is content to exist without the two last, which alone bear any resemblance to the first ... I shall still be a gay shadow ... bodily liberty is as dear to me as the mental.'

This was Horace's male menopause. He declared that he was through with people and society. It was not the French whom he was travelling to see: 'I have much more curiosity for their habitations than their company ... I go to see French plays and buy French china.' Paris for Horace in his forty-eighth year was what Byzantium was to be for Yeats, a symbol of arts and eternity.

It took only a Channel crossing with a favourable wind to blow away most of this depressed nonsense. According to the *Memoirs*, Horace had left Henry Conway after a cousinly row. Conway was 'vexed and his pride hurt, he employed Lady Ailesbury to tell me in his presence that he looked on my behaviour as deserting him, and himself dropped many peevish accents.' Horace told Montagu at the time that he was not going to France 'to know their ministers, to look into their government, or think of the interest of nations'. None of these claims was true; he and Conway had parted the best of friends. If Montagu, with whom Horace kept up a gloomy chain of correspondence throughout this period, could have read the letters Horace was writing to Conway at the same time, he might have wondered if he was dealing with a split personality. No sooner was Horace in Paris than he was addressing Conway as 'Biau [an old French affectionate form of 'beau'] Cousin' and penning one of his most sprightly anecdotes of travel. A mile or two outside Calais, he had encountered a coach-and-four with

> a lady in pea green and silver, a smart hat and feather, and two *suivantes*. My reason told me it was the Archbishop's concubine; but luckily my heart whispered that it was Lady Mary Coke. I jumped out of my *chaise* – yes, jumped! Fell on my knees and said my first *ave maria gratia plena*! We just shot a few politics flying – heard

that Madame de Mirepoix had toasted me t'other day in tea –
shook hands, forgot to weep and parted.

The rest of the letter was equally cheerful, listing calls in Paris on
those of the nobility whom he had cultivated in parties at
Strawberry – the Duc de Nivernais and the Comte de Guerchy. He
had been delighted by 'the most glorious works' of Raphael, da
Vinci, Titian, Giorgione and Correggio which he had viewed at
the Marquis de Marigny's town house. Conway must visit Paris
and admire at some future date the new Dépôt des Archives as a
marvel of utility and invention.

As for Horace's determination not to look into government 'or
think of the interest of nations', he was once more revelling in the
role of Horace Walpole, secret agent, in a return to his spying days
at Rome for Horace Mann. This time the reports which he made
to Conway, as Foreign Secretary, were remarkably prescient. For
the government's sake, he mixed with the intellectuals he despised
and was able to warn Conway, from the tedious hours he had
spent in their company, that the *'Philosophes'* were 'men, who
avowing war against popery, aim, many of them, at the subversion
of all religion, and still many more at the destruction of royal
power', thus foreseeing the French Revolution twenty-four years
before it broke out. He also continued his stream of wise counsel
to Conway on English colonial affairs: 'Pray put the colonies in a
good humour,' he urged, writing from what he had learnt about
French opportunism on the other side of the Atlantic, 'I see they
are violently disposed to the new administration.' Conway followed his advice, had the Stamp Duty repealed, and by that action
gave the first British Empire at least a few years' breathing-space
before the American colonies broke away.

As of old, Horace delighted in the secret rituals of spying. He
sent Conway 'a most curious paper' on the *'Philosophes'*, but
warned him that 'I should not like to have it known to come from
me, nor any part of the intelligence I send you: with regard to
which, if you think it necessary to communicate it to particular
persons, I desire my name be suppressed, but would not have anybody else think I do anything here but to amuse myself.' This was

written in October, when he had been only a month abroad. In November came a turn of emotional events as remarkable as any since that meeting with Lord Lincoln in Reggio. In two letters, one following swiftly upon the other, dated 20 and 22 November, and both subsequently destroyed, Henry Conway, despite his position of Secretary of State for the south, just one step away from being Prime Minister, wrote to Horace complaining that he was tired of it all and asking Horace to come away to Naples with him, which was exactly what Horace had been urging him to do only a year ago.

What occasioned this extraordinary turn-about is a mystery. But then Conway's whole personality remains mysterious. How close had his relations with Horace really been since their time at Eton? He was the soldier who seems to have enjoyed his garden more than his wars, the Governor of Jersey who happened to be absent from his island on the only occasion when it was invaded by the French, yet was so admired by the islanders that they gave him an entire prehistoric stone circle as a leaving present. His political rise had been astonishing. Few men seemed ever to have got close to him. Even Horace, his best friend, said that 'his soul was good, virtuous, sincere; but his temper was chill, his mind absent.' Was he so absent-minded that he only registered Horace's appeal to fly a whole year later? If that was the case, then November 1765 was much too late. Horace was a changed man from the 'outed' lover of October 1764. 'Pray stay where you are,' he wrote back severely, 'and do some good to your country – or retire when you cannot – but don't put your finger in your eye and cry after the sugar plums of Park Place. You have engaged and must go through, or be hindered.' Then, with that same chill of temper which he accused Conway of showing, Horace reverted smugly to his own situation: 'I determined, whenever our opposition should be over, to have done with politics; and you see I have adhered to my resolution by coming hither ... You have life and Park Place enough to come, and *you* have not had five months of gout.'

It was an old man's letter. To be fair, Horace had suffered another and even more severe attack of gout in Paris in October, far from the security and comforts of home. But to turn down

Henry Conway's appeal in this icy language, to reject the romantic exile for which he had been appealing only a year before, was very mature, very responsible and not remotely the whimsical, passionate Horace of old. Possibly he was irritated at the thought of all his covert intelligence and his 'most curious paper' going to waste in Whitehall. Certainly by this time in late November, with his 'flying gout' briefly at rest, Horace had begun to establish a routine of sorts for himself in that mannered and wearily sophisticated society. Of his two avowed objects in making the visit, French china and French plays, only the china had come up to expectation. He was to buy avidly, confessing when he left in April 1766, 'I have not a farthing left in the world'. But a visit in September to the Italian comedy at the Comédie-Française had proved emotionally disturbing. It was to Montagu, not Conway, that he unburdened himself with an account of the performance, picking up on the theme of lost youth and dreary age:

> Harlequin, my passion, makes me more melancholy than cheerful. Instead of laughing I sit reflecting, how everything loses charm when one's own youth does not lend it gilding. When we are divested of that eagerness and illusion with which our youth presents objects to us, we are but the CAPUT MORTUUM of pleasure. In short, I have done with the world, and only live in it, rather than in a desert.

Not only plays but also the French obsession with 'philosophy, literature and free-thinking' bored and alarmed Horace as he drifted into the conservatism of middle age. He found 'philosophers so overbearing and underbred'; 'free-thinking is for oneself, surely not for society' and 'literature is very amusing, when one has nothing else to do.' For relief, he turned to his own kind of people. One day's entry, taken at random from his Paris journal, reveals the pattern of his life. For 22 November 1765 it runs:

> To manufacture of French china with Duke and Duchess of Richmond etc. After dinner to Mme de Boufflers, Baron d'Holbech, and Lady Fife; none at home. To Mr Craufurd. To Lady Berkeley's assembly, Lady Aston, Lady St George, and Mrs Matthews there. Supped at Mme du Deffand's with Mmes de la Valliere, Valentinois, Bentheim, Lambert, Chevalier de Botteville, Pont de Vegle, Courte, d'Usson and 2 more.

There is the Proustian parade of noble names, the hints – 'none at home' – of occasional frustration, and other names, Mr Craufurd and Mme du Deffand, which, when followed up, reveal histories of emotional complexity with both sexes. Horace had arrived, by introductions and by Strawberry Hill hospitality returned, at a high social level. But for all his professed determination to avoid fellow countrymen, these records include almost as many English as French. He had even invited 'Tozhy' Cole to join him in Paris for three of the six months he was to spend there. Cole was Horace's gesture towards sobriety and old age. He had been his companion in drawing lessons in the days before Horace went up to Eton. Now he was a High-Church parson and an antiquary with a living in Cambridgeshire and close university contacts. Horace had recently come to rely on his advice in the running battles which he was waging with the Society of Antiquaries. In Paris they visited the churches and monasteries of the city together on those afternoons when Horace was not out shopping. His mornings were usually spent in bed recovering from very late night parties with old ladies. It was these strange revels with the senior citizens of the *ancien régime* which made Horace's five visits to Paris more infamous than celebrated, more ridiculed than admired by friends in England. But since the emotional affair which they sparked off was to endure until the death of Madame du Deffand in 1780, a whole fourteen years of psychic energy misplaced, they need to be set into perspective.

Horace was rising fifty when he left England proclaiming, to the contentedly decrepit George Montagu, that youth was the only time that mattered and old age was a disaster. That had been his mood in August. By next January he was writing to Lady Hervey to say that 'though the fountain of youth is not here, the fountain of age is, which comes to the same thing. One is never old here, or never thought so. One makes verses as if one was but seventeen.' Being Horace, he had to exaggerate a little: 'the first step towards being in fashion is to lose an eye or a tooth ... it is charming to totter into vogue.' All this was in a city which he had earlier described as 'the ugliest, beastly town in the universe', dismissing its citizens' 'boasted knowledge of society' as 'talking of their suppers, and every malady they have about them or know of'. For relief from the aggressive atheism of the *'Philosophes'* he had returned to a place of youthful inspiration, telling Thomas Gray, who would have remembered it well, 'I go and compose myself at the Chartreuse where I am almost tempted to prefer Le Soeur to every painter I know'. He had seen 'the Hôtel de Soubise, de Luxembourg, de Maurepas, de Brancas and several others, especially the boasted Hôtel de Richelieu, and could not perceive any difference, but in the more or less gold, more or less baubles on the chimneys and tables; and that now and then Vanloo has sprawled goddesses over the doors, and at other times, Boucher.' So even the mannered French classicism was a bore to someone accustomed to Strawberry Gothic.

Any normal man of his disenchanted disposition might have seized the opportunity of a foreign capital, notorious for pleasure, to have a love affair with someone young and beautiful, female or male. What Horace did to transform his attitude to France and the French was to fake a mildly funny, gently rude, letter from the King of Prussia to Jean-Jacques Rousseau. Spite was behind it. Rousseau had just gone to England with Hume as his chaperone and Horace was sick of hearing Hume's praises sung in every Paris salon. Also Horace was suspicious of the natural emotions which were Rousseau's stock-in-trade: 'you have made yourself sufficiently talked of by Singularities little worthy of a great Man,' Horace sneered, 'Show your Enemies that you can sometimes have common Sense, that will grieve them without doing you much Harm.' The letter was aimed at making Rousseau look a little foolish, pretending that the King of Prussia was more sorry for him than sympathetic and was urging him to give his self-pity a rest.

The device was far more effective than it deserved. Parisian society was either outraged or amused; Rousseau was furious, thought that Hume had written it and staged a quarrel with him; but socially Horace was made. Initially he had found that 'the disadvantage of speaking a language worse than any idiot one meets is insurmountable: the silliest Frenchman is eloquent to me, and leaves me embarrassed and obscure'. But once the letter had been written on 28 December it went round like wildfire and Horace's halting French was no longer a handicap. Instead he was, for a month at least, the lion of the salons; he toured all the famous hostesses, appraising and appraised: Mesdames Geoffrin, du Deffand, de Mirepoix, de Boufflers, de Rochfort and the Maréchale de Luxembourg. Thomas Gray was given an excited account of their varying personalities, a 'Which' survey of all the gossip shops: Geoffrin 'has little taste and less knowledge'; Boufflers is 'always sitting for her picture to her biographer'; Mirepoix was 'false, artful and insinuating beyond measure'.

To Horace, this world of influential, sophisticated old women was very Heaven; and to understand its charm for him it has to be remembered that it was only Twickenham to the power of ten. He had always been addicted to old ladies, to feminine sensibility without the sex drive. When he was at Strawberry he spent almost every evening with either Lady Suffolk, who had been, briefly and dysfunctionally, the mistress of George II but was now in her seventies, or with Kitty Clive, who would talk a little bawdy, reminisce about her stage career and play cards by the hour. Now, in Paris, he chose the salon of Marie du Deffand, Marquise de Chastres, who combined in one person the desirable characteristics of both Suffolk and Clive. Twenty-one years his senior, a famous wit and letter-writer, a correspondent of Voltaire and the Holy Roman Emperor, she was, Horace told Gray, very warm in dispute, 'her judgement on every subject is as just as possible; on every point of conduct as wrong as possible'. Unlike her rivals she was 'still anxious to be loved', but, Horace added hastily, anxious not to give the wrong impression, 'I don't mean by lovers.' Her marriage to the Marquis de Chastres had lasted only four years but she had the supreme sexual cachet of having been the mistress, back in the 1720s, of that famous lecher, Philip, Duc d'Orléans and Regent of France. That she had only been his scarlet woman, *'la grande pécheresse'*, for a mere fortnight added a comic zest to the distinction. The bizarre and tragic element to the relationship into which Horace entered with this alarming old dragon was that, since 1752, she had been blind. She fell headlong in love with the sound of Horace, with his stumbling French, his whimsical, argumentative ways, his originality; and until she died, fourteen years later, she was to woo him in over four hundred passionate dictated letters. Typically, Horace developed a friendly relationship with her male secretary.

Madame du Deffand called Horace *'mon tuteur'* and he called her *'ma petite'*; she told him 'you behave like the Grand Turk. Like him you are a tyrant, but at the same time you are magnificent. It is this second quality that impels me, against my will, to write to you.' If it is difficult to recognize Horace in such a description, then perhaps the affinity between this unlikely pair is explained by the names which Madame gave to her successive lapdogs. She called them Bedreddin, Kismi, Fanny, Diane and Tonton. This sounds more Horatian than 'the Great Turk'. Tonton was bequeathed to Horace, along with her papers, in her will and Horace cared fondly for the grossly fat little dog until its death.

There still remains much to account for. When Horace joined her salon it was in social decline. The *'Philosophes'* had deserted her for a rival salon set up by her protégé, Julie de Lespinasse. All Deffand had going for her was her conversation, her passionate enthusiasm for life and an excellent cook who prepared good suppers twice a week. George Selwyn, who at this time was deeply involved with young Lord March, son to the Duke of Queensbury, had recommended Madame to Horace, which in itself says little for the salon's tone. On his first visit Horace heard that the dying Dauphin had had *'une évacuation foetide'* and Madame had called out, 'Oh! I had forgot to mention that he threw down his chamber pot, and was forced to change his bed.' In that respect her apartment in the convent of the Filles de St Joseph on the rue St Dominique was coarser in tone than Lady Suffolk's Marble Hill House at Twickenham.

At first, Horace cultivated her principally for her memories. She is 'delicious', he told Selwyn, 'that is as often as I can get her fifty years back ... I sup there twice a week, and bear all her dull company for the sake of the Regent.' The company was not only dull; it was antique. The President Hénault, Madame's official *cavaliere servante*, was eighty, but there were a few young English, including

Lord Ossory and Mr Craufurd, a Scots laird's son. There was also, on occasion, the lively, attractive Duchesse de Choiseul, wife to Louis XV's chief minister and related by marriage to Madame du Deffand. Everyone was polite to Horace: 'they humour me and fondle me, and are so good natured, and make me keep my chair, and rise for nobody, and hand out nobody, and don't stare at one's being a skeleton'; and he was collecting *bons mots*, such as *'se marier est bien, y réfléchir est mieux'*, anecdotes of the kind that the English like to think typically French. When, for instance, M de Plessis-Chatillon lamented his first wife's death to his second wife, she said, *'Je vous assure, Monsieur, que personne ne la regrette plus que moi'*. ['Take my word for it Sir, no one regrets that more than I do.'] That went into a letter, along with the Bailli de Chabrillon's comment when Horace told him that the aged Countess of Desmond had broken her neck in gathering apples: *'Elle était fort attachée au péché original!'* ['Of course, she was always very keen on original sin!']

This style of society might be endured for one visit but what has to be explained is that Horace, who admitted, 'Ever since I stopped being a young man, I have had a terrible fear of being a ridiculous old one,' came back to it in 1767, 1769, 1771 and 1775 for four more encounters with his 'dear old blind lady', and replied conscientiously to that torrent of her epistolary love, though only six scraps of his replies have survived his own censorship. It may, as Wilmarth Lewis has suggested, have been a case of finding a substitute for the well-loved mother who had died when Horace was twenty. Then again it is possible that he cultivated Madame for the same reason that he had written *Otranto* – to counter the reputation for homosexuality that Guthrie's 'outing' had given him in England. There is also the Sévigné factor. Madame de Sévigné, the great French letter-writer of Louis XIV's reign, had always been Horace's literary heroine and model. His Green Closet at Strawberry had been dedicated to her writings and mementos, and when the Duchesse de Choiseul wished to give him particular pleasure she gave him a supposed Sévigné original manuscript and a snuff-box inset with a miniature of Sévigné. Madame du Deffand had some claim to be considered as the Sévigné of the eighteenth century and Horace might have thought that he would gain immortality by being involved with her in a grotesque courtship that would endure down the centuries. This would explain the whole episode as part of the Horace Walpole public relations campaign: alms for oblivion.

The question has to be asked whether Horace, at this stage of his life, had a heart or a vanity. There is his own celebrated analysis of his post-Guthrie mood in France: 'the dead have exhausted their power of deceiving . . . I almost think there is no wisdom comparable to that of exchanging what is called the realities of life for dreams.' He wrote that confession in a letter to Montagu of January 1766 just as he was settling into the relationship with Madame du Deffand, but did not mention her by name. Instead, he explained that 'Old castles, old pictures, old histories, and the babble of old people make one live back into centuries that cannot disappoint.' The mood was elegaic, but how did Madame fit in with it? Something of Horace's dangerously detached state of mind is indicated by his often quoted 'Craufurd' letter.

January 1766 was the month when young Mr Craufurd left Paris for England. Soon he was writing back, in a letter which has not been allowed to survive, to propose a loving friendship with Horace. That, at least, is what must be assumed from Horace's icy reply of 6 March. After an opening page on the falsehood, spite, meanness, malice, barbarity and injustice of 'our good old friend's' hangers-on, Horace turned the North wind of his rhetoric onto the unfortunate Craufurd, who is known to have been small in stature and was, one would guess, physically unattractive. The letter went on:

> . . . to keep your friendship within bounds, consider my heart is not like yours, young good, warm, sincere, and impatient to bestow itself. Mine is worn with the baseness, treachery and mercenariness I have met with. It is suspicious, doubtful and cooled.

A few months later he was to attempt to quieten Madame's protestations by telling her '*Je suis refroidi*'. Now he picked up an old theme,

I laugh that I may not weep. I converse with Mesdames de Mirepoix, Boufflers and Luxembourg that I may not love Madame du Deffand too much – and yet they do but make me love her the more. But don't love me, pray don't love me.

Then he was off in the kind of self-indulgent posturing which explains why Lord Byron was to rate Horace Walpole among the 'greats': 'I think one had better be dead than love anybody,' he sneered, and ended 'if you would converse with me through the grate at Strawberry Hill, I desire no better, but not a word of friendship.' If a man had addressed a woman in such terms it could reasonably be interpreted as a covert invitation to conduct an affair after a few provocative and ritual insults.

That was not the last of Mr Craufurd. Nothing can be taken at face value where Horace is concerned. Next year, after who knows what stratagems and contrivances, Horace and Craufurd were together again and Madame, who must have been worldly wise about middle-aged English bachelors from her friendship with George Selwyn, was gloating over the reunion like a manipulative old witch:

I'm very glad that you're good friends again. I have never found that an age difference is any obstacle. The spirit never grows old . . . As I believe M. Craufurd is exempt from the passions I think he'll suit you admirably. Go on! Love each other. St John the Evangelist is my favourite saint. He is always writing, 'Love each other my children', and I say the same to you. To you *'dont je serais la mère,'* and to him, *'dont je serais la grand-mère'*. My age never worries me.

As April came round, Horace's favourite season at Strawberry Hill, he noted 'my lilacs pull hard' and made his farewells. He left Paris on 17th and was in London on 22nd. On 30 April Madame was already replying to his first letter with an artless enthusiasm which must have been quite new to Horace:

I can say, without a word of exaggeration, that if everyone shared my opinion of you, you would be the first man, not just in England, but in the universe. That's not flattery! It is your spirit; only in you are such talents and such extreme goodness united.

It was the start of a mental bombardment of literary lust and adulation that would result, next Christmas, in Horace's last great original, *The Mysterious Mother*. But for a time it may have been a relief to catch up with Henry Conway's political fortunes, to enjoy the lilacs and give grand French passions a rest.

CHAPTER ELEVEN

Horace as the constant lover

With a volley of urgent love letters, sometimes two a week, following after him, Horace came back to the sobering realities of London and problems. For two years he had protested to all and sundry that he was tired of politics and determined to quit the whole dirty game, but now, when he should have been relaxing under his lilacs at Strawberry, he found that the Rockingham administration was looking very frail. Towards Rockingham himself he was indifferent, but the political causes for which Horace had suffered public humiliation in the recent past were in peril and therefore his cousin Henry Conway was, as usual, in need of support.

Perhaps that rude and unsympathetic letter which Horace had written to Conway in November had done something to stiffen his political will. Certainly Rockingham's oddly assorted team of reformers and time-servers had recently proved both idealistic and effective. In February they had repealed the Stamp Act and given Britain a breathing space with the colonists of New England; and now, in April, Parliament had declared general warrants to be illegal. These should have been triumphs for Conway and have reflected some credit on Horace, for all his absenteeism.

But there were difficulties. The colonists had sensed their strength; so too had the mobs which had rioted in London for Wilkes and liberty. There was also still a strong feeling in Parliament that the colonies should pay something towards the cost of the British troops stationed over there. What Parliament had not appreciated was that the colonies no longer needed British troops now that the French had been evicted. Naïvely, the British supposed that if the colonists would not pay the direct taxes imposed by the Stamp Act then perhaps indirect taxes could be devised to fall on their imported luxuries, tea from India being the most obvious item. Meanwhile the King, no wiser but much more experienced, was only waiting for a chance to bring in a Prime Minister who would be his creature. The Marquis of Rockingham was living on borrowed time.

Appreciating the situation, Horace sat down and wrote in two days his most effective political satire, *An Account of the Giants lately discovered.* For someone who never dreamed of crossing the Atlantic, Horace was impressively perceptive, not only about the rights of the colonists, but about the future potential of their state. The 'imperial presidencies' of the twentieth century would not have surprised him; he foresaw 'twenty empires and republics forming upon vast scales all over the continent'. He possessed that outsider's ability to stand back critically from any subject, except the sinecures from which he drew his own income, and speculate on its validity with an open, ranging mind. Science fiction would have come naturally to him. Back in 1748 he had written to Conway prophesying that 'it will be as common to remove oaks 150 years old as it is now to transplant tulip roots.' Futurity would enjoy 'pocket spying glasses to see all that is doing in China, with a thousand other toys, which we now look upon as impracticable'. Only his 'tame tigers taught to fetch and carry' still elude us.

So it was as an outsider supporting what was basically a ministry of outsiders that Horace wrote, in June 1766, his *Account of the Giants.* Its approach was Swiftian. An inventive narrative of the discovery of a strange new tribe, a race of Patagonian Giants mounted on horseback, was followed by an outrageous proposal expanded as if it were obvious common sense. The giants must be enslaved and made subject to the parliament of Great Britain. 'The invaluable liberties of Englishmen are not to be wantonly scattered over the globe ... If giants once get an idea of freedom they will soon be our masters instead of our slaves.' This was prescient indeed. 'What have we to do with America,' Horace asked, 'but to conquer, enslave and make it tend to the advantage of our commerce? Shall the noblest rivers in the world roll for savages? Shall mines teem with gold for the natives of the soil? And shall the world produce anything but for England, France and Spain?' It was all good rumbustious rhetoric and on the strength of his *Giants* alone Horace has merited at least one life-size statue somewhere in the United States, perhaps outside the Library at Farmington. But admiration has to be tempered by recognition of his impertinence in adapting Rousseau's concept of the noble savage only a few months after ridiculing Rousseau in that pretended *Letter from the King of Prussia.*

Again and again his *Account of the Giants* loses its precise focus upon the colonists of New England and becomes confused with Horace's long-standing loathing of the slave trade. That was a subject on which, in 1755, he had lectured Bentley at some length. Now, with his giants, he returned to 'that wise maxim of our planters, that if a slave lives four years he has earned his purchase money, consequently you may afford to work him to death in that time.' This was good libertarian polemic but it was hardly relevant to Massachusetts. It would have been seen more as an attack on the southern states with their slave economies than as a defence of the rights of all the states.

Inevitably, the Irish question was raised as well, though in a flippant Horatian fashion. Speaking of the great utility that might be drawn from these enslaved giants, Horace suggested 'that a moderate importation of them might be tolerated for the sake of mending our breed'. But not, he hastened to add, 'for second husbands to dowagers. Ireland is already kept in a state of humiliation . . . we check their trade . . . matrimony is their only branch of commerce unrestricted, and it would be a most crying injustice to clog that too.' In Horace's letters to Mann the sexual attraction of Irish studs for middle-aged English widows is a recurring joke.

None of these sideways cuts obscures the power and honesty of Horace's attack upon the evils of colonialism and capitalist exploitation: 'Europe has no other title to America, except force and murder, which are rather the executive parts of government than a right.' At such points, Horace Walpole is not an old-style Whig; he is a Radical.

Written at the end of June, the *Giants* came too late to give Rockingham any useful support though it may have helped Conway. The King had already demonstrated his lack of confidence in Rockingham by promoting army officers without reference to him and in July 1766 the Marquis resigned. Conway stayed on to lead the Commons under Pitt, now Earl of Chatham and Prime Minister. *An Account of the Giants* was published on 25 August and Conway, who could have resigned as a gesture of support to his lost leader, considered it worth staying on to fight his cause. He survived for more than a year, finally resigning as Secretary of State in January 1768, when Lord North succeeded him on his last step before becoming the Prime Minister who would preside over the dissolution of the first British Empire.

Even before his *Giants* was on the streets, the devious and increasingly detached Horace had begun to write his *Memoirs of the Reign of George III*, for posthumous publication, like his *Memoirs of the Reign of George II*. His writing pace was leisurely, much interrupted by other projects, and it would not be until 1768 that he would come to deal with the events of 1765 and 1766 and write a deliberately wounding sketch of his best friend, Conway. But it seems from the critical tone of the early part of the *Memoirs* that he had Conway in his sights from the beginning.

These later *Memoirs*, quite apart from their importance as a controlling factor in the way historians of the nineteenth century interpreted the eighteenth century, are a revelation of Horace's Machiavellian past. He claimed that 'personal dislike to the Bedford faction' had been the prime cause of his opposition to Grenville's ministry in 1765. A few chapters earlier, however, we find him hurrying across London in his 'chariot' one Sunday evening because a mob of Spitalfields silk-weavers had injured the Duke of Bedford with a paving stone and laid siege to Bedford House. Fearlessly, Horace ploughed through the crowd, braving a hail of dirt and stones, to park amongst the Horse Guards in the court of Bedford House. All this simply to express aristocratic sympathy and solidarity with a duke whom he apparently detested. A little further back, Horace's letters have radiant accounts of happy parties at Strawberry Hill with the Duke and his family.

It comes then as no great surprise to learn that according to the *Memoirs* the letters which Horace had written at the time had been a smokescreen. Conway had cruelly disappointed Horace in June–July 1765 by not offering him a position in the Cabinet which he could then have rejected, or by confirming him in the sinecures on which he depended for financial security. In those weeks of political free-for-all, Horace claimed that 'disinterestedness was my ruling passion,' yet he fully expected that Conway would remember the hint he had dropped earlier: that the sinecures should in future be made cast-iron proof against any interference by maliciously-minded ministers. 'It was not,' he noted arrogantly, 'in my nature to repeat such a hint ... a haughtiness I maintained throughout my life'. The hint was not remembered so Horace received nothing in the usual share-out of benefits upon a change of government. Conway did, however, see to it that his own future income was made quite secure. In retrospect, Horace decided that he had been hard done by. 'Such a failure of friendship,' he complained, 'or to call it by its true name, such insensibility, could not but shock a heart at once so tender and proud as mine'. To which a fair response would have been that tender and proud hearts had no business getting involved in eighteenth-century politics. If you wanted a favour you asked for it at the right time, but at the 'right time' in 1765 Horace had been high on drugs administered by his apothecary. He decided that Conway's 'heart was so cold that it wanted all the beams of popular applause to kindle it into action', and unfortunately there would have been no popular applause for any favours given to Horace.

The two friends had in reality been trapped in a subtle moral dilemma. Horace was sensitive enough to see that Conway had acted with truly Roman probity: 'His temper hurt me, but I forgave his virtue, of which I am confident, and know it was superior to my own.' It was Horace who had this time the expectations not of a reforming Radical, but of an old-style unregenerate Whig, his father's true son. To his great credit he was able to be frank about his venality when writing to posterity if not to his contemporaries. There is all the sadness of a disillusioned old man in his summary of the changed friendship:

> We have continued to this day on an easy and confidential footing; but conscious that I would not again devote myself for him, I have taken strict care never to give him decisive advice when it might lead him to a precipice.

Yet there is abundant evidence in the *Memoirs* that even after his return from France in April 1766 Horace saw himself as the mastermind of British politics and pushed Conway towards at least one precipice. 'The night I arrived,' he reported wearily, 'the Duke of Richmond came to me to entreat Mr Conway to go on without Mr Pitt.' Horace agreed and Conway, though 'very ill and sick of the fatigue', remained in office. A short time later, the Duke of Grafton having resigned, 'I resolved to try to make the Duke of Richmond Secretary of State.' Horace had become friendly with Richmond in Paris where he had succeeded Hertford as ambassador. Now, with superb condescension, Horace noted that Richmond was 'apt to be indolent if not employed: the Secretary of State's Seals might inspire him with more taste for business.' He dropped a word to Rockingham who, always according to Horace, eagerly agreed. Together, Rockingham and Horace overcame Conway's scruples at appointing Richmond, who was his stepdaughter's husband, as the other Secretary. Despite the King's intense disapproval, the appointment was made.

Three months later Rockingham was sacked. Horace reported airily 'in truth I believe the Seals which I had obtained for his Grace [Richmond] were a mighty ingredient towards the fall of that Administration.'

Was all this fantasy or was Horace really the king-maker his *Memoirs* make him out to have been? If he had the political skills to raise Conway and Richmond to secretaryships of state and Hertford to the viceregency, could he, if he had been treated as an honoured partner, have projected cold, honest, handsome Henry that one stage further to be Prime Minister? In a Britain run by a tight group of friends and foes, it may have been a possibility and all the retrospective resentment which the *Memoirs* pour over Conway could be regret at a great opportunity lost. On the other hand, the *Memoirs* may be well-informed invention designed to make Horace appear a far more influential figure than he actually was. In the event, Henry Conway failed to make any warm, venal gesture. Thereafter Horace Walpole was in permanent political retreat.

While one male relationship was growing less intense, one female relationship remained, one-sidedly at least, most ardent. Rousseau had said of Madame du Deffand that he preferred her hatred to her friendship, and in this first year after leaving Paris Horace was so splendidly distressed by the pressures which the Deffand correspondence laid upon him that he wrote the first three acts of a tragedy in which an oversexed and frantic French countess commits incest, under cover of darkness, with her noble, and of course guiltess, son.

Freudian interpretations of literature are not fashionable, but a subtle Viennese psychiatrist is not needed to point out the obvious connections between Madame du Deffand and Horace and the Countess of Narbonne and her son Edmund in *The Mysterious Mother*. If the play had been, like so many contemporary tragedies that reached the English stage, inept rubbish, it could be dismissed here with a brief mention. Not only was its inspiration and its writing closely bound up with Horace's emotional life in the years between 1766 and 1780, but the play itself is tantalizingly near to being a masterpiece, though flawed in its last two acts and ultimately only performable as a curiosity.

It was begun on Christmas Day 1766, and the first three of its five acts were written quickly. To understand why its author felt compelled to such a theme it is only necessary to study the Deffand correspondence of the preceding months. The letters are all in French as Madame spoke very little English, and one has a sense of being in the same room as the woman, subject to a passionate and unstoppable flow of sensitive perceptions, pitiful vulnerability, embarrassing honesty and endless demands for response. They are not so much letters as aggressive journals of the heart. As she herself advised, opening a ten-page outpouring on 4 September, 'Read this letter in separate stages, there is enough here for eight days' reading'; and Horace the reader was always, in between the paragraphs of witty gossip and cultural chat, subject to pressure, to warnings and to emotional demands. Even now, two centuries later, the emotional blows come thudding home:

> I have decided not to write to you any more. It is not that you are bad for me, quite the reverse, but I am afraid that in your present state of health it would be debilitating for you even to receive a letter from me.

> Ah! Do not wear yourself out anymore with attacks on friendship. Why are you forever reminding me of all those things which you have said and written to put me off liking you?

> You claim that I am hard to please. You could not say anything more hurtful. It is like telling me that I bore you, that I pester you and that as a result our correspondence has become a burden.

> No! No! Don't give me up, if I've done wrong you must forgive me, and in any case if I meant no harm then I can have done none.

> The Sultan's Queen Mother comes to receive the orders of her lord and master. She implores his highness to moderate the blows or at least to soften them in silk wrappings. His slave meanwhile will try to moderate her writing style.

> Ah! What a mistake to have friends abroad and be dependent on the whims of wind and water.

> *Mon tuteur!* They have poisoned you! I am sure of it! Those hot potions which you've taken, that wine which they prescribed for you against common sense, it is all calculated to kill you off.

Always in the correspondence there is an insistence on replies, on some return:

> But I must keep getting news from you, not just once a week, but twice by every post and when any other opportunity offers. Even if it is just four lines, in French or English, it makes no difference but I must get news of you regularly. That is one response which you cannot refuse because it is absolutely essential to me.

Sometimes, when Madame herself was worn out, knowing

Horace's susceptibilities, she would get her secretary Wiart to put in a request for her: 'Please send us,' Wiart would write in prim officialese, 'twice a week a bulletin on the state of your health.' On very rare occasions Madame would pen only a brief note: 'You are very lucky. Today I am not in the mood for gossip. *Adieu mon tuteur, je crois que je vous aime toujours.*'

In page after page, 'paper has to put up with everything; it puts up with just being plain white paper, it puts up with insults, with outrage' – her letters read like some terrible punishment on Horace for the emotional pressures which he had laid, all those years ago, on Lord Lincoln. The roles were reversed and yet he must to some degree have enjoyed it, as Lincoln had enjoyed it. What if his lover was not only of the wrong sex but seventy years old to his forty-nine? To have a Marquise, mildly infamous and mildly celebrated, hopelessly in love with him, was flattering when any idea of lusting after other men had become ridiculous and dangerous. Madame made herself at least half acceptable by presenting herself as a mother. But that second proposition stirred Horace's innermost neuroticisms. Most of his replies have been destroyed to conceal his inadequate French or his unseemly emotions, but it appears that their usual appeal was less for emotion and more for Parisian gossip.

As the years went by and he fell into a pleasant routine of two-yearly visits, the incest threat would fade and Horace would learn to cope with an old French lady's excessive fondness. To be loved for the sound of your voice builds the self-esteem whether or not you fully return that love, and there was never the slightest sugges-tion that he ever bedded her. As late as 1769 when he was describ-ing his visits to Montagu there is something very close to love, or at least to loving admiration in his own words. She is 'my dear old friend . . . she makes songs, sings them, remembers all that ever were made . . . affectionate as Madame de Sévigné she has none of her prejudices, but a more universal taste; and with the most deli-cate frame, her spirits hurry her through a life of fatigue that would kill me.' Obviously Horace had no notion where, if anywhere, it was all leading – 'what is next year but a bubble that may burst for her or me?' – and he seemed still dreamily bemused by what he had let himself in for.

To form plans and projects in such a precarious life as this, resembles the enchanted castles of fairy legends, in which every gate is guarded by giants, dragons etc. I sit contented with the beggars at the threshold, and never propose going in, but as the gates open of themselves.

That he had become, in late middle-age, a social figure in the capital city of the arch-enemy was a stroke of luck he was happy to accept. The gates had opened. But he still described Madame as 'the best and sincerest of friends, who loves me as much as my mother did!' so there remained that note of the forbidden relationship. His mother may have been thirty years in the grave, but she had been the dominant emotional influence of his childhood. Madame du Deffand had revived that mother-love, but she saw him more as a lover than a son. Horace resented that and wrote *The Mysterious Mother* to exorcise the threat.

The play is a brilliant fusion of Racine and Shakespeare, with the classical unities and declamations of the one expressed in a convincing pastiche of the other's blank verse. It opens with darkness, fear and superstition, like a cross between Hamlet and Macbeth, in the setting – a castle by a large monastic church – of *Otranto*. Florian, a soldier friend of the exiled Count Edmund, confronts the aged porter at the gate of Edmund's mother's castle to try to unravel the mystery of the Countess's long years of penance. In these first acts Horace was writing in good Shakespearean form as the porter jeers at Florian:

> Thou know'st my lady then? – Thou know'st her not.
> Can'st thou in hair cloths vex those dainty limbs?
> Can'st thou on reeking pavements and cold marble,
> In meditation pass the livelong night?
> Can'st mortify the flesh my rosy minion?

It is soon established that women are a bad influence:

> I never knew a woman
> But loved our bodies or our souls too well
> They tease us to be damned or to be saved

but that the Roman Catholic church, personified by two wicked friars, is an even worse influence. Horace was riding his two pet hates at the same time as he was conducting a non-sexual love affair with an old lady who lived in an apartment within a Roman Catholic convent. Nevertheless:

> The church is but a specious name for empire
> And will exist whenever fools have fears.
> Rome is no city; 'tis the human heart.

If the refined and well-travelled Horace could write with such venom, it becomes easy to understand the zest with which the underclasses of London would soon be throwing themselves into the anti-Catholic orgy of the Gordon Riots.

With the scene set, the play piles up an effective tension of half-suppressed truths and ugly insinuations as Adeliza is introduced. She is a pure young girl, convent-educated, but actually the result of a night of dreadful passion between the Countess and her son Edmund, who thought at the time that he was having intercourse with a local girlfriend and who still remains ignorant of the truth. Adeliza is already both his sister and his daughter. Soon, if the wicked friars Benedict and Martin have their way, she will also be his wife. Horace did nothing by halves, but it is intriguing to speculate what kind of future this well-crafted sensationalism might have had on the stage in Protestant England. He did tell Montagu in 1768, immediately after the last two acts had been written, 'I wish to see it acted', but never repeated that wish.

When the monstrous Countess of Narbonne appears, she is devoted to penance, good works and long soliloquies, a subliminal reminiscence perhaps of Madame du Deffand's recent correspondence. Confusingly, Horace begins to associate her with the Protestant faith, which blurs her image of vice and wicked passions. This may explain why he paused for a year in the writing between the third and fourth acts and why he never succeeded in convincing the reader of her motivation. But already the play had fine dramatic touches that would have worked well on the stage. In one scene a choir of young children enters singing, to counterpoint the villainy of Friar Benedict, and in another a crisis is interrupted

by the apparently ghostly cry of 'Forebear!' offstage which resolves
into another choir, this time of holy friars singing,

> Forebear! forebear! forebear!
> The pious are heaven's care
> Lamentations ill become us,
> When the good are ravished from us.

Then both the poetry and the plausibility of *The Mysterious
Mother* go into decline. Horace admitted that the last two acts were
'not now as much finished as I intended'. After his return to Paris,
in the summer of 1767, he would have taken the measure of
Madame's affections, found them to be at an acceptable moral
level, and no longer felt the literary drive to express her as the
Countess of Narbonne. In the play, the Countess's unforgivable sin
is explained as a temporary aberration, sexual frustration following
the death of her husband as he was returning after a long absence.
Horace realized that this was a central weakness in the plot, but
claimed 'it makes her less hateful than if she had coolly meditated
so foul a crime. I have endeavoured to make her very fondness for
her husband in some measure the cause of her guilt.' It only shows,
in fact, that a dramatist should not attempt to put on stage emotions which he has neither experienced nor observed.

Madame du Deffand drew Horace Walpole into novel experiences and uncharted emotional territory very late in his life, but it
was a mutually advantageous affair. For an ageing, self-centred
homosexual to win the intense affections of an intelligent French
woman with an apartment in the heart of Paris, a good cook and a
wide circle of fashionable acquaintance in the most sophisticated
society in Europe, was luck. For a blind old lady to meet a sensitive, witty man, twenty years her junior, infinitely entertaining and
conversant with the inner workings of the British establishment,
was equal luck. For Horace, the only difficulty, which was in itself
a mental widening, was the matter of adaptation to the formalities
of an intense relationship with a foreigner of the opposite sex.
While in no sense of the word bisexual, he was, nevertheless, able
to make that adaptation; *The Mysterious Mother* is psychic litter left
by the wayside: almost a great drama written to purge his own

unease at the imbalance he sensed in their relationship.

He had fifty copies of the play printed in 1768 on his private press for distribution to friends. Chute liked it, Gray approved it. Montagu introduced 'the boys', a group of young squires, to the play and it was a roaring success: 'They would have got it by heart.' Montagu read the part of the Countess, which in itself must have been an experience. The vicar in the party 'looked grave but they threw him his Ten Commandments and a bottle of port and amused themselves without'. At that point Horace began to backtrack. 'I am sorry those boys got at my tragedy,' he wrote. 'I beg you would keep it under lock and key; it is not at all food for the public – at least not till I am food for worms.' 1768 was the year when he resigned his seat in Parliament and appears to have been looking forward to a quiet life and a blameless reputation just when he could have been projecting himself as a dangerously innovative playwright.

What he had written was a high Romantic drama, a *'Sturm und Drang'* masterpiece before *'Sturm und Drang'* had got under way in Germany. He sensed that he had made a breakthrough, but sensed also that it was a breakthrough before its time and in the wrong country. Dodsley printed more copies in 1781 for further private distribution. The play was much discussed, usually in terms of shock and horror, and when a pirated Dublin edition was being produced in 1791, Horace carefully corrected it and thanked the publishers for the compliment. But in a lifetime of successful public relations *The Mysterious Mother* has to be written off as a book too far. Horace funked the publicity and never really reaped the possible fame.

His state of mind at the time of writing is a study in itself. Between the third and fourth acts he broke away from incest for a year to attempt to whitewash murder. This was one of his most ingenious journalistic strokes, perfectly calculated to catch the attention and enrage every dry-as-dust antiquary in Britain. In his *Historic Doubts on the Life and Death of King Richard the Third*, begun in late January 1767 and published in February 1768, Horace set off a controversy which has rattled on well into the twentieth century. The idea of the book is far superior to its treatment. Horace began by listing the chain of supposed murders by which Richard, Duke of Gloucester made his way to the throne. The man was already a legend, a royal serial killer, as a result of Shakespeare's treatment. He was said to have murdered Edward, Prince of Wales; King Henry VI; his own brother, the Duke of Clarence; lords Rivers, Gray, Vaughan and Hastings; his two nephews, King Edward V and the Duke of York; and finally his own Queen, after which he was proposing to marry his niece, before death intervened on the field of Bosworth.

What is significant in all this is that Horace chose this appalling catalogue of crimes to give himself a rest from writing an account of how a young man was duped into marriage with his own sister –daughter. Again it is the stuff of *'Sturm und Drang'*, emotional sensationalism, antiquarian studies crossed with the revelations of the tabloid press. The Romantic movement was stirring behind both the play and *Historic Doubts* and it was Horace who was doing the stirring, as Lord Byron was later to acknowledge when he described him as 'the father of the first romance, and of the last tragedy in our language, and surely worthy of a higher plane than any living writer be he who he may'. Coleridge, on the other hand, described *The Mysterious Mother* as 'the most disgusting, detestable, vile composition that ever came from the hand of man ... No one with a spark of true manliness, of which Horace Walpole had none, could have written it.' Interestingly, Coleridge had already picked up, in the 1830s, an awareness of Horace's sexual apartness and was using it against him.

Horace, the chameleon writer, always took on the style appropriate to his material: his letters entertain, his play is in pastiche Shakespearean blank verse, the *Memoirs* read like lucid plausible history, and the *Historic Doubts* is a convincingly dry imitation of antiquarian research, overloaded with pseudo authorities and marred by special pleading on every important issue, as for instance:

> he acted as most princes would have done in this situation in a bar-barous and lawless age yet we must not judge of those times by the present.

Nor ought the subsequent executions to be considered in so very strong a light as they would appear in if acted in modern times.

To judge impartially therefore, we ought to recall the temper and times we read of. It is shocking to eat our enemies; but it is not so shocking in an Iroquoi as it would be in the King of Prussia.

After one entirely arbitrary execution, Horace remarked airily that 'trials had never been used with any degree of strictness, as at present'. An intelligent reader is left with the impression that perhaps there had been up to ten unusual deaths, but there had been in every case many other potential murderers around in addition to Richard of Gloucester, and if he had indeed been behind some of the deaths, they were 'more the crimes of the age than of the man'. As usual, Horace threw in a provocative disclaimer as to any serious purpose. He was only a gentleman dabbling in a genre: 'If any man as idle as myself, should take the trouble to review and canvas my arguments, I am ready to yield so indifferent a point to better reasons.' This was like a red rag to a bull for half the Society of Antiquaries in 1772. Letters came in, replies were published and Horace's 'discovery' of a supposed Coronation roll of King Richard proving that his nephew King Edward V walked in the procession in fine garments was rightly rubbished. Horace became involved in counter- and counter-counter-replies that echoed the Guthrie papers of 1765, all the more spitefully as Guthrie himself became involved. Horace was urged to consult Guthrie's *History of England*. He replied tartly that he 'consulted the living works of dead authors, not the dead works of living authors'.

What can be said for claim and counter claim is that critical scholarship was coming to life in historical studies, and that Horace was the author who had brought some life to very dry bones. The danger lay in the notoriety he achieved among a more than usually malicious group of scholars. He himself behaved intemperately, resigning from the Society of Antiquaries when that learned body set up an enquiry into the authenticity of Dick Whittington's cat. The whole dispute, ingenious and eye-catching as it proved to be, was something of an expense of spirit and, intellectually, the eighteenth-century equivalent of how many angels can pirouette on a needle point.

The danger was soon demonstrated. Late in March 1769, when Horace, unusually, was not at work on a book, a brief letter and lengthy enclosure from a Thomas Chatterton was passed on to him from a bookseller in the Strand. The enclosure claimed to be a copy of 'The Ryse of Peyncteynge yn Englade, wroten bie T. Rowlei. 1469 for Mastre Canynge'. It was a substantial piece of prose followed by twelve lines of poetry, this last supposedly written in the late twelfth century by an abbot of a Bristol monastery in praise of King Richard Coeur de Lion. It was, of course, a fake composed by a seventeen-year-old scrivener's clerk in collusion with a Bristol surgeon and antiquary, William Barrett. The clerk was Thomas Chatterton, a poet immortalized by his life and death more than by his poetry. He was to become the archetype of the Romantic tragic genius, unappreciated while alive, valued only after his suicide in August 1770. Chatterton, rather than Guthrie, was to become Horace's worst piece of bad luck.

When this 'Ryse of Peyncteynge' was discussed later, the experts said that Horace had been rather foolish to be taken in by it. These wiseacres were forgetting its conjunction with the letter. The two together were a clever combination. The letter was simple, humble and naïve.

> Being versed a little in antiquitys, I have met with several Curious Manuscripts among which the following may be of Service to you in any future Edition of your truly entertaining Anecdotes of Painting – In correcting the mistakes (if any) in the Notes – you will greatly oblige
> Your most humble Servant Thomas Chatterton
> Bristol March 25th Corn Street.

In sharp contrast, the enclosed passage lay like some rich treasure, like perhaps a sketch by Francesco Salviati that an expert spies, or thinks he spies, lying amidst the junk on some stall in the Portobello Road and snatches up from the stallholder without querying the price. Unlike the letter, it was long, richly obscure in its vocabulary, but helpfully annotated. It contained a dramatic anecdote perfect for inclusion in the next edition of Horace's *Anecdotes of Painting* and, most tempting prize of all, appeared to confirm, on fifteenth-century monkish authority, Horace's theory in the *Anecdotes* that oil paints were invented by the English before the Flemings. It had to be genuine; vanity demanded it.

No one as dim and self-deprecatory as the letter-writer could possibly have composed the 'Ryse of Peyncteynge'. Ever the confident gentleman amateur, Horace read them once and rushed off an eager reply of thanks to ask for more of T. Rowlei. He even failed to notice that the poem was not supposed to be by fifteenth-century Rowlei, which would have been just plausible, but by a twelfth-century abbot, which was totally implausible as the Middle English in which it was written had not at that time emerged as a language. Haste and greed for an antiquary's bargain made Horace briefly a gull. As soon as he received Chatterton's second letter with more 'Historie of Peyncters', he realized that a joke was being played on him by some fellow antiquaries in Bristol. The letter he then wrote to Chatterton has not survived but was apparently condescending enough to infuriate Chatterton, who was a moody, disagreeable genius unlikely to appreciate a joke turned back upon him. The copied lines 'wroten bie T. Rowlei' were returned. Horace had no further contact with Chatterton, who came to London to make his fortune and committed suicide very painfully in a fit of depression. His legend grew, his works were published and the antiquaries settled down to one of their futile controversies as to whether there had really been a monk called Rowlei or whether the entire invention had been Chatterton's. The literary world indulged itself in a pang of guilt at having ignored a national treasure.

But then in May 1777 an eccentric Bristol antiquary, George Catcott, who could quite possibly have been one of those who put Chatterton up to sending that first letter to Horace, published a malicious, lying article in the *Monthly Review*. This stated that Chatterton had contacted Horace in London, asked for his help, and been spurned; the implication being that Horace Walpole, more than any other man, was responsible for the death of a great poet.

This disgraceful accusation was widely believed and was the foundation for the bad reputation which had gathered around

Horace's name by the beginning of the next century. Probably the process of vilification was cumulative. First came Guthrie's accusations of unnatural love, then Horace deliberately trailed his coat at fellow antiquaries with a provocative theory shoddily supported. Having set himself up as a villain of scholarship inclined to scorn and scoff, he was wide open to Catcott's lies. In 1779 and 1782 Horace printed, first privately then publicly, his defence, protesting with justice that he was 'perhaps the first instance of a person consigned to judgement for not having been made a fool of'; but truth rarely catches up with lies. He had also played his own part, in a decade much given to literary hoaxes, by publishing *Otranto* in its first edition as the work of a sixteenth-century Italian, Onuphrio Muralto.

What was most regrettable about this Chatterton controversy was that it tended to obscure the very real scholarly advance made by Horace's *Anecdotes of Painting*. A second edition of the first three volumes had come out in 1765. These were almost entirely the work of George Vertue, and Horace, who had ordered Vertue's chaotic research notes, gave Vertue full and generous credit. To enliven the volumes he added his own observations and gleanings, including that fateful speculation on the English origins of oil painting which had left him open to Chatterton's bait. If Horace had not bought Vertue's notebooks from his widow and painstakingly ordered them, the foundations of future English art history would have been lost. For the reign of Charles I alone, the *Anecdotes* cover sixty-five artists and craftsmen; the range is encyclopaedic and Horace's throw-away criticisms – Hilliard: 'void of any variety of tints'; the Wilton Van Dyck of the Pembroke family: 'I cannot but observe how short he falls of his model Titian' – are refreshingly controversial even now, when it has become heresy to lavish anything but praise on Elizabethan miniatures or that loosely composed and ill-related group in the Double Cube Room at Wilton. At least Horace cannot be accused of an insular narrowness of judgement.

Unfortunately the same cannot be said of the fourth volume of the *Anecdotes*, written in 1770–1 and published in 1780. This covered his own times and owed little to George Vertue. William Kent's Gothic work, which had been Strawberry's inspiration, was given mean and ungenerous treatment as the author fell into the trap of scholarly authenticity. Was Strawberry the cradle of the Gothic Revival or the deathbed of Gothick? Then Horace over-praised the English Palladian revival as having 'established the throne of architecture in Britain', an illogical comment from some-one who avoided the style in his own building activities.

With many years still ahead of him, the creative and significant part of Horace Walpole's life was almost at an end. There were still personal family excitements: his widowed niece and ultimate heiress, Lady Waldegrave, one of his brother Edward's illegitimate brood, proved the flexibility of the social system by secretly marry-ing the King's brother, the Duke of Gloucester, in 1766, openly declaring the marriage in 1771. Horace, the supposed republican, was gratified and grovelled tactfully to his royal relative. His nephew, the 3rd Earl of Orford, went mad in 1773, leaving Horace to attempt to rescue the estate. Returns of lunacy resulted in the sale of Sir Robert's picture collection in 1779 to the Tsarina, a doubtful bargain at £45,000.

More woundingly, in 1770, George Montagu had, without warning, dropped Horace socially for ever, apparently at a nod from his patron, Lord North, who disapproved of Horace's intelli-gent regard for the New England colonists. Montagu had brought out the best in his friend as a letter-writer because they were both males with a shared Etonian schoolhood and both felt sensitively for the past. But with a more supportive family circle he had never needed Horace's friendship as much as Horace had needed his. The Countess of Upper Ossory, who took over Montagu's role, was a poor substitute. She had first attracted Horace socially because she was the Duchess of Grafton; but then, after her divorce, remarriage and lonely exile in Bedfordshire, he felt sorry for her. She, for her part, valued his letters for their news of the London society which she had lost, but she had nothing to offer Horace in return.

Friends were dying off: Lady Suffolk in 1767, Lady Hervey in

1768, and then in 1771 Thomas Gray. This last should have been a disturbing reminder of mortality, but to Horace it was at first an excitement, as if a door had been opened into a locked room where he could now go in and rummage, eager to find new poems to publish and a reputation to build even higher. When no new work of any significance was found, he took over his dead friend's image instead, like a personal possession, ensuring that when William Mason wrote Gray's biography Horace was the final authority and the account of the quarrel at Reggio was glossed over. When Madame du Deffand was dying she spared her uneasy lover the emotional strain of her deathbed. In her very last letter she wrote, 'amuse yourself as best you are able my friend and don't get upset about my condition. We have come to the end of our relationship and will never see each other again; but because it is always some comfort to know that one is loved you will regret my passing.' Horace's immediate concern, as with Gray, was to get hold of her papers.

In 1772 he began his last burst of building and added the Great North Bedchamber to Strawberry, not so much as a place in which to sleep as an additional area for the display of his growing collection. Sited over the kitchen and servants' hall and refrigerated, like the Holbein Chamber, by three outside walls, it was never a functional room in the normal sense, but it completed the sequence of show rooms. While his writings, apart from the letters, fell away, his pleasure in Strawberry and his pride in what he had gathered there were constants. The Great North Bedchamber was not quite his last addition to the fabric. In 1776 the Beauclerc Tower would improve the silhouette of the Round Tower. But in 1774 Horace must have considered his castle complete enough and, to ensure that its visitors should miss nothing of their formative experience, he published the first edition of *A Description of the Villa of Mr Horace Walpole*, in itself both a summary and a full stop.

CHAPTER TWELVE

The house, the garden, the man

Anyone who takes the trouble, on a winter morning when the leaves are off the trees, to walk along Waldegrave Road in Twickenham, will find that the north or entrance front of Strawberry Hill is virtually unchanged in its appearance from views commissioned in Horace's lifetime. It is rarely photographed. The south front with the original villa and Gallery, which has been altered far more, losing most of its original three-dimensional quality and being overshadowed by nineteenth-century additions on a different scale, gets all the attention. Looking at the north front, it is easy to see why. The place is a charming shambles, alive with interesting features and afterthoughts but, for all that, in design terms, a disaster. Who else but Horace would have created or evolved (the appropriate verb is hard to select) an entrance front which is really the back-kitchen and dustbin front and where the main door is tucked away down a narrow passage flanked by blind windows? To build such a design disaster on a limited income required will-power and a talent for improvisation; but then to bring dukes and ambassadors hurrying along to inspect it and finally one morning to turn away the Queen because the owner was still in bed, was a real achievement. Though it has to be added that Horace's dourly republican Swiss servants were not aware, when they turned a couple of unheralded visitors away one morning, that they were German relatives of the young Queen Charlotte who was waiting around the corner in her coach.

One chapter away from the end of this book, the time has come to be ruthlessly honest about Strawberry Hill and respectfully honest about Horace. Neither the house nor its creator have anything to fear from direct criticism; both were prodigies of innovation but both raise questions of taste, and taste is highly subjective, not a matter for final judgements. Neither Horace nor his house are to everybody's liking. The important thing is that they were, and to a limited extent still are, influential.

What is seen on the entrance side of Strawberry is really two houses, though a casual passer-by could be forgiven for thinking it the domestic backside to a terrace of four. First comes the windowless rectangular outline of a low tower; then, up a passage between blank walls, is the main door under a crow-stepped gable and the only convincingly Gothic window of the whole hit-or-miss elevation. The projecting bay of the Holbein Chamber is followed by a shapeless recession leading to the servants' hall, over which the Great North Bedchamber is perched as an obvious afterthought. Then comes the most eccentric feature in a succession of structural improvisations: a bulbous projecting extrusion with side apses swings out upon little support. This is the Tribune, Strawberry's mock-shrine. Recessed behind it rises the Round Tower, the only castle-like feature of the whole composition. This is coarsely detailed and out of scale with everything else because the Waldegraves added an extra storey to Horace's Round and Beauclerc towers in the nineteenth century. Nothing has been demolished on this north side and, apart from the false note of authority added to the Round Tower, nothing has been altered. Strawberry always was as episodic and its separate additions as unrelated as they now appear.

Horace prepared carefully and assiduously for posterity in his letters and in his two sets of *Memoirs*. He intended to control the way in which future generations interpreted his contemporaries. But was his construction of Strawberry carried out with the same eye to futurity? Did he suppose that the house could influence architects as his *Memoirs* could influence historians? Strawberry has certainly shaped building design as much as any of its great classical contemporaries. Horace, a natural journalist, had an interest in chaos, but did it extend to house building? Pinnacles were tumbling off the parapets in strong winds before the walls had been standing twenty years and he seems not to have expected the house to last much longer than his own lifetime. 'Poor Strawberry must sink in *Faece Romuli*', he wrote in 1778, 'that melancholy thought silences me.' By that time Strawberry had served its turn as a publicity gimmick, social and political, and had become for Horace only a summer home. He had moved from Arlington Street in 1778 to another plain classical house in Berkeley Square, next door to the Duchess of Beaufort. Meanwhile Strawberry had become a favourite venue for the many local dowagers, and it had already acquired a stylistic life of its own. The whole point of his going Gothic back in the early 1750s had been to be unique, to set a trend, to give the impression of having created a style even though he was only a follower. He certainly noticed during his later tours of England that a Gothic Revival was under way, but his competitive comments on other houses phased into a resigned awareness that, in a creation like Lee Priory in Kent, James Wyatt had outpointed Strawberry in both authenticity and profile. When he began to build, Horace was consciously setting a precedent for Gothic theatricality as opposed to 'correct' classical taste.

As was natural to a son of the builder of Houghton's Palladian sumptuosities, he was aware of conventional classicism, but he was bored by it. Strawberry, both inside and out, was deliberately nonconformist. Horace as a sexual, and in some ways a social, outsider, associated Houghton's symmetries with the tedium of his father's bucolic friends and relatives: with long hours of drink, heterosexual smut and post-mortems on the massacre of pheasants. The style of Strawberry was an intensely personal statement of apartness and he also intended it to seduce.

There were, before Horace presented society with this alternative style, definite functional and economic disadvantages to building in the classical manner. It had the prestige of Greece, Rome and the Renaissance behind it and its symmetry was in itself visually satisfying. But it offered wrap-around façades that failed to express the functions within – reception, sleeping, dining and purging.

Because it projected all-inclusive symmetry from the start of a building operation, it made piecemeal development and improvisation difficult. Strawberry escaped most of these limitations. It could be built in sections as funds became available and it gave outward form to many of its inner functions; there was the Tribune-chapel, a Gallery for receptions, a Library tower and a master bedroom. Only the cachet of Greece and Rome was missing, and Horace had thought his way through that deficiency in his 1759 'Book of Materials':

> If two Architects of equal genius and taste, or one man possessing both, and without the least degree of partiality, was ordered to build two buildings, one in the Grecian and one in the Gothic style, I think the Gothic would strike most at first, the Grecian would please the longest. But I believe this approbation would in some measure flow from the impossibility of not connecting with Grecian and Roman architecture the ideas of the Greeks and Romans. If one has any partiality to old knights, crusaders, the wars of York and Lancaster, then the prejudice in favour of the Grecian building will be balanced.

Horace had that 'partiality' and, with the rise of the Gothic novel, from his *Otranto* to Sir Walter Scott's *Waverley*, that 'partiality' became general. Not only had Horace raised, presented and advertised in Strawberry an acceptable icon of the Gothic close to London, but he had set in train a literary genre which would give the style associations as rich as classical legend, with the bonus of being ancestral in its connotations and patriotic. In Strawberry, assertive individualism thumbed its nose at conventional design and then – this was Horace's impudence – demanded to be admired. The building of this house, and its subsequent publicizing as an appropriate frame within which fashionable society could enjoy the usual pleasures of life, was the most destructive design event of the century. After Strawberry there were few stylistic limits. Eclecticism was in for the next hundred years.

How then, behind that irresolute entrance front, which faced visitors as they drove up in their carriages, did Strawberry work? It could hardly have been by those irregularities alone that a new generation of house builders was won over. An earlier chapter has considered the visual shock administered by Strawberry's first reception area, the narrow pinched entrance route and then the shadows and bright colours of stained glass playing upon attenuated Early English arches. But between 1756, when that first area of Strawberry was complete, and 1774, when Horace printed 100 copies of his *Description of the Villa of Mr Horace Walpole*, he had added an entire second house, twice as large as the first. This contained his expanding collections. It had no other purpose, apart from a rare grand reception, than to give visitors something to visit while preserving his own privacy in Strawberry Mark I. This new Strawberry Mark II, extending to the west of the original villa, anticipated exactly what the twentieth-century 'heritage' and 'stately home' industry has found paying visitors require: a picture gallery, a drawing-room, a special exhibit not always open for viewing, a chapel, a state bedroom, access to grounds with ornamental features and, above all, a celebrated resident who might, with luck, be encountered leaving the private sectors of the house.

Horace offered all this at Strawberry without charging for entrance. London's polite population was on his doorstep and the visitors flocked in. They came by pre-booked ticket in parties of no more than four in any one day, unless they were French, the favoured nation, in which case seventeen could, on occasion, be squeezed into smaller rooms like the Tribune. Children were not allowed and the season lasted from 1 May to 30 September. The index on the Yale *Correspondence* devotes nine pages to the names of the most notable visitors, but over the years there were at least 10,000, all of whom had to be reasonably well-off and therefore have the potential to build themselves. That was how Gothic was sold to the nation.

Strawberry on display sold something else equally insidious to standards of accepted taste. It sold the decoration of a room as an uninhibited ego-trip. Each room on show had an underlying decorative theme, but in every case this was overlaid by unmitigated Horace: his ancestors, his friends, his historical fads, his travels and his collections. Every wall was crowded with evidence of his personality, a glorious junk-shop of presents, knick-knacks, objects of virtue, valuable paintings and bizarre curios. There was no evidence of unifying taste or selectivity; the whole house set a persuasive precedent for the eclecticism that ran riot in the next century.

One theme underlying Horace's patronage of the arts and the decorative overlay of Strawberry was his partiality for lady artists, preferably ones with an unhappy marital record. It was as if, after his quarrels with Bentley and Müntz, Horace despaired of controlling men and found it easier to relate to creative women. Henry Conway's daughter Anne was a lesbian sculptress whose work Horace admired and purchased; Lady Diana Beauclerc, whose 'soot paintings' (a mixture of charcoal and watercolour) featured prominently in several rooms of Strawberry, had divorced her first husband, Lord Bolingbroke. Another of Horace's women friends was the notorious writer and impresario Lady Craven, whose liaisons had scandalized not only England but half Europe. So Horace was no moral prig. On the contrary, he preferred women with a shadow over their reputations; Lady Ossory and Kitty Clive might be included in this category.

As Strawberry Mark II represented Horace's mature decorative taste, it will be described before the private apartments where the collections were more acquisitive and sentimental than thematically deliberate. What the average visitor's tour of Strawberry Mark II covered after the shock of the Paraclete and the Armoury ('tread quietly, please, the master of the house is working in his library across the landing') was the Star Chamber, Holbein Room, Gallery, Tribune, Great North Bedchamber, Round Drawing-Room, then down the back stairs to the Great Cloister and so out to the grounds. The only feature missing from a modern stately home visit was tea and cakes and, with the kitchen in the ground floor of the Round Tower next to the Great Cloister, Horace's housekeeper, who conducted all these tours, would have lost an opportunity if she had not offered some refreshment.

Atmospherically, the Star Chamber was an extension to the Paraclete and the Armoury. Its window was entirely of painted glass, unlike those in the other rooms which had coloured glass only in their top lights; its theme was rough, archaic furniture. The

Holbein Room came next; as its name suggests, it presented the artist in the context of late-medieval, Tudor and Elizabethan paintings; Cardinal Wolsey's hat hung there near a chair made for one of the last Abbots of Glastonbury. A dark 'Trunk' passage with 'panelled Perpendicular' Gothic walls and ceiling led dramatically to the brilliant lighting and colour, crimson damask, gilt net-work over radiantly reflecting mirrors of the Gallery; an undeniable *coup d'oeil* to quell any latent criticism.

Here the heavyweight exhibits were gathered: two granite tables from the Farnese gardens, a Roman sepulchral altar and Horace's prize, the Boccapadugli eagle: 'one of the finest pieces of Greek sculpture in the world, the boldness and yet great finishing of this statue are incomparable, the eyes inimitable.' In all instances, it is helpful to accept Horace's evaluations and attributions without argument, though this by no means implies agreement. There were many busts and urns and, although the walls were not as ideal for the hanging of pictures as Richard Bentley had originally intended, a Giorgione and a Rubens hung beside a group of Carolean portraits.

The Tribune or Chapel introduced another clever change in lighting to a golden gloom within a domed, four-apsed square. This was Horace's shrine to his mother, a 'lady chapel' of sorts, built almost thirty years after her death. Her statue, copied in bronzed plaster from that over her memorial in Westminster Abbey, stood in one niche; in the other four Venus, Flora, Apollo and Antinous kept up a judicious balance of the sexes and sexual preferences. An altar, copied from that to Edward III's children, was set with candlesticks, sconces and ivory vases – a prototype for nineteenth-century Anglo-Catholics. Where Christianity was concerned, Horace was determined to have his cake but not to eat it. He admitted everything to his High Church friend William Cole:

> I like Popery as well as you, and I have shown I do. I like it as I do chivalry and romance. They all furnish one with ideas and visions, which Presbyterianism does not. A Gothic church or convent fill one with romantic dreams – but for the mysterious, the Church in the abstract, it is a jargon that means nothing or a great deal too much, and I regret it and its apostles from Athanasius to Bishop Keene.

His religious sensibility, as witness this Tribune, resembled that of the later Oxford Movement, but he had been trapped at Cambridge into a smug deism by Conyers Middleton and into a cynical worldliness by another don, John Whaley. A revived Gothic, at first playful but increasingly serious, was his neurotic release from the tension. 'As to orthodoxy,' he told Cole severely, 'excuse me if I think it means nothing at all but every man's own opinion.' A very real dread of 'Enthusiasm', in the form of Methodism or the Countess of Huntingdon's Connection, drove him to claim a stoic morality: 'does it import whether profligacy is baptized or not? I look to motives not to professions.' The Tribune suggests that if an intelligent Jesuit had cornered him he would have 'turned' easily enough. Not that a casual visitor would have noticed the psychic profile of those five statues and the altar to the dead children behind the dense accumulation of oddments anywhere in the house: all the Walpoles in miniature; hair of Edward IV; Roman earrings; an Egyptian duck; two phalli; crucifixes; a silver tea kettle; a Charles I mourning ring, 'very rare'; smelling bottles in purple glass; a boy's head in wax on copper; Christ in the sepulchre, after Raphael. It was a chapel to the irrelevance of taste and the unimportance of aesthetic values.

Strawberry's tourist circuit plumbed the nadirs of taste in its two latest additions, the Great North Bedchamber, raised over the servants' hall, and the Round Drawing-Room over the kitchens, both indicating by their siting that they were never intended for serious regular use. They were decorated like film sets with tawdry richness; both were hung with Horace's favourite crimson Norwich damask, the bed of one and the chairs in both rooms were covered in Aubusson tapestry flowers on a white ground, some chairs were of ebony, some painted white and gold. The state bed, a necessary set piece, was topped with plumes of white ostrich feathers.

These dreadful apartments sometimes hosted appropriately terrible fêtes, like that of 11 October 1778 which was thronged with dowagers and old maids 'with silver beards down to their girdles'. For this, 'the illumination of the Gallery surpassed the Palace of the Sun' and a climax was the arrival of the fat old comic actress

Kitty Clive, 'in the full moon, nothing could be more striking'. The state bed 'looked gorgeous, and was ready strewed with roses for the hymeneal'. It was a bed that 'would become Cleopatra on the Cydnus or Venus if she was not past child bearing'. There was a distinct element of kitsch Hollywood finery about these last rooms of Strawberry and Horace's language matched the camp vulgarity of the decor. Between them, those two masters of ill-advised eclecticism – Horace Walpole and Robert Adam – had designed for the Round Drawing-Room with its theme of the love of Queen Elizabeth and Robert Dudley, the ugliest object still surviving in the house. This was a chimneypiece in pseudo-Cosmatesque decorative mosaic inlay, modelled more or less on the work which Henry III's Italian craftsmen applied to the shrine of Edward the Confessor in the Abbey. Neither Gothic nor Cosmati nor in any eighteenth-century style, it exemplifies the way in which eclecticism breeds a spirit of 'anything goes' and individual whims supplant a national stylistic consensus. Horace could not resist the lure of borrowing and mixing. After reading Swinburne's *Travels in Spain* in 1779, he wanted to write a 'Moorish Novel': 'by taking the most picturesque parts of the Mahometan and Catholic religions and with the mixture of African and Spanish names, one might make something very agreeable'. But by this time, fortunately, he had almost taken his leave of publications. 'The last years of one's life are fit for nothing but idleness and quiet, and I am as indifferent to fame as to politics'.

Adjoining the Round Drawing-Room, screened off by a curtain, was his literary shrine, the Beauclerc Tower, added in 1776 and hung in blue Indian damask. Here were Lady Diana Beauclerc's 'sublime' series of 'soot paintings' drawn in the same year to illustrate *The Mysterious Mother*. Horace had paid £500 for them. Only select visitors were admitted to this sanctum where a copy of the 'forbidden' play lay in the drawer of a black cabinet to enable connoisseurs of the exotic erotic to study Diana Beauclerc's drawings alongside the text.

In the private rooms of the original villa, Strawberry Mark I, the same thematic approach to the furnishings was carried through beneath the welter of decorative objects. The Library and the China Closet were self-descriptive and on the ground floor two rooms followed conventional contemporary practice. The Refectory or Great Parlour had the principal family portraits and the Waiting Room, the original hall, was predominantly white and grey with busts. Venice was the theme of the Little Parlour. It should have been the *sala terrena* of the house, as it opened onto the garden, but Müntz had painted the convolvulus upon trellis-work proper to such a room in the China Closet next door. The oddly named Beauty Room, a ground-floor bedroom, was lightly erotic in theme with a Hermaphrodite in bronze and portraits of queens, kings and their mistresses. Upstairs, the Red Bedchamber ran to paintings of old people and grotesque figures. The Blue Bedchamber featured Horace's family and the Eccardt portraits of his close friends; the Green Closet, crammed with 123 objects, allowed landscapes to predominate.

That left the two most intimate rooms: the Breakfast Room on the first floor and Horace's bedroom immediately above it. Although they both had some painted glass to catch the morning sun, both rooms were notably un-Gothic, which implies that in private retirement Horace was indifferent to his Gothic legend. In the Breakfast Room, the lady artists were generously repre-sented: Mrs Damer's terracotta of Prince Paris, a Beauclerc of boys, Margaret Bingham's water-colours and Mrs Delaney's paper flower mosaics. There was a 'daintee boy' in enamels with verses, twenty-four Hilliard, Oliver and Petitot miniatures and any number of portraits of Sir Kenelm Digby's family, including one of Lady Digby lying dead. Before her marriage she had been a celebrated courtesan, which may account for Horace's interest in her.

'Mr Walpole's Bed Chamber' had the celebrated death warrant of Charles I labelled 'Major Charta' hanging by the bed, but was otherwise acceptably sentimental, with paintings of Patapan and a cat, a copy of Batoni's portrait of Chute, a Rembrandt of an old lady, Horace's own barely competent copies of Watteau which he had painted during his last happy years with his mother, and twelve drawings of comedians. Conyers Middleton's face was predictable, but not that of his spiritual opposite Dr Ashton, with whom Horace was supposed to have quarrelled years before precisely because Ashton had publicly branded Middleton an 'infidel'. He favoured both rooms chiefly for their outlook to the east over his carefully 'natural' grounds.

While his house was strikingly, even perversely original, the forty-five acres of Horace's gardens were laid out with conventional restraint. They formed a rough triangle with the house, offices, printing-house and greenhouse in the top corner. Public roads bounded the area on its left and right side, though the kitchen garden, tea-room and little library lay outside the triangle just across the road from the main house. Horace was never obsessed with privacy and in his short treatise *On Modern Gardening* (1780) described it as 'comic to set aside a quarter of one's garden to be melancholy in'. While disparaging a hermitage as an 'ornament whose merit soonest fades', he did, however, build himself a chapel, modelled on a chantry tomb at Salisbury: a harsh linear design, typical Chute-work, which survives now in a car-park. Lawns bordered the house on the south and east, ending on the eastern, river side, in a broad green terrace above a field for cows. From his first occupancy of Strawberry, Horace had conceived the place as a *ferme ornée* inspired by Southcote's grounds at Woburn Farm in neighbouring Esher. Like Woburn Farm, Strawberry's grounds had a serpentine walk. This ran along the left-hand and bottom sides of its triangular area through a planting of trees which was thin on its inner side, to afford views across to the house, thicker on its outer side. But at all times Horace was anxious to preserve the open outlook of the house east to the Thames, south to Richmond Hill and north-east to Twickenham village and Eel Pie Island.

Most of the garden's ornaments – the Chapel in the Wood, Shell bench, Gothic Gate and bridge – lay on the serpentine walk which began at the greenhouse and stables just north of the house. There was also a gently curved path through the grounds leading to the meadows and Little Strawberry Hill where first Kitty Clive and, after her death, the Berry family lived in Strawberry's version of a dower house.

Horace despised formality in gardens. In his *Modern Gardening* he quotes Sir William Temple's celebrated description of an ideal garden of paved terraces and steps at Moor Park, Hertfordshire with a curl in his lip, as conceived by someone 'born in and never stirred out of Holbourn'. To Horace, the greatest invention in garden history had been the ha-ha because it allowed private grounds to merge imperceptibly with the trees, fields and gentle hillsides of the country. South-eastern England was Arcadia to Horace. Every time he returned from his French visits, he rhapsodized about the contrast between the beauty of Kent and the chalky aridities of France. Yet it was Fragonard's country glimpses which were his ideal and he saw gardens essentially as settings for Rococo-style *fêtes champêtres* where ladies laugh together, music is played among the trees and cows are milked to provide warm syllabubs, hence the *ferme ornée*, to give a rustic illusion. If only Horace could have become familiar with Marie Antoinette they could have made butter and cheese together very happily in the dairy of the Petit Trianon: two old relics of Rococo aesthetics.

Instead, he had his own equally Rococo memories of a May day's entertainment for the French at Esher back in 1763, 'the scene transporting, the trees, lawns, concaves, all in the perfection in which the ghost of Kent would joy to see them'. They had 'a magnificent dinner', but 'cloaked in the modesty of earthenware' for bucolic simplicity. Horace's verses, translated into French, were recited in the belvedere over coffee. Then the ladies made a circle of chairs before the mouth of the grotto 'which was overhung to a vast height with woodbines, lilac and laburnums, and dignified by those tall shapely cypresses. On the descent of the hill were placed the French horns; the abigails, servants, and neighbours wandering below by the river – in short it was Parnassus as Watteau would have painted it.'

By 1765 Horace had, by industrious planting and following the advice of the nurserymen who abounded in polite Twickenham, achieved his own Parnassus at Strawberry.

I am just come out of the garden in the most oriental of all evenings, and from breathing odours beyond those of Araby. The acacias, which the Arabians have the sense to worship, are covered with blossoms, the honeysuckles dangle from every tree in festoons, the syringas are thickets of sweets, and the newcut hay of the field in the garden tempers the balmy gale with simple freshness, while a thousand sky-rockets launched into the air at Ranelagh or Marybone illuminate the scene and give it an air of Haroun Al Raschid's paradise.

Slip that passage in among the letters of John Keats and few would notice the transposition. Horace could evoke the sensuous richness of the Romantics as well as their Gothic glooms; it is after reading such lines that Wilmarth Lewis's ostensible reason for despair at ever writing a biography of Horace can be understood. Horace wrote it all so well himself.

Trees, untrimmed and naturally spreading, were a passion with him. Indeed if the grounds of Strawberry had a fault it was that they had more the air of an arboretum than a park. There was none of Kent's strategic clumping of trees to focus the eye. Instead there was a thin scatter all over the grounds (as opposed to the 'lawn' and the 'field'). Each tree was given room to achieve its natural space, the more conical Norfolk Pines standing uneasily alongside the rounded forms of native species. Flowers were tolerated chiefly for their scent. As the passage just quoted indicates, Horace revelled in perfumes and if a tree, like an acacia, had a sweet scent, he ignored the fact that it had a weak outline and was covered in spines. When possible, the house itself was overwhelmed with tuberoses: house, garden and grounds thus working as a Gothic, not a classical, Arcadia.

Visitors flocked to Strawberry for two reasons. First, for its Gothic oddity, which would have impressed most middle-income visitors as being within their financial range, reassuringly manageable in scale, soothingly verdant yet distinctive. Secondly, they came for the overwhelming evidence of its celebrated owner's taste and personality. If Horace sometimes allowed himself to be glimpsed opening the Library door and civilly passing the time of day, all parties would be gratified. Horace claimed hypocritically to be weary of these admirers: 'I shudder when my bell rings at the gate.

241

It is as bad as keeping an inn, and I am often tempted to deny its being shown, if it would not be ill-natured to those that come.' But he never stopped issuing the tickets and was personally affronted if his rooms and collections were treated brusquely. 'Three came to see this house last week,' he told Mann crossly in July 1783, 'and walked through it literally while I wrote eight lines of a letter; for I heard them go up the stairs and I heard them go down exactly in the time I was finishing no longer a paragraph.' To make matters worse, the offenders were French; they had obviously despaired of the house after seeing the Gallery and returned contemptuously to their coach.

It is apparent from his letters to Cole that Horace regularly made himself pleasant to complete strangers. An undemanding acquaintance at that level satisfied his taste for animation without commitment. To young 'confirmed bachelors' like Mr Craufurd who kept trying to scrape up a friendship, Horace maintained a nervous hostility: 'you are not the most amiable of men,' he told him, 'and I have nothing to amuse you with; for you are like electricity, you attract and repel at once.' So either Craufurd was a particularly intractable personality, or Horace had still not come to terms with his homosexual nature. 'I live at this time of year,' he continued in the same letter, 'with nothing but old women. They do very well for me, who have little choice left, and who rather prefer common nonsense to wise nonsense, the only difference I know between old women and old men.' Here was Horace pretending, 'What am I but a poor old skeleton, tottering towards the grave?' He told Craufurd sourly that, though he was always employed, 'I must say I think I have given up everything in the world, only to be at liberty to be very busy about the most errant trifles.' But then he transformed the whole guarded letter with an enchantingly funny account of being swept down the flooded Thames with an hysterical woman in a ferryboat navigated by drunks. It is easy to understand why, despite rebuffs, Craufurd persevered.

Like many frail old homosexuals, Horace preferred to lavish his affection upon dogs rather than on dangerous young men. He responded with particular warmth to small, tetchy dogs with chronic illnesses. He was himself, on gouty days, being carried from room to room in Strawberry by his superior Swiss servants as early as 1770, when he still had twenty-seven years to live. The power of pain to limit his ambitions and widen his sensibilities in later life should never be underestimated. He appears, paradoxically, to have clung to youth and at the same time to have embraced old age eagerly and early, possibly as early as that fit of gout in July 1765 when he was not yet fifty. Horace inclined to cherish his own limitations and could express them freely through his pets. 'My poor Rosette is dying,' he wrote to Lady Ossory, who did not like dogs:

> She relapsed into her fits the last night of my stay at Nuneham; and has suffered exquisitely ever since. You may believe I have too – I have been out of bed twenty times every night, have had no sleep, and sat up with her till three this morning – but I am only making you laugh at me: I cannot help it, I think of nothing else. Without weaknesses I should not be I, and I may as well tell them, as have them tell themselves.

A week later Rosette was dead and Horace had penned an epitaph beginning:

> Sweetest roses of the year
> Strew around my Rose's bier
> Calmly may the dust repose
> Of my pretty faithful Rose!

This shamelessly sentimental verse ended with the wish that he and his dog might be united in Heaven. It is not unusual for men to grow more religious as they grow older, but Horace in his sixties fell into a mood closer to that of Matthew Arnold in 'Dover Beach': one of helpless sadness at the 'melancholy, long, withdrawing roar' as the 'Sea of Faith' retreated from Christian Europe, helpless because he himself had no faith yet loved faith's Catholic forms and its evidence in churches, monasteries and art.

After revisiting his beloved Chartreux in Paris again in 1771 he wrote despairingly to Chute of 'the consciousness that the vision is dispelled, the want of fervour so obvious in the religious', of a solitude that proceeded 'from contempt, not from contemplation'.

The buildings appeared 'like abandoned theatres destined for destruction. The monks trot about as if they had not long to stay there; and what used to be holy gloom is now but dirt and sadness. There is no more deception than in a tragedy, acted by candle-snuffers.' He was nostalgic for a successful 'deception', his word for faith, and the emptiness of reason swept in on him. 'One is sorry to think that an empire of common sense would not be very picturesque', would in fact result in a world he would hate. All his adult life he had stood, or thought he stood, for 'common sense' against the faith he now seemed to value more. It was the dilemma of a natural Romantic conditioned by the Age of Reason.

The Boston Tea Party and the war with the American colonists brought out all Horace's 'common sense' instincts once again. From the first signs of trouble he foresaw disaster. 'A war on our own trade is popular!' he wrote incredulously as Lord North rode on into ruin. 'Both Houses are as eager for it as they were for conquering the Indies.' That was in February 1775. By September he was in Paris with a pro-American Madame du Deffand in good form and his radical views had clarified. He told an apprehensive Mann:

> I am what I always was, a zealot for liberty in every part of the globe and consequently I most heartily wish success to the Americans ... If England prevails, English and American liberty is at an end! If the colonies prevail, our commerce is gone – and if at last we negotiate, they will neither forgive nor give us our former advantages.

Intoxicated by his treasonable free-thinking, Horace related how the French 'talk of our tyranny and folly with horror and contempt, and perhaps with amazement'. No longer mortified by hearing his country deprecated, he felt positively comforted at finding 'the sentiments of the rest of the world concur with and confirm mine'. He believed France would not enter the war but that England would sink deeper into conflict. In his new pro-French mood, he wrote with deluded optimism, 'this country is far more happy. It is governed by benevolent and beneficent men under a Prince who has not yet betrayed a fault; and who will be as happy as his people if he always employs such men.' The 'Prince' was Louis XVI. So much for the political prognostications of the hopeful *bien pensant*.

CHAPTER THIRTEEN

The women gather round

'Icannot make news without straw,' Horace wrote despairingly to his new friend and companion Mary Berry as he was preparing in 1791 for his annual retreat to Strawberry for the summer. That was only one of the problems limiting the range of his letter-writing in the last two decades of his life. He had little first-hand contact with decision makers and events. He suffered acutely from 'the gout' and supposed, like most invalids, that his friends would want to read every detail of his aches and pains. Most damaging though was the quality of his correspondents. A great letter sequence is love at third hand. It is a contact, even a conflict, certainly a tension between two minds, and in most of Horace's last letters, polished and informative as they are, this element of tension is missing. It survives in his letters to the Revd William Mason, the biographer of Gray, but he quarrelled with Mason in 1784 and in 1787 he lost his old friend and fellow antiquary Lord Harcourt, at whose Oxfordshire seat, Stanton Harcourt, he had spent many pleasant days and with whom he had kept up an amiable if intermittent correspondence for thirty-six years. The element of tension surfaced in a new correspondence with the blue-stocking, Hannah More, feminist, educationalist and forerunner of Victorian pietism. But as her real aim was to bring Horace to Jesus, there was an unreal quality to their exchanges.

To preserve the immediacy of his letters, Horace should never have quit Parliament in 1768 but remained as a back-bencher; to preserve their tension, he should not have chosen the Countess of

Upper Ossory, that improbably titled and rather dull lady, to succeed Montagu as his principal correspondent. Wilmarth Lewis
loved the Countess. Virtually none of her own letters had survived
to create problems and distractions for an editor, and because she
was a titled lady, if a divorcee, there were no indecencies to disturb
a scrupulous editor. 'The earlier letters to Montagu are gayer,'
Lewis allowed, 'the letters to Lady Ossory are perhaps more studied, but Walpole's self-consciousness here is that of the mature
artist, and I believe now, forty years after my introduction to him,
that he is at his best as a writer and as a person [obviously a moral
matter there for Lewis] in these letters to Lady Ossory'.

Everyone to their taste; it is true that even in his late years
Horace could, when writing to a man, strike out a little. 'You talk
of bad weather in your last,' he wrote to Mason, 'it has lasted here
to this instant: there is not a leaf big enough to cover a caterpilla's
pudenda.' But with another man he could take issue over literary
judgements, as he did with Mason and Cole, or over political loyal-
ties as he did with Lord Harcourt. Lady Ossory and Mary Berry
appear to have been content to receive studied accounts of receptions and love affairs, that had been reported to Horace by a second person, but give nothing in return. The reader begins to pine
for a little anger and criticism, for the guard to be let down occasionally.

John Chute's death in 1776 had provoked a real reaction from
Horace, both selfish and disturbingly honest about that selfishness.
This was because he was writing to Mann, not to Ossory: 'how self
prides even in our grief . . . my loss is irreparable. To me he was the
most faithful and secure of friends, and a delightful companion. I
shall not seek to replace him.' Yet even as he wrote that down, an
alternative had flashed into his mind. All those years he had been
writing to Mann, keeping him in his ministry at Florence despite
changes in government patronage, securing a baronetcy for him,
even the Order of the Bath; why not call for a return – bring Mann
back from Italy to take the place of Chute? 'You could be that
resource,' he suggested tentatively, 'but I must not think of it, I
must not be selfish.' But he had thought of it, he had been selfish.
Mann had been put on the defensive, shown his duty to his best

friend. 'I will go take a walk,' Horace artfully concluded, 'shed a tear and return to you more composed.' He was to end his days surrounded by ministering women, but not by choice. In his later years he had tried to persuade three male friends – Montagu, Cole and Mann – to come and live near him. One of them, of course, George Montagu, did move into London, where Horace spent at least half the year, but as soon as he had settled in neighbourly proximity to Horace's comfortable house in Berkeley Square, he cut his friend dead.

In these later years Horace's casual genius was by no means spent. He could still react brilliantly when a great event occurred on his doorstep. His letters on the Gordon Riots to Mann, Lady Ossory and Mason are among his greatest, four or five in one week – London burning, drunken apprentices challenging the upper classes to show a light at their doors to signal their Protestantism, the House of Lords in uproar, peers preparing to fight their way out of the chamber with their swords. Horace loved it as he, the man of peace, loved all disasters and thrived on wars. As General Conway ran down the street to a fire, Horace, usually carried from room to room by servants, limped after him on his cane to catch 'Haymarket and Piccadilly illuminated from fear' and the crash of 'bushels of half pence which fell about the streets' as the toll houses were sacked by the mob. He was still young enough to admit an absolute error of analysis: 'I allow all you can think of my littleness of mind,' he told Mason, 'how short sighted my penetration is.' In his last letter he had declared confidently 'that national lethargy would doze into despotism', and now a week later the capital was in turmoil. But Horace was still warm enough at heart to allow, 'I did feel joy for the four convicts who were released from Newgate within twenty four hours of their execution!' Those were the words of a true outsider, even of an anarchist, though it may have helped that the mob had only been persecuting Catholics and that Horace had earlier advised against Rockingham's over-liberal bill which had provoked it all. English Catholics lacked the aesthetic appeal of ritual and great churches which made their brethren across the Channel acceptable to Horace.

In 1782 William Cole died after taking thirty drops of laudanum, a heavy dose, every night for a month. 'I had such a sound sleep as surprised me and relieved me,' he reported after the first experiment. He was no real loss: a pleasant old bore who had encouraged Horace to exchange symptoms of 'flying gout' regularly, and fixated his friend upon the collection of 'heads' – prints of the famous and semi-famous to the number of some four thousand, like two excited schoolboys over their cigarette cards. There had always been a competitive undertone to their letters. Cole would snub Horace for some inaccuracy in heraldry; Horace would poke unkind fun at Cole's churchmanship. When they exchanged gifts of china, manuscripts and prints, it was done in a careful equilibrium of gratitude. Time and again Horace tried to persuade Cole to take a living nearer to him. Cole often pretended to an interest but never seriously intended leaving his flat Cambridgeshire acres. Without Cole's sly nagging, Horace would never have wasted his time over replies on the Richard III and the Chatterton controversies.

Kitty Clive had died in 1785, leaving Little Strawberry Hill vacant, and an empty place at Horace's Twickenham card-table; in 1786, Horace Mann had died weeping over Horace's last letter. Almost as if there had been no interruption, Horace continued to write his news letters to Mann's nephew, another Horace. But it was to take him a little longer, three years to be exact, to fill Kitty Clive's place.

In 1788 a new family settled in Twickenham and were an instant social success. The Berrys were a widowed father and his two daughters, Mary the beauty and Agnes the artist. They were not wealthy, but an air of distinction clung to them because Mr Berry had forfeited an inheritance by refusing to make a second marriage. Instead he had educated his daughters to be attentive listeners and consequently Horace was quickly ensnared. It was at about this time that women began to close in on him. In addition to being a well-known wit and literary figure, Horace was worth £91,000 and had no obvious heir. The Berry sisters soon became emotionally necessary to him for cards, conversation and sympathy. Mary Berry was a handsome woman with a confident, decided manner of speaking. She had fine dark eyes 'very lively when she speaks, with a symmetry of face that is more interesting for being pale'. Horace found her 'an angel inside and out'. Agnes was plain and dabbled in water-colours which Horace patronized rather as he patronized Anne Damer's sculpture. Horace mentioned their father as an afterthought, as 'a little merry man with a round face'.

Horace's nearer female relatives began to keep a wary eye on these potential fortune-hunters. Possibly as a way of keeping a check on her, Anne Damer, Henry Conway's only child, began an intense relationship with Mary Berry. Hannah More was also establishing an emotional closeness with Mary, but by a different approach. Her *Memoirs* read:

> Spoke boldly to Miss Berry. Made her promise to read some of the evidences of Christianity, and the New Testament. Oh Lord! Do thou follow with thy blessing her resolves, and show her the truth 'as it is in Jesus'. Open the blind eyes! Spent two mornings with Lord Orford, for him I offer the same fervent petition.

Lord Orford was Horace, newly ennobled as the fourth and last Earl of that uncertain line. Only ten years earlier he would have been outraged at the notion of even one morning spent in Evangelical 'enthusiasm'. Old age was mellowing him. There is something dramatically appropriate in Horace's last years being crowded with proto-lesbians, when he himself had only shown a sexual interest in men.

The outbreak of the French Revolution in 1789 had, for Horace, more dramatic irony than dramatic appropriateness, for it turned him from a dilettante Radical into a raging reactionary. It was not the storming of the Bastille that transformed him. Indeed his concern in the revolution's early days was that the batteries of cannon, which he imagined were mounted on the walls of that fortress, might be turned with terrible effect upon the innocent cit-izenry as they demonstrated for liberty, his favourite cause. What shook him to the core was the news that 'Monsieur d'Olan, a wor-thy man, and nephew of my dear friend Madame du Deffand, has been taken out of his bed, to which he was confined by the gout, at Avignon, and hanged by the mob!' The disturbing detail was that touch of the gout. Change Avignon to Twickenham and it could have been Horace himself. As for Madame, 'I have said for this year that I am happy she is dead; and how much that reflection is fortified!' But if only she had still been alive and Horace had felt impelled to rush as Pimpernel on crutches to her rescue, what an authentic *Tale of Two Cities* would have resulted: Horace's character sketch of Danton, his impressions of Philippe Egalité, revolutionary fashions in women's wear and a first-hand account of the proceedings of the National Assembly!

Amazingly it could all easily have happened if he had not been so crippled. In 1790 the Berry sisters and their merry, round father set off for the Continent and moved with superb detachment through Italy in tension and France in ferment; only returning to Horace late in 1791. It was the great missed opportunity of Horace's life: Madame Defarge in place of Madame du Deffand. Instead, desperately worrying about his 'angel's' safety, he lay at home dictating counter-revolutionary rant to his new friend, 'My dear Saint Hannah'. His poor crabbed fingers were so knotted with chalk stones that Kirgate, his printer, had often to act as secretary, but 'I know not how to stop', Horace admitted, 'when I talk of these ruffians'.

Even when he was writing an austere scholarly letter to Sir William Hamilton in Naples on the qualities of perspective in Etruscan vases, he became caught up in a chain of associations – Naples, Queen of Naples, sister of the Queen of France, Marie Antoinette – and he was off again:

> No Christian martyr was ever tortured so inhumanly for three years together – nor is there on record any memorial of such over-savage barbarities as have been committed by that atrocious and detestable nation! – a nation as contemptible as it is odious – and when La Fayette called them *cowardly cannibals*, he gave but a faint idea of half their detestable qualities.

On their safe return Horace installed the Berry family in Little Strawberry Hill and sank contentedly, with their backing, into querulous old age. Horace had become the 4th and last Earl of Orford rather too late to enjoy the title. He never revisited Houghton or even took his seat in the House of Lords, claiming gloomily that he was the poorest earl in England. Friends continued to predecease him. That connoisseur in executioner's techniques, George Selwyn, died in 1791, the year of Horace's ennoblement. 'Him I really loved, not only for his infinite wit, but a thousand good qualities,' Horace wrote elegaically, before Selwyn was actually dead. It was the end to a series of *bons mots*, recorded reverentially over the years by Horace, but which only serve, like Shakespeare's puns, to record the odd transience of humour. Lord Lincoln, who had, since his uncle's death in 1768, been the 2nd Duke of Newcastle, died in 1794; Henry Conway in 1795. Neither the former, Horace's passion, nor the latter, his greatest friend, received any written farewell. Before his death Conway, by longevity, had become one of Britain's least famous Field Marshals.

Death came for Horace on 2 March 1797 at his London house in Berkeley Square. Some accounts describe him at the end as a pathetic, bemused old man. His last letters tell a very different story. Compare the manipulative letter which he wrote to Mary Berry on 7 August 1796:

> Can you wonder at a heart so affectionate as mine being wounded by some (I am willing to hope unmeant) expressions in your last letter? Mortified as I have been by finding so little return of a friendship that had been the principal occupation of my whole life, and conscious of having no address, felicity or art of attaching those whom I most wished to please; and decayed in spirits and in every agreeable light, I naturally dread being grown a burden to those I chiefly cultivate.

with his last letter to Lady Ossory, written on 16 January 1797, just over a month before his death. She had praised him for his style and asked for more London news, but he replied with ruthless realism, 'I see nobody that really knows anything, and what I learn comes from the newspapers that collect intelligence from coffeehouses; consequently what I neither believe nor report.' The letter continued, harsh and wholly unsentimental:

> At home I see only a few charitable elders, except about fourscore nephews and nieces of various ages, who are each brought to me

about once a year to stare at me as the Methusalem of the family, and they can only speak of their cotemporaries [*sic*], which interest me no more than if they talked of their dolls, or bats and balls.

Then with a characteristic brilliant change of mood he swung into a passage as moving as the death of Falstaff, as carefully contrived as Dickens's death of Little Nell:

Oh my good Madam pray send me no more such laurels, which I desire no more than their leaves when decked with a scrap of tinsel and stuck on twelfth-cakes that lie on the shop-boards of pastry-cooks at Christmas. I shall be quite content with a sprig of rose-mary thrown after me, when the parson of the parish commits my dust to dust. Till then, pray, Madam, accept the resignation of your Ancient servant, Orford.

How proper for the natural journalist to have written his own epi-taph; but it would be intriguing to know how long he had been considering its wording: the homely imagery of tinsel on a cake and the dying fall of the rhetoric. The parson of the parish com-mitted his dust to dust 'in a private manner, agreably to his partic-ular directions'. The *Gentleman's Magazine* reported 'Lord O was never married, and as far as we can learn, his chief mistress, through his life, was the Muse'.

Inevitably Horace's last will and testament was not a simple thing, but twenty-two pages long with seven codicils. Even so it made no mention of his principal, but spiritual and metaphorical bequest, which was one of a confidently exotic life-style with Gothic overtones, an example of precedents suitable to a wealthy sexual outsider. This he left to William Beckford of Fonthill, a man already disgraced by the kind of sexual scandal, in Beckford's case with the young Lord Courtenay in 1784, from which Horace had escaped with Lord Lincoln in 1741 and been tainted by in 1765 with Henry Conway and the Guthrie writings. Beckford was to relive Horace's life but angrily, more openly, in a more defiantly flamboyant register. Possibly, sensing a too eager disciple, Horace kept a discreet social distance from the son, though he had got on well with his father, Alderman Beckford.

With his worldly, as opposed to his spiritual, goods, Horace had been explicit, foreseeing every eventuality. Houghton went to the Cholmondeleys, his sister Mary's family; they still retain the estate. Strawberry was offered to the Duchess of Gloucester, but she preferred the alternative of £10,000, so the castle-house went to Mrs Damer for her lifetime with £2000 a year for its upkeep. That unpleasant woman, who had made jokes in his last days about Horace and his cat vomiting on the carpet and then eating the vomit for their supper, tired of the place and let it go prematurely to the Waldegraves, the family of his neice Maria by her first marriage. The Waldegraves cared for Strawberry and made extensive additions. It is now St Mary's University College and Horace's original buildings are a treasured feature of the campus, open occasionally, as in Horace's time, to visitors. Robert Berry and his daughters were given 'box O' of Horace's printed works and manuscripts 'to be published at their own discretion and for their own emolument'. In 1798 they published a handsome five-volume edition of Horace's *Works*, which sold well. All letters to living friends were to be returned to them. The wretched Damer and Horace's half-sister, Lady Maria Churchill, Sir Robert's illegitimate daughter, destroyed all theirs, leaving two great blanks in the glorious Proustian edifice of Horace's world.

Most excitingly of all, 'a large wainscot chest marked on the outside lid with a great A' was only opened in 1810, when the current Lord Waldegrave had reached his prescribed twenty-fifth year. He was hugely disappointed to find 'it was not stored with silver, gold or precious jewels' but with Horace's two *Memoirs*, those of George II and George III, and some Waldegrave papers. When consulted, Lord Holland, Henry Fox's grandson, read the *Memoirs* and urged that they 'throw a great light on history ... and are too valuable to be withheld from the public ... One or two disgusting, unimportant anecdotes might be suppressed and some coarse epithets not suited to our present taste.'

John Murray gave £2000 for the papers, published an edited two-volume version of *George II* in 1822 and made a profit. But Lord Holland's nervous reservations were ominous. By ensuring that no one mentioned in the *Memoirs* would be alive when chest A was opened, Horace had thrust his lively, charming, biased writings forward into a hostile environment, into an age that preferred to believe in heroes, an age of averted eyes and hypocritical decencies.

In 1833 Macaulay, the historian, wrote an attack on Horace in the *Edinburgh Review* as earthy and entertaining in its images as the best of Horace's own writing, and far more sustained in its venom and contempt than anything that Horace himself ever wrote, unless his scattered references to the Duke of Newcastle could be gathered into one anthology.

Macaulay, as much a tabloid journalist as Horace, opened with a rousing knockabout assault, better calculated to sell the *Works* than to damn them. Horace's writings were, he claimed, like Strasburg pies:

> But, as the *pâté-de-foie-gras* owes its excellence to the diseases of the wretched animal which furnishes it ... so none but an unhealthy and disorganised mind could have produced such literary luxuries as the works of Walpole.

Horace had been 'the most eccentric, the most artificial, the most fastidious, the most capricious of men. His mind was a bundle of inconsistent whims and affectations.' This is fair enough. Intelligent contemporaries of Horace and thoughtful readers of his work have always sensed that he was a homosexual of a certain type, whether open or concealed, and this is Macaulay's embarrassed way of saying so. But then he accuses Horace of having 'played innumerable parts, and over-acted them all' – the misanthrope, the philanthropist, Radical, snob and reformer. This is the core of Macaulay's attack and betrays a psychological crudity most damaging in an historian.

For the sake of his argument, Macaulay pretended to believe that Horace had traduced a set of heroes. He raged at him for describing Pitt as 'a strutting, ranting, mouthing actor – Charles Townshend, an impudent and voluble jack-pudding – Hardwicke, an insolent upstart, with the understanding of a pettifogger, and the heart of a hangman – Lyttelton, a poor creature, whose only wish was to go to heaven in a coronet.' If we were to believe all this, Macaulay protested, 'England in his time contained little sense and no virtue.' The truth is that Charles Townshend, Lord Hardwicke and George, 1st Baron Lyttelton, were only a cluster of competitive politicians manœuvring for power as the Pelham dynasty showed signs of faltering in 1754. As for the great Mr Pitt, while it was true that he sometimes postured and strutted his part, Horace had this to say in honest patriotic appreciation: 'we see St James's Street crowded with nabobs and American chiefs, and Mr Pitt attended in his Sabine farm by eastern monarchs, and Borealian electors, waiting, till the gout is out of his foot, for an audience.' That was sufficient recognition, even by Macaulay's standards, for a successful imperialist who was, after all, only a flawed and infirm human being. Horace had no conception of heroes, that was one of his great virtues.

Macaulay knew that there were elements of truth in all those descriptions and that none of the Whig politicians had been of legendary stature. The only man he should have defended from Horace was Newcastle and he never mentioned him. When he complained that Horace was a set of masks within masks, he was protesting about human nature and Horace's unguarded honesty over his motivation. A popular historian may well find the complexities of truth to be inconvenient for the generalizations he is seeking to put before the average reader. Horace was offering facts, not popular history, hence Macaulay's irritation. Macaulay grumbled because Horace 'scoffed at Courts, and kept a chronicle of their most trifling scandal', but Horace had been typically honest about this common paradox: he was, he said, 'a quiet republican, who does not dislike to see the shadow of monarchy like Banquo's ghost, fill the empty chair of state'. Horace was a hypocrite, Macaulay claimed, because he posed as a lover of peace yet never once spoke against war in his twenty-six years as an MP. Where would Macaulay the historian have been without wars to carry his own narrative? Most sane people are repelled by slaughter, but most sane people respond eagerly to an interesting disaster. As Horace, openly again, told Bentley when Bentley had anticipated Macaulay's attack, 'I see no blame in thinking an active age more agreeable to live in than a soporific one.'

With just one shaft, Macaulay did strike home at Horace's weakest point, more by accident than perception, for he failed to press his thrust home. Horace, he said, 'loved mischief: but he loved quiet,' and it was in this contradiction, between his essential sexual or emotional privacy, his quiet, and his pleasure in faction, that Horace was vulnerable. That was how Guthrie traumatized him for a year or more, replying to Horace's attack on the Grenville ministry in 1764 by a counter-attack on Horace's affection for Henry Conway, his love of inner privacy. Horace took his revenge by destroying Grenville's ministry, but even so that humiliation may have ruined Horace's pleasure in politics and led ultimately to the resignation of his seat.

For the rest, Horace was invulnerable because he was open. He described himself as one who had 'a propensity to faction, and looked on the mischief of civil disturbances as a lively amusement.' He never claimed to be a historian: 'I write casual memoirs; I draw characters; I preserve anecdotes which my superiors, the historians of Britain, may enclose into their weighty annals or pass over at their pleasure.' Macaulay's essay was more a protest at the ignobility and diversity of the human condition than anything else; if he had lived another thirteen years, to 1870, he might have choked on Leslie Stephen's judgement that 'The History of England, throughout a very large part of the eighteenth century, is simply a synonym for the works of Horace Walpole'. That generous admission explains Macaulay's sense of claustrophobia as he tried to reshape the past into an acceptable Victorian pattern while in the multiple grip of Horatian sources; but Stephen still misses the whole truth.

Horace had, in his letters, invented a new art-form which has still not been given a name. It demanded a lifetime of dedicated detachment. It occupied a literary ground somewhere between *War and Peace* and *A la recherche du temps perdu* – life as a prolix novel. Horace Walpole wrote the portrait of an entire social class over four imperial decades, a portrait flawed by his own nervous censorship but still convincingly inclusive. His strength, possibly even his greatness, was that he wrote as a sexual, aesthetic and social outsider yet never became alienated. He was confident that he belonged.

As for Macaulay's more general condemnation of the triviality of

Horace's interests, it would not stand up for a moment if launched in the late twentieth century. 'To preserve from decay the perishable topics of Ranelagh and Whites – to record divorces and bets, Miss Chudleigh's absurdities, George Selwyn's good sayings – to decorate a grotesque house with pie-crust battlements.' Macaulay is scorning the stuff of social history and failing to see the source of the Gothic Revival triumphant in his own day.

What Macaulay failed to recognize was Horace's extraordinary psychic stature. He did not launch a Gothic Revival, he made one popular. He did not invent the Gothic novel, he simply wrote the first wildly popular example of the genre. Far more than Edmund Burke, with his theory of the sublime and the beautiful, or William Blake, with his recognition of Satan as creator, Horace was the man who released the fabled Monsters of the Id. He sent them rampaging down the decades to wreak havoc upon Macaulay's nineteenth century and our twentieth.

It is not irrelevant that *Otranto* is a silly novel, and *The Mysterious Mother* a ridiculous play; both of them are tissues of amusing improbabilities. That was their strength and their danger. Three-quarters at least of Freud's perceptions lie implicit in their nonsense. Most Gothic novels subsequent to Horace were written for the Minerva Press by women and read in the lending libraries by women. Why then do they continue Horace's theme of young girls threatened in gloomy places by male violence and male lust? Only because the theme, which homosexual and entirely unthreatening Horace had lighted upon, was deeply relevant to women, both fascinating and horrifying. But rape was not the only monster he released – a boy's ambiguous love for his mother, a mother's for her son, an older man's impatience with an ageing wife and his drive to renew his lusts with young girls, the power of guilt to rear up even through several generations and throw down the very structure of a state – to all these Horace gave an acceptably trivial, easily readable form: mental poisons in sweet lemonade.

It was exactly the same with his house and its interior. No one would ever take Strawberry Hill seriously. That was its insidious attraction: to hold tea parties in a necromancer's castle. Like his

Otranto, it had an incompetent charm, it was affordable and it was copyable. It preached a lesson in taste like that of Rabelais's Thelema – 'Do what you will' – you are the arbiter. Add a tower here, a wing there, ignore symmetry, express your own life-style, the Monsters of your own Id. Live in a church if that amuses you, climb winding stairs to bed, greet the morning sun through Gothic tracery. It was all a huge liberation and, let there be no underestimating its force, Strawberry was the source-spring of all that great outpouring of eclectic design which is called 'Victorian'. Outside a house and inside a house, personal taste, or its absence, triumphed because Horace's Strawberry was the ultimate ego-trip, not only for individuals but even nations. It was a gate thrown open in the walls of accepted taste and one the more tempting in that it allowed the building classes the additional luxury of functional planning once the confines of symmetry had been rejected for the attractions of the Picturesque. Soon, in parks and suburbs up and down the country, and finally on the Thames at Westminster, Strawberry's children would be flaunting their towers, battlements and spirelets. After Horace, the Deluge.

Select Bibliography

Adams, C.K. & Lewis, Wilmarth S., 'The Portraits of Horace Walpole', *Walpole Society*, vol 42, 1970

Barrell, John, *The Birth of Pandora and the Division of Knowledge*, Macmillan, London, 1992

Barrell, Rex A., *Horace Walpole and France*, Carlton Press, New York, 1978

Beckett, John, *The Rise and Fall of the Grenvilles*, Manchester University Press, 1994

Black, Jeremy, *Britain in the Age of Walpole*, Macmillan, London, 1984

Black, Jeremy, *British Foreign Policy in the Age of Walpole*, John Donald, Edinburgh, 1985

Black, Jeremy (ed.), *British Politics and Society from Walpole to Pitt 1742–1789*, Macmillan, London, 1990

Brewer, John, *Party ideology and popular politics at the accession of George III,* Cambridge University Press, 1976

Browning, Reed, *The Duke of Newcastle*, Yale University Press, New Haven & London, 1975

Chase, Isabel Wakeling Urban, *Horace Walpole: Gardenist,* Princeton University Press, 1943

Clark, Kenneth, *The Gothic Revival: An Essay in the History of Taste*, John Murray, London, 3rd edition, 1962

Colley, Linda, *In Defiance of Oligarchy: The Tory Party 1714–60,* Cambridge University Press, 1982

Conner, Patrick, *Oriental Architecture in the West,* Thames & Hudson, London, 1979

Craveri, Benedetta, *Madam du Deffand and her World* (trans. Teresa Waugh), Halban Press, London, 1995

Select Bibliography

Crook, J. Mordaunt, 'Strawberry Hill Revisited', *Country Life*, 7, 14 & 21 June 1973

Crook, J. Mordaunt, *The Dilemma of Style: Architectural Ideas from the Picturesque to the Post-Modern*, John Murray, London, 1987

Davis, Terence, *The Gothick Taste*, David & Charles, Newton Abbot, 1974

Dobson, Austin, *Horace Walpole: A Memoir*, Dodd, Mead & Co., New York, 1890

Eastlake, C.L., *A History of the Gothic Revival* (1872); ed. J. Mordaunt Crook, Leicester, 1970; revised 1978

Evans, Bertrand, *Gothic Drama from Walpole to Shelley*, University of California Press, Berkeley & Los Angeles, 1947

Fothergill, Brian, *The Strawberry Hill Set: Horace Walpole and his circle*, Faber & Faber, London, 1983

Girouard, Mark, *Life in the English Country House*, Yale University Press, New Haven & London, 1978

Gray, Jennie, *Horace Walpole & William Beckford: Pioneers of the Gothic Revival*, Gothic Society monograph, Gargoyle's Head Press, Chislchurst, 1994

Greenwood, Alice Drayton, *Horace Walpole's World*, Bell & Sons, London, 1913

Greer, Germaine, *The Obstacle Race*, Secker & Warburg, London, 1979

Guillery, Peter, 'Strawberry Hill: Building and Site; Part One: The Building', *Architectural History*, vol 38, W. S. Maney, Leeds, 1995

Guthrie, William, *Address to the Public on the late Dismission of a General Officer*, London, 1764

Guthrie, William, *A reply to the Counter Address being a vindication of a Pamphlet entitled Address to the Public on the late Dismission of a General Officer*, London, 1764

Guthrie, William, *A Question of some late dismissions truly stated by a friend to the army and the constitution*, London, 1764

Gwynn, Stephen, *The Life of Horace Walpole*, Thornton Butterworth, London, 1932

Halsband, Robert, *The Life of Lady Mary Wortley Montagu*, Clarendon Press, Oxford, 1956

Halsband, Robert, *Lord Hervey: Eighteenth-Century Courtier*, Clarendon Press, Oxford, 1973

Harfst, Betsy Perteit, *Horace Walpole and the Unconscious, An Experiment in Freudian Analysis*, Arno Press, New York, 1980

Select Bibliography

Hazen, A.T., *A Bibliography of Horace Walpole*, Yale University Press, New Haven & London, 1948

Hibbert, Christopher, *The Grand Tour*, Thames Methuen, London, 1987

Hill, B.W., *British parliamentary parties 1742–1832: from the fall of Walpole to the First Reform Act*, Allen & Unwin, London, 1985

Holmes, Geoffrey & Szechi, Daniel, *The Age of Oligarchy: Pre-industrial Britain 1722–1783*, Longman, London & New York, 1993

Hussey, Christopher, *English Country Houses: Early Georgian 1715–1760*, Country Life, London, 1955

Jacques, David, *Georgian Gardens: The Reign of Nature*, Batsford, London, 1983

Jestin, Loftus, *The Answer to the Lyre: Richard Bentley's Illustrations for Thomas Gray's Poems*, University of Pennsylvania Press, Philadelphia, 1990

Judd, Gerrit P., *Horace Walpole's Memoirs*, Bookman Associates, New York, 1959

Kallich, Martin, *Horace Walpole*, Twayne Publishers, New York, 1971

Kelch, Ray A., *Newcastle, A Duke Without Money: Thomas Pelham-Holles 1693–1768*, Routledge & Kegan Paul, London, 1974

Kelly, Linda, *The Marvellous Boy: The Life and Myth of Thomas Chatterton*, Weidenfeld & Nicolson, London, 1971

Ketton-Cremer, R. Wyndham, *Horace Walpole*, Longman, London, 1940

Ketton-Cremer, R. Wyndham, *Thomas Gray: A Biography*, Cambridge University Press, 1955

de Koren, Anna, *Horace Walpole and Madame du Deffand: An Eighteenth Century Friendship*, D Appleton & Co., New York, 1929

Lees-Milne, James, *Earls of Creation: Five Great Patrons of Eighteenth-Century Art*, Hamish Hamilton, London, 1962

Lees-Milne, James, *William Beckford*, Compton Russell, Tisbury, 1976

Lewis, Wilmarth S. (ed.), *The Yale Edition of Horace Walpole's Correspondence*, 48 volumes, Yale University Press, New Haven & London, 1937–83

Lewis, Wilmarth S., 'The Genesis of Strawberry Hill', *Metropolitan Museum Studies*, vol 5, part 1, 1934, New York, 1936

Lewis, Wilmarth S., *Horace Walpole*, Rupert Hart-Davis, London, 1961

Lewis, Wilmarth S., *A Guide to the Life of Horace Walpole (1717–1797) Fourth Earl of Orford, as Illustrated by an Exhibition Based on the Yale*

Edition of His Correspondence, Yale University Press, New Haven &
London, 1973

Lyte, H.C. Maxwell, *A History of Eton College 1440–1910*, Macmillan,
London, 1911

Marshall, Dorothy, *Eighteenth-Century England*, Longman, Harlow,
1962

McCarthy, Michael, *The Origins of the Gothic Revival*, Yale University
Press, New Haven & London, 1987

Mehrota, K.K., *Horace Walpole and the English Novel: A Study of the
Influence of 'The Castle of Otranto' 1764–1820*, Blackwell, Oxford,
1934

Melville, Lewis, *Horace Walpole (1717–1797) A Biographical Study*,
Hutchinson, London, 1932

Meyerstein, E.H.W., *A Life of Thomas Chatterton*, Ingpen & Grant,
London, 1930

Plumb, J.H., *Sir Robert Walpole: The Making of a Statesman*, Cresset
Press, London, 1956

Plumb, J.H., *Sir Robert Walpole: The King's Minister*, Cresset Press,
London, 1960

Rogers, Pat, *Literature and Popular Culture in Eighteenth-Century
England*, Harvester Press, Brighton, 1985

Rogers, Pat, *Eighteenth-Century Encounters: Studies in Literature and
Society in the Age of Walpole*, Harvester Press, Brighton, 1985

Rowse, A.L., *Homosexuals in History: A Study of Ambivalence in Society,
Literature and the Arts*, Weidenfeld & Nicolson, London, 1977

Sabor, Peter (ed.), *Horace Walpole: The Critical Heritage*, Routledge &
Kegan Paul, London, 1987

Sherrard, O.A., *Lord Chatham: A War Minister in the Making*, Bodley
Head, London, 1952

Smith, Michael Quinton, *St Mary Redcliffe: an architectural history*,
Redcliffe, Bristol, 1995

Smith, Warren Hunting (ed.), *Horace Walpole: Writer, Politician and
Connoisseur*, Yale University Press, New Haven & London, 1967

Snodin, Michael, 'Strawberry Hill: Building and Site; Part Two: The
Site', *Architectural History*, vol 38, W S Maney, Leeds, 1995

Spector, Robert Donald, *The English Gothic, a bibliographic guide to
writers from Horace Walpole to Mary Shelley*, Greenwood Press,
London, 1984

Starr, H.W. & Hendrickson, J.R. (eds), *The Complete Poems of Thomas
Gray*, Clarendon Press, London, 1966

Select Bibliography

Summerson, John, *Architecture in Britain 1530–1830*, Penguin, London, 6th edition, 1977

Toynbee, Paget, & Whibley, Leonard (eds), *Correspondence of Thomas Gray*, Clarendon Press, Oxford, 1935

Toynbee, Paget, 'Horace Walpole's Journals of Visits to Country Seats', *Walpole Society*, vol 16, 1928

Taylor, Donald S. (ed.), *The Complete Works of Thomas Chatterton*, Clarendon Press, Oxford, 1971

Walpole, Horace, *The Works of Horatio Walpole, Earl of Orford*, London, 1798

Watkin, David, *The English Vision: The Picturesque in Architecture, Landscape & Garden Design*, John Murray, London, 1982

Worsley, Giles, *Classical Architecture in Britain: The Heroic Age*, Yale University Press, New Haven & London, 1995

Index

Adam, Robert, 122–3, 237
Ailesbury, Caroline, Countess of (née Campbell; Henry Conway's wife), 166–7, 180, 197
Alexander, Daniel, 177
Algarotti, Francesco, Count, 33
Alnwick Castle, Northumberland, 123
Alps: HW in, 48–50
Amelia Sophia Eleanora, Princess, 137, 157–9, 171
America see North America
Anson, George, Baron, 157, 163
Anspach, Margravine of see Craven, Elizabeth, Countess of
Arnaud, François Baculard d', 188
Arnold, Matthew, 243
Arundel Marbles, 35
Ashton, Thomas: at Eton, 11; at Cambridge, 17, 28; and HW's Grand Tour, 44; reveals Gray's criticisms to HW, 74; and Gray's reconciliation with HW, 113; Eton Fellowship, 114–15; portrait at Strawberry Hill, 239
Augusta of Saxe-Gotha, Princess Dowager (George III's mother), 193–4

Barrett, William, 224
Barry, Sir Charles, 123
Bateman, Richard, 120
Beauclerc, Lady Diana, 234, 237
Beauvau, Charles Just de Beauvau-Craon, Prince de, 59
Beckford, William, 123, 253
Bedford, John Russell, 4th Duke of, 137, 170, 212–13
Bentheim, Marie-Lydie de Bournonville, Gräfin von, 196
Bentley, Richard: and Strawberry Hill designs, 7, 116, 123, 126–8, 133–43,

146, 148, 235; taste, 116–17, 128, 130; illustrates Gray's poetry, 125, 128–9, 132–3; friendship with HW, 128–31, 141, 177; appearance, 129; background and career, 129; debts, 129–31, 138, 141; in Jersey, 136, 138–40; correspondence with HW, 139–41; radicalism, 140; sends Müntz to HW, 142; leaves HW and Strawberry Hill, 147–9, 151–2, 155–6, 234; HW's ill behaviour towards, 150; literary career, 152–4; death, 155; given sinecure, 155; HW supports, 155; letter from HW on Pelham's death, 159; and HW's execration of slave trade, 211; and Macaulay's attack on HW, 256; *Epistle to Lord Melcomb*, 153; 'Patriotism', 155; *Philostrate*, 154; *The Wishes*, 153–4
Bentley, Mrs Richard ('Hannah Cliquetis'), 131, 139–41, 148, 151–5
Berkeley, Norborne, 122
Berkeley Square, London: HW's house in, 231, 248
Berry family, 239, 249, 251
Berry, Agnes, 249–51
Berry, Mary, 246–7, 249–52
Berry, Robert, 239, 249, 254
Bisham Abbey, Buckinghamshire, 126
Blake, William, 258
Blakeney, General William, Baron, 156
Bland, Henry, 13
Bodmer, Johann Jakob, 189
Bologna, 62
Boston Tea Party (1773), 244
Boufflers, Amélie de, 203, 207
Bourchier, Cardinal Thomas, Archbishop of Canterbury: tomb, 148–9
Brawne, Fanny, 30
Bromwich, Thomas, 149

265

Index